ZULU!

Dr Edmund Yorke is senior lecturer in Defence Studies at the Royal Military Academy at Sandhurst and has written and researched extensively on the Zulu War. He was the historical consultant for the recent History Channel/Discovery Channel television documentary on Rorke's Drift. His other books include *Mafeking: The Story of a Siege* and *The New South Africa: Prospects for Domestic and International Security*.

ZULU!

The Battle for Rorke's Drift 1879

EDMUND YORKE

TEMPUS

This edition first published 2005

Tempus Publishing Limited
The Mill, Brimscombe Port,
Stroud, Gloucestershire, GL5 2QG
www.tempus-publishing.com

British Library Cataloguing in Publication Data.
A catalogue record for this book is available from the British Library.

ISBN 0 7524 3502 7

Typesetting and origination by Tempus Publishing Limited
Printed and bound in Great Britain

Contents

Dedicated with love to my wife, Louise, and my parents and family for enduring nearly four decades of 'Zulumania'.

Preface

This book constitutes the first fully referenced, single-volume history of the battle of Rorke's Drift. The aim throughout this work has been not merely to construct an analytical narrative of the main events, but through extensive deployment of contemporary eyewitness accounts, to bring a new intimacy and understanding to this heroic conflict. Hopefully, this work will also throw some fresh light upon both the origins of the war and the overall military, strategic, political and social significance of this epic siege. Inevitably, this work, due to the paucity of Zulu oral source material, has been 'Anglocentric', but full use has been made of most existing African sources, notably the James Stuart Archive, to achieve some (if limited) balance in this analysis of the siege.

Many individuals have contributed to the evolution of this book. My gratitude must first be extended to the librarians, archivists and staff of the Universities of Oxford (Rhodes House) and Cambridge; the National Army Museum, London; the Royal Regiment of Wales (South Wales Borderers) Museum, Brecon, Wales; the Public Record Office, Kew, Surrey; the Royal Logistical Corps Museum, Surrey; the Army Medical Corps Museum, Aldershot, Hampshire and the Royal Military Academy Sandhurst (especially Sarah Oliver, Anne Ferguson, Diane Hillier and Peter Thwaites, Curator). Major Martin Everett, curator of the Brecon Museum, was particularly generous with his support, and my good friend and colleague, Principal Librarian Andrew Orgill, RMAS, proved an indispensable source of advice, expertise and encouragement throughout the project.

I would also like to thank Sophie Bradshaw and the staff at Tempus for all their hard work on the new edition.

I gratefully acknowledge the inspiration provided by the works and commentary of seven leading experts in the Anglo-Zulu war field – namely Professor John Laband, John Young, F.W. Jackson, Ian Knight, David Rattray, Donald Morris and the late Frank Emery. Ian Knight has proved a steadfast correspondent over many years and John Young's friendship and generous pictorial support has also been crucial to the preparation of this book. John Laband's many seminal works, in particular his erudite chapters on the Zulu perspective of the Rorke's Drift action, have proved a great source of stimulation. His co-edited (with Ian Knight) nine-volume work *Archives of Zululand,* has provided a plethora of source material, especially useful for scholars unable to visit South Africa on a regular basis. Captain Andrew Banks, RMP and Philip Barlow (late 3 Para) also provided excellent pictorial support from their private collections, and Philip Barlow's generous loan of documents from the recently discovered papers of Major Wilsone Black was a wonderful unexpected bonus to the volume. My gratitude is also owed to the relatives of Lieutenant Chard VC, notably Mr Peter Booth and Jane Woodward, who so kindly donated photographs of John Chard's personal artefacts.

The author also owes a great debt of gratitude to the word-processing and secretarial staff of the Royal Military Academy, who generously gave their free time to this project (especially Elaine Allen, Pauline Medhurst, Carol Nightingale and Yoland Richardson). Yoland Richardson provided exceptional unstinting support and proved enormously patient and supportive during the final stages of the project.

Over the past decade, several colleagues and hundreds of boundlessly enthusiastic cadets and captains, who it has been my privilege to tutor, have been a continued and great source of inspiration. Drs Duncan Anderson, Dr Christopher Duffy, Dr

Stephen Badsey and Matthew Bennett MA have either shared my enthusiasm, or provided constructive support at in-house seminars. Dr Francis Toase, my Head of Department, has always been an enthusiastic supporter and great facilitator of this project and my thanks are also extended to the Director of Studies, Matthew Midlane MA and the Commandant, Major-General Trousdell CB, for continuing to promote the already high academic reputation of the Academy.

Above all, I must reserve my greatest appreciation for both my dear family and special friends Jennifer Wheeler and Alison Foskett, who have been an unfailing source of love and encouragement during the genesis of this book over the past two years.

The opinions expressed in this work are entirely my own and do not represent or reflect the opinions of the Ministry of Defence or the Royal Military Academy Sandhurst.

I

Road to War:
The Storm-Clouds Gather,
1877-9

As it happened, a letter urging the postponement of all operations for war with the Zulus reached me some days too late to
enable us to recede with any regard to either safety or honour.
The aid you are now sending us, will, I hope, enable us to settle
the Zulus finally, speedily and with the least possible bloodshed,
but it is really not possible, without some loss of life, to render
innocuous to his neighbours a savage with 30 or 40 thousand
armed men at his absolute command, whose system of government and personal pleasure rest equally on bloodshed, who was
never known to forgive, never observe a promise, who believes
himself the greatest potentate on earth and whose outposts are on
one side of the river fordable for eleven months of the year, and
our farmers on the other?

Sir Bartle Frere, High Commissioner South Africa, to Mr Herbert,
Under-Secretary of State Colonies, 23 Dec 1878, in J. Martineau, Life
of Sir Bartle Frere, *p.266*

The causes of the 1879 Anglo–Zulu War continue to be the subject of considerable academic debate.[1] For some historians, the

war was essentially a result of an almost subconscious desire by the imperial metropole and local settler governments to exploit and incorporate the virgin Zulu labour pool into the rapidly expanding mine and farm industrial complex of South Africa. For others, it was essentially a question of security – a necessary pre-emptive strike against a volatile, highly militaristic and allegedly barbarised African state which posed a major strategic threat to local under-populated white societies and constituted a deep affront to the principles of 'white civilisation'. Of the officials directly involved in this 'war policy' against the Zulu-men, such as Sir Theophilus Shepstone, Lieutenant-General Frederick Thesiger (Lord Chelmsford) and Sir Michael Hicks Beach, Colonial Secretary, it has been Sir Henry Bartle Frere, the British High Commissioner for South Africa, who has been largely blamed for the prosecution of the Zulu War and the subsequent destruction and break-up of the Zulu nation. Thus leading historians have described Frere as an aggressive unprincipled expansionist, 'a man of tenacious character and grave and lofty if ill calculated aims',[2] and a man who 'by his high-handed conduct plunged the country into an idle and indefensible war against the Zulu'.[3]

This chapter, by critically evaluating the key events leading up to the outbreak of war, will seek to throw fresh light upon the conduct of Sir Bartle Frere. It will focus especially on the support afforded him at the very heart of the Colonial Office, support which continued well after the official government veto on the Zulu War, and which continued even after Frere felt compelled, for good military and strategic reasons, to exceed his instructions and promote and execute what he considered to be a necessary preventative war against the Zulu.[4]

The Strategic Background, 1877-9

The political and strategic situation in South Africa that confronted the British government in the late 1870s could only be described as deeply depressing. In many respects, South Africa was undergoing a familiar, periodic turbulence which had already earned it the reputation of being one of Britain's most difficult and complex colonies. By January 1878, the ailing brain-child of Colonial Secretary Lord Carnarvon's grand confederation scheme, aimed at establishing a modern, unified, self-governing and above all loyal and economical dominion of the Empire, was facing disintegration. Strenuous efforts over the preceding decade to achieve political unity had made little headway, for, although three out of the five of the white settler states – the Cape, Natal and Griqualand West – were under British government rule by 1876, no two communities had expressed a willingness to unite and no two constitutions were alike. Old inter-colonial, often commercial jealousies, such as those existing between the Cape and Natal, between Griqualand West and the Cape and even between the Eastern and Western Provinces of the Cape, continued to remain potent obstacles to confederation. The other white settler colonies – the two Boer Republics, the Orange Free State and the Transvaal – remained extremely hostile to the idea of British rule. It was a hostility dating back to the 'Great Trek' of the 1830s, when hundreds of Boer families trekked north and east to escape the pressures of British authority, especially new tax and anti-slavery laws. The Orange Free State remained solidly independent from British rule and was already benefiting economically from the earlier great diamond field discoveries of the 1860s. By contrast, the under-populated Transvaal was facing bankruptcy and imminent collapse under the pressure of hostile African tribes, and was in danger of creating a serious security vacuum for white settlerdom in the region.

The state of African affairs was similarly unprepossessing. The Cape-Xhosa war was in full swing and others were perceived to be imminent. The diamond discoveries in Griqualand West and the Orange Free State during the late 1860s and 1870s, and the consequent insatiable demand for black labour, had hastened the break-up of tribal societies. The resultant economic and social disquiet lay at the heart of African unrest, which the new South African High Commissioner Sir Bartle Frere was destined to inherit across many of the provinces' borders. There were, as Lord Carnarvon himself remarked, 'clouds gathering all round the horizon',[5] and no cloud could be more ominous and threatening than that of the Zulu 'thunder cloud' overshadowing the isolated, under-populated and consequently highly vulnerable colonies of Natal and the Transvaal. Friction and war between these groups of European settlers and the most powerful African polity in sub-Saharan Africa had been a recurring feature of southern African history for the previous half-century. Major conflict between the two peoples again dated from at least the 1830s, when migrating Boer trekkers had first clashed with Zulu *impis* (regiments) as they pushed deep into the southern African interior. The great Zulu empire, forged by war out of a few disparate Nguni clans by Chief Shaka, had by the 1870s come to dominate the south-east region of the South African empire, deploying up to 40,000 warriors. Nevertheless, up to the late 1870s, the tiny British colony of Natal (established in 1845), despite its precarious strategic position within Zululand, had maintained relatively amicable relations with successive Zulu chieftains, and imperial forces had not been drawn into any full-scale conflict with the Zulu. Indeed, as we shall see, the British settlers were already rivals of the Boers and had often seemed to be friends if not allies of the Zulu. As even Sir Bartle Frere was later to admit, the Zulu and their current chief Cetshwayo, were

> always anti-Boer and therefore philo-Natal, and one sees a good deal of the feeling for him thus engendered among people here, some of whom would sooner see us join the Zulus to teach the Boers manners, than join the Boers to prevent the Zulus from murdering.[6]

Catalyst for War – The Transvaal Annexation (April 1877)

In April 1877, a single legal act had made the Zulu a more potent threat than ever before to the peaceful conditions that Carnarvon had recognised as an essential prerequisite of any successful South African Confederation. The annexation of the Transvaal by the British Administrator, Sir Theophilus Shepstone, an act sanctioned and carried out on behalf of Carnarvon, has been recognised by virtually all historians as a primary catalyst for the Zulu War. B.C. Pine, a former governor of Natal, described it as 'the immediate cause of the Zulu War'. The annexation of what was, admittedly a chronically insolvent and collapsed state, effectively destroyed what Pine described as the 'system of checks and balances' whereby Natal had been safeguarded from Zulu attack by the existence of an independent Transvaal as a counterpoise or buffer. The change of flag in the Transvaal made it impossible for Natal to pursue its hitherto successful but risky policy of employing the long-standing enmity between Boer and Zulu to secure for herself immunity from Zulu aggression.[7] As Shepstone reported:

> hitherto the relations of the Amaswazi Zulu with Her Majesty's Government had been from circumstances of those of distant neighbours but by that recent change they had become either adjoining neighbours or subjects.[8]

For the newly arrived High Commissioner, Sir Bartle Frere, long regarded as the primary author of the Zulu War, this new, critical strategic situation was one for which he had no direct responsibility. Frere had only arrived at the Cape at the end of March 1877, and it was not until 10 April that he had formally taken up his post as governor of South Africa and High Commissioner for Native Affairs. The first news of Shepstone's action was not telegraphed to him from Kimberley until 16 April, while the official report and copies of the proclamation failed to reach him in Cape Town until 30 April. The annexation, in Frere's own words:

> was an act which in no way originated with me, over which I had no control, and with which I was only subsequently incidentally connected...[9]

The political and strategic implications of the annexation of the Transvaal were dire. As Sir Bartle Frere reported to General Ponsonby, Queen Victoria's secretary, in an elegant allegorical phrase, demonstrating his fine command of the English language:

> the fact is that while the Boer Republic was a rival and semi-hostile power, it was a Natal weakness rather to pet the Zulus as one might a tame wolf who only devours ones neighbours

sheep. We always remonstrated, but rather feebly, and now that
both flocks belong to us we are rather embarrassed in stopping
the wolf's ravages.[10]

The Zulu 'wolf' was now at Natal's door, and the two nations
were propelled onto a collision course, precipitating a tense face-
to-face confrontation with Zulu power along a far wider strategic front. According to a keen contemporary observer, Sir H.
Rider Haggard,[11] this made Cetshwayo suspiciously hostile to the
apparent concerted attempt at the encirclement of Zululand by
his former British friends. Sir Bartle Frere's ability to deal with
this expanded complex situation enjoyed the full confidence of
the Home Government. Frere had come from India to South
Africa with an awesome reputation as an imperial statesman, even
as a 'troubleshooter'. C.W. De Kiewiet observed that 'no South
African Governor had come so rich in a varied experience'.[12] A
man perceived to be of the highest honour and integrity, he had,
for nine years, been Chief Commissioner in Scinde, where his
courageous administration during the Indian Mutiny had moved
none other than Sir John Lawrence to observe:

that probably there is no Civil Officer in India, who for eminent
exertions, deserves better of the Government than Mr H.E.B.
Frere.[13]

He had been governor of Bombay and a member both of the
Viceroy's Council and of the Council of India. More significant
than anything else, Frere had established a high reputation for his
robust views and minutes on Indian frontier policies during the
1860s and 1870s. In stark contrast, Frere's new political master,
Colonial Secretary Sir Michael Hicks Beach, possessed virtually no
experience in colonial administration, and even his arch-defender
and biographer, Lady Hicks Beach, was forced to concede that he
became Colonial Secretary 'with no special knowledge of South
African affairs'.[14] It boded ill for a minister in charge of one of
Britain's most difficult and complicated colonies. He was a loyal
Disraelite and, as C.F. Goodfellow remarked:

it was probably his loyalty, as much as his ability which had produced his elevation to the Cabinet while still Chief Secretary for
Ireland in November 1876.[15]

His great inexperience clearly showed in his early correspondence with Frere. During the first exchange of letters between
the two men, an ill-at-ease Hicks Beach readily confessed that
he was a 'poor substitute for Carnarvon' and, rather reminiscent
of a pupil addressing his schoolmaster, informed Frere that 'I have
been doing my best to make myself acquainted with my new
work and more especially with South African Affairs.'[16] Frere
was immediately given wide discretion to complete Carnarvon's
confederation policies. In one letter, Sir Michael assured Frere of
his 'anxiety to co-operate with you in every possible way',[17] and
stated that he 'hardly feels in a position to express any opinions on
South African affairs'.[18] Frere was encouraged to act on his own
initiative and was promised 'support and co-operation in your
difficult position which you have a right to expect from anyone
here'.[19] Twelve months later, Frere might well have wondered
why such support was not forthcoming!

Frere was now plunged into a virtual political vacuum as he
proceeded to grapple with the twin problems of implementing
the Confederation and addressing the new security problems of
Natal and the Transvaal. A number of incidents on the British
Transvaal and Natal borders hastened the two empires along the
road to war over the next twenty months. At the centre of tension was the long-standing and urgent problem of the border
dispute between the Zulus and the Transvaal Boers, a problem
now reluctantly inherited by Britain. The dispute stemmed from
a Boer claim to a strip of land located in the south-east corner
of the Transvaal, territory also claimed by Cetshwayo, paramount
Zulu Chief since 1873. With annexation, this problem was now
a major British problem, and in February 1878, in response to
frequent Zulu protests, the Natal governor, Sir Henry Bulwer,
established a commission to arbitrate.

Sir Bartle Frere and the Zulu 'Frankenstein'

By that time, Sir Bartle Frere had decided that in the strategic interest of achieving a modern 'civilised' confederation, prolonged physical security and, with it, hopefully the loyalty of both British and Boer white interests in South Africa, the Zulu Empire would have to be dismantled. In this decision, he had been deeply influenced by Theophilus Shepstone, the new Administrator of the Transvaal. Initially, he had been a friend of Cetshwayo, having attended his coronation in 1873. In October 1877, however, after meeting with Cetshwayo's envoys on the frontier to seek a final settlement to the border dispute, he had been met by them in an allegedly 'self asserting, aggressive and defiant spirit'.[20] Thereafter, Shepstone took an increasingly anti-Zulu and pro-Boer stance in his communications with Frere. By December 1877 he was openly accusing Cetshwayo of violating his coronation promises of 'good government' and the Zulu of acting as a catalyst for all African unrest:

> one thing is certain that if we are forced into hostilities we cannot stop short of breaking down the Zulu power, which after all is the root and real strength of all native difficulties in South Africa.[21]

With reference to the boundary dispute, he expressed his belief that this 'difficulty is a preconcerted matter and that Cetshwayo really believes in his power to overcome us all without much difficulty'.[22] Such reports convinced Frere by June 1878 that the Galeka and Gaika risings, the earlier war with Sekukuni, were the result of a general conspiracy headed by the Zulu 'incubus'. In a crucial dispatch to R.W. Herbert, Under-Secretary at the Colonial Office, sent in mid-March 1878, he expounded these deeply-held beliefs:

> I do not think I ever expressed to you my conviction which has been gradually and unwillingly growing, that Shepstone and others of experience in the country, were right as to the existence of a wish among the great Chiefs to make this war a general and simultaneous rising of Kaffirdom against white civilisation.

Frere continued:

> this conviction has been forced on me by a hundred little bits of
> evidence from different quarters... and... there was a wide spread
> feeling among them, from Secocoeni to Sandilli, that the time
> has come for them all to join to resist the flood of new ideas and
> ways which threaten to sweep away the idle, sensuous, elysium of
> Kaffirdom such as Gaika and Chaka and Dingaan fought for and
> enjoyed...[23]

There were more sinister ulterior motives beyond this security
problem presented by the Zulu. Cetshwayo's warrior army of up
to 40,000 males represented a 'virgin', untapped labour pool, presenting a golden opportunity to 'modernise' the Zulu. A break-up
of the Zulu Empire would clearly serve the rapacious needs of the
mines and farms of white settlerdom. In Shepstone's words:

> had Cetshwayo's 30,000 warriors been in time changed to labour-
> ers working for wages, Zululand would now have been a pros-
> perous peaceful country instead of what it now is, a source of
> perpetual danger to itself and its neighbours.[24]

But for Sir Bartle Frere, it was, above all, a security problem. He
knew from his bitter experiences, particularly during the Indian
Mutiny but also in the Sind, the Punjab and Afghanistan, where
'native conspiracies' were seen to be rife, that a robust forward
policy was essential – there could be no uncertainty as to whether
European or 'native' power was the strongest. In his concept of a
robust 'Pax Britannica', a civilised and uncivilised power could not,
he held, exist peaceably side by side as European nations could,
unless the uncivilised power distinctly recognised that it was the
weaker of the two, and that it must in essentials conform to the civic
standard of right and wrong of the other. Thus in an 1863 minute,
Frere defined the English 'frontier system' as 'a reserve of physical
force amply sufficient to enforce its moral obligations whenever an
appeal to physical force was inevitable'.[25] This was not as arbitrary
and ruthless as it seemed, as he also stressed that force should only

be employed when conciliatory methods such as attempts at open diplomacy and good neighbourliness had been exhausted.

For Frere and other leading officials, the events of the past two years (1876–8), including the period before Frere had arrived, had already undermined any concept of 'good neighbourliness' with the Zulu. In late 1876, an official protest sent to Cetshwayo by the normally 'Zulu-phile' Natal governor, Sir Henry Bulwer, concerning the slaughter of a number of Zulu maidens as punishment for marrying into traditionally celibate Zulu regiments, had led to an aggressive warning from Cetshwayo against interference in Zulu internal affairs.

Consequently, Bulwer sent a strongly-worded dispatch to Carnarvon, in which he described Cetshwayo as expressing 'a great desire for war' and stated that information had reached him that Cetshwayo 'had not only been preparing for war but that he had been sounding the way with a view to a combination of the native races against the white men'.[26] The fact that these words were written by one of the formerly staunchest pro-Zulu politicians in Natal is indicative of the deterioration now occurring in Anglo-Zulu relations. Missionary reports of the persecution, even murder, of their Zulu converts further convinced Frere of the need for decisive action. Evidence also of gunrunning to the Zulu by unscrupulous (mainly Portuguese) traders in the Delagoa Bay region, and of the apparent increased German infiltration into the region, increased Frere's security fears.

By the spring of 1878, it confirmed to Frere that the success of his 'Grand Design', the final push to confederation, rested on the elimination of the Zulu menace. If Frere's policy was, in Goodfellow's words,

> no more than Carnarvon's policy pricked from a canter to a gallop by the presence in South Africa of a man who combined the authority to initiate with a capacity to execute,[27]

it did, nevertheless, reflect a new sense of dynamism and spirit of optimism. In the spring and summer of 1878, these forward policy moves received the wide and unqualified support of both

the inexperienced Hicks Beach and his senior, more experienced
Colonial Office officials. In March 1878, Hicks Beach gave Frere
even greater support and powers of discretion, agreeing

> that the presence of a considerable force in Natal with some...
> augmentation of that in the Transvaal could not be without its
> useful effect on Cetshwayo.[28]

As Bulwer negotiated the boundary dispute between the Zulu
and Transvaal Boers, Hicks Beach agreed that they should be
'pushed on', and that the 'dwellers in the disputed territory be
protected from aggression...'.[29] One month later, Hicks Beach
actively supported a military build-up: 'the movement of troops to
the Transvaal and Natal especially the former, seems very desirable
in order to impress both the Boers and the Zulus'.[30]

By June 1878, Frere was entrusted with even greater authority by Hicks Beach and told that not only should he personally
supervise the Boundary dispute, but 'when you do arbitrate, your
arbitration must be upheld at whatever cost'.[31] The Commission's
findings published in June 1878, ruling in favour of the Zulu, were
an unwelcome surprise, but did not deflect Frere from his broader
concept of breaking up Zulu power, and he effectively reserved
decision on the matter. Home Government support continued
for both his formal Zulu policy and a wider extension of British
control under Carnarvon's confederation concept. When, for
instance, he extended imperial control over Pondoland and the
St John's River, he received constant encouragement and even
praise for his bold initiatives. On the annexation of Pondoland, for
instance, one senior Colonial Office official, Pearson, wrote:

> I think Sir Bartle Frere was right in acting upon his own judgement
> without waiting for authority from home as a weak Governor
> might have done... the occasion came at a critical time when hesi-
> tation or delay might have been attended with serious results.[32]

Such words of encouragement must have again rung in Frere's ears
as he faced censure for his Zulu war policies a mere six months

later. Another official, Edward Wingfield, similarly expressed the hope that:

> Natal will be sensible of the importance of securing a position of commanding influence over Pondoland in the event of war with the Zulus and will appreciate the steps taken by Sir Bartle Frere for that purpose.[33]

Further reports of Russian and German involvement in the region 'show that there is no lack of willingness on the part of the Zulu or their European friends', and the kidnapping and murder of two Zulu women who had fled across the border by the sons of Sihayo, a significant Zulu chieftain, further convinced Frere that the Zulu problem, their 'war fever', must be 'at once grappled with'.[34] In September, while 'on the spot' in Natal, Frere dramatically reported that the people of Natal were now

> slumbering on a volcano and I much fear that you will not be able to send out the reinforcements we have asked for in time to prevent an explosion… the Zulus are now quite out of hand.[35]

A war with the Zulu was imminent, and Home Government support remained solid during the rest of September. In mid-September Wingfield, scribbled on one of Frere's dispatches: 'it seems only too probable… that a Zulu war is imminent'.[36] His senior, Under-Secretary Herbert, went even further:

> It seems certain that there is to be a Zulu war and I see little to hope for except that the resistance of the natives may be weak and the operation soon over.[37]

Frere accordingly continued with his war preparations, assisted by his Commander-in-Chief of South Africa, Lieutenant General Lord Chelmsford.

An Imperial Betrayal?
Frere and the Outbreak of War with the Zulu

On 5 October 1878, Frere suddenly received a bombshell telegram from Hicks Beach which effectively reversed his Zulu
policy and vetoed any prospect of a Zulu war. In one astounding
sentence, Hicks Beach declared:

> I am led to think the information before me that there could still
> be a good chance of avoiding war with the Zulus.[38]

Further confirmation and amplification of the Cabinet decision
to veto a Zulu war arrived in another telegram of 12 October,
and in an official dispatch of 17 October 1878.

The motives lying behind this *volte face,* which placed Frere in
an impossible strategic situation, were brutally revealed in Hicks
Beach's frank private letter to Frere on 10 October 1878. He
reported that 'considerable exception was taken to the great expense
being incurred'.[39] Reinforcements would not be forthcoming.
Hicks Beach had told Frere only part of the answer. Troubles in
Europe and Asia, notably the crisis with Russia over Afghanistan,
had turned the Cabinet against any diversion of resources to a Zulu
war. But it was the cost factor, always a restraining issue in South
African affairs, that lay at the heart of Prime Minister Disraeli's
motivation for his abrupt decision in early October 1878, particularly in view of the chronic trade depression at home. Disraeli
had earlier deprecated the heavy expenditure of Carnarvon (or
'Twitters' as he preferred to call him), particularly after the Cape-
Xhosa or Ninth Kaffir war of September 1877 to June 1878. In
one letter to Lady Bradford at the end of September 1878, he had
written '…if anything annoys me it is our Cape affairs… I fear a
new war. Froude was bad enough and has cost us a million; this
will be worse…'.[40] Valid as these reasons might have been for
the dramatic reverse of policy by Disraeli and his Cabinet, they
took little account of the precarious strategic crisis in South Africa
and the extent to which Frere had been militarily and politically
committed to a Zulu war by mid-October 1878. Throughout the

spring and summer of 1878, troops and equipment had been slowly moved up to the Transvaal and Natal borders, a policy of strength fully supported, as we have seen, by Hicks Beach and the Colonial Office. By this time, Chelmsford had also drawn up plans for a Zulu campaign and, by the end of October, reported reciprocal hostile Zulu activity: 'the assembly of a large number of Zulu regiments at the Kings Krael... which... must undoubtedly be considered as a menace either to Natal or to the Transvaal'.[41] Natal – with scattered European communities of no more than 25,000 including a resident population of 300,000 Africans, of whom two-thirds were Zulu refugees – was extremely vulnerable. Two strategic factors were unavoidable for both Frere and his military and political advisers. Firstly, the extreme mobility of the enemy promised a full-scale attack without warning, the dangers of which Frere was acutely aware of from his Indian Mutiny experience, when several European garrisons, notably at Delhi and Cawnpore, were massacred. Moreover, recent South African history provided glaring examples of such potential catastrophe. Only four decades earlier, the Cape governor, Sir Benjamin D'Urban, had his New Year's Eve dinner ruined by news of wholesale massacres of scores of European settlers by up to 10,000 African assailants who had swept across the border. The Zulu had also demonstrated such surprise tactics in 1838, when they overwhelmed the Boer wagon-train encampment at Weenen and massacred men, women and children alike. Moreover, Frere had only a few thousand regular troops to defend hundreds of miles of frontier which, after April 1877, included the Transvaal-Zulu border. The Natal front alone was 200 miles long. Defensive war was impossible – a pre-emptive strike or preventative war was in Frere's view absolutely essential. One other key strategic factor demanded immediate action – the condition of the Tugela and Buffalo rivers. After January 1879, the rivers would be fordable and Natal highly vulnerable to such sudden Zulu attack.

A third factor which convinced Frere of the necessity to commence an immediate war with the Zulu via an ultimatum was the chronic slowness of communication. Direct telegraph com-munication between Britain and South Africa was not

established until 25 December 1879 – until then it took several
weeks for an exchange of letters and dispatches, and the partial telegraph system only reduced this time by a week or so.
Critics have argued that this technical problem enabled Frere
to exceed his instructions and conceal his plans for war with
the Zulu. Because of the time delay, Frere felt obliged to act, as
to have postponed would have been fatal in view of the critical strategic situation by December 1879. As he later put it to
Hicks Beach: 'a full explanation... would have involved four or
five months delay. I felt quite sure we could not have kept the
peace here as long'.[42] There was one other major strategic factor.
Faced with increasing Boer discontent in the Transvaal over the
British annexation and a potential war, Frere felt that in order
to avoid a 'two-front war', the Zulu question must be settled
first (especially as one of the principal Boer demands had always
been a containment of the Zulu menace; a swift resolution
might yet appease them). In a letter to Hicks Beach, Frere thus
stressed that postponement of the Zulu problem could result in
an immediate Boer rebellion, which, by tying down resources,
would leave Natal open to Zulu attack, or perhaps – even worse
– a war against the Boers with the Zulu allied with the British
against their hated Boer enemy. As Frere put it:

> Such Zulu allies would have been worse for us than a Zulu inroad
> into Natal – it was a simple solution 'risking a Zulu war at once
> or incurring the risk of still worse – a Zulu war a few months
> later, preceded by a Boer rebellion'.[43]

It was an opinion shared by Shepstone, who had already cyni-
cally abandoned Cetshwayo in favour of his Transvaal Boer
constituents.

Hicks Beach continued to pursue a weak and vacillating policy,
in one despatch assuring Disraeli of 'throwing as much cold water
as possible upon... evident expectation of a Zulu war',[44] and in
another agreeing to send reinforcements so as to 'avoid blame'
for 'not supporting him [Frere]'.[45]

Ultimatum

Further border incidents (fully communicated to Hicks Beach and the Colonial Office), notably the kidnapping of two European surveyors by the Zulu on the Tugela river and Zulu threats against German settlers at Luneburg in the Transvaal (see map, p.99), spurred Frere on to the brink of war. By the end of October, 'the time for verbal discussion and diplomatic argument has passed'.[46] By mid-November, moreover, there was a distinct shift of approach in the Colonial Office. Before news of Frere's ultimatum had arrived, probably influenced by the news of these serious border incidents, one official, Pearson, minuted strongly in favour of Frere's war policy: 'I cannot help feeling that there could be a very grave danger in any peace arranged with Cetewayo [*sic*] which would leave his power untouched.' Sharing Frere's strategic worries, he continued:

I cannot but believe that now when we have the opportunity the action which will in the end be best for all interests, whether Imperial or Colonial, European or native, finally or otherwise, will be to enforce such terms upon Cetewayo as would at least render him less threatening in the future.[47]

His senior, Herbert, Under-Secretary for the Colonial Office and the most experienced 'South African' official, also gave strong support, scribbling on one of Chelmsford's despatches his appreciation of the critical military situation: 'the position is no doubt a difficult one and an invasion of Zululand may not be very economical of time and money but necessary for safety'.[48] In January, before receiving news of the outbreak of war, Herbert wrote:

Sir Bartle Frere is evidently convinced that war cannot be avoided and it could be dangerous rather than advantageous to evade or postpone such a permanent settlement with the Zulus... and I fear it must be admitted that Sir Bartle Frere has good grounds for insisting that the Zulus will not keep quiet any longer and should not be allowed to attack us when less prepared than we now are.[49]

The strong support from local leading colonial officials in South Africa (Bulwer and Shepstone, as well as men such as Mr Brownlee, a former 'Native Affairs minister' of Cape Colony) undoubtedly influenced the Colonial Office's growing support for Frere – again a contradiction of imperial policy and of the veto on war. The general support of Bishop Colenso of Natal, later a fierce critic of the Zulu War, which he described as 'the most enormous piece of wickedness',[50] later converted the one remaining critic amongst the six South African officials in the Colonial Office. Mr Edward Fairfield thus minuted:

> the adherence of the Bishop to the view that the military system of Cetshwayo and the compulsory celibacy established by law ought to be broken down is extremely important for Sir Bartle Frere or anyone wishing to take up his defence.

Recording that, in 1874, Bishop Colenso came right across the world to protest about the injustice done by the Natal government to Langelibilile and Patili, he stressed 'if he now acquiesces in the main policy of Sir Bartle Frere his adhesion is a much telling event in the controversy'. [51]

Above all, between October 1878 and early January 1879, even Hicks Beach suddenly experienced a similar 'road to Damascus' conversion. Practically ignoring or conveniently not remembering Frere's earlier dispatches on the critical political and strategic situation, he greeted the news of Frere's ultimatum to the Zulu on 7 November as 'constituting proposals which I do not understand... nor do I at present see the necessity for an ultimatum'.[52] Hicks Beach continued: 'we entirely deprecate the idea of entering on a Zulu war in order to settle the Zulu Question'.[53] Within a month, however, before news of war had even arrived, and as supportive memoranda flooded in from South Africa for Frere's policies, Hicks Beach distinctly changed his tune. Reporting that Frere and Thesiger (Chelmsford) 'seemed confident' and the 'Zulus divided and passive',[54] Hicks Beach was persuaded to support a seemingly short, cheap and therefore politically acceptable war. Frere was now to be judged not according to his political principles, but according to the government's political expediency. As Hicks Beach put it to Disraeli: 'there is I hope a good prospect of the war being short and successful like the Afghan campaign'. That support was conditional upon military success was, however, made abundantly clear in one crucial sentence:

> So that on the whole, although Frere's policy especially in the matter of cost, is extremely inconvenient to us at the moment I am sanguine as to its success and think we shall be able without much difficulty to defend its principles here.[55]

Frere's political fortunes would now rest on the ability of his military subordinates 'to finish off the affair easily and quickly'.[56] As we shall see, the terrible disaster at Isandlwana, nine days later, was to change all this and reveal the underlying hypocrisy of Hicks Beach and other members of Her Majesty's Government.

The Zulu Response to the Ultimatum

If Frere was fast becoming a victim of the machinations of the imperial metropole, the ultimate tragic victims were clearly going to be Cetshwayo and the Zulu nation. The terms of Frere's thirty-day ultimatum delivered to Cetshwayo's *indunas* on 11 December 1878 beside the 'Ultimatum Tree' on the banks of the Tugela river were predictably impossible to comply with without destroying the very foundations of Zulu society. Two demands in particular struck at the political, social and economic heart of the Zulu polity – one calling for the immediate dismantlement of the Zulu military system, the second for complete submission to British 'supervision'. Both effectively signified the end of Zulu independence.[57]

Cetshwayo's predictable resistance to such devastating proposals was probably stiffened by ominous signs of internal crisis within his own kingdom. By 1879, Cetshwayo was a leader under pressure, encircled by white colonial rule and betrayed by his erstwhile friends, Bulwer and Shepstone. It is probable also that, as further north in Swaziland, small but significant numbers of young Zulu males were crossing the Transvaal–Natal border, tempted by the cash wages available in the towns and farms. This tendency would clearly ultimately undermine the highly central-ised and militarised Zulu state. The earlier 1876 killings of Zulu maidens as a punishment for marrying into traditionally celibate regiments, and the 1878 border incident when two women were murdered, may also been indicative of growing social stresses within the tightly controlled Zulu nation. Even Frere, determined as he was to break Zulu power, empathised with Cetshwayo's deep predicament:

> He is now wholly surrounded by Natal and the Transvaal, the Swazi, the Portuguese and must sooner or later succumb. The only prospect was to stand and fight.[57]

In fact, Cetshwayo adopted a passive but firm posture, similar to the one he exhibited towards the governor of Natal two years earlier over the issue of the murder of Zulu maidens. Then, he had remonstrated:

> Why does the Governor of Natal speak to me about my laws? Do I go to Natal and dictate to him about his laws. I shall not agree to any laws or rules from Natal and by doing so throw the great kraal which I govern into the water. My people will not listen unless they are killed; and while wanting to be friendly with the English I do not agree to give over my people to be governed by laws sent to me by them… Go back and tell the English that I shall now act on my own account and if they wish for me to agree… it will be seen that I will not go without having acted. Go back and tell the white man this and let him hear it well. The Governor of Natal and I are equal. He is Governor of Natal and I am Governor here.[58]

Cetshwayo allowed the ultimatum to expire. His understandable act of defiance was now to cost the lives of thousands of his Zulu warriors. On 11 January 1879, with no Zulu reply and with an expiry of the thirty-day ultimatum, the first British troops crossed over the border into Zululand. War had begun.

2

Preparations for War:
The Two Opposing Armies

The preparations for invading Zululand had taken months. In 1879, the British army remained a largely cumbersome, hierarchical machine, but one which was well used to victory over 'native enemies' in Africa and elsewhere.[1] The army's extended imperial role as guardians of huge tracts of territory, particularly in Africa and India, had deeply moulded its character and its organisation, which differed greatly from other contemporary armies on the continent. Rather than constituting an army in the context of a large field force organised into divisions and corps under a systematic chain of command, it was distinguished by small 'penny packet' formations, often only of battalion size and scattered throughout the Empire. Highly mobilised and specialised in order to deal with a wide variety of small colonial wars, it relied heavily on overwhelming superiority of equipment, expecting only minute casualties and easy victories. The British army was so imperially orientated (with up to fifty battalions based in India after the mutiny of 1857) that it played little role in influencing events in Europe. In 1846, for instance, barely 10,000 men could be found at home to meet a perceived imminent French threat. Improvisation was the order of the day, and without the collective high-level command structure of, for instance, the French and German armies, military success often depended on the perceptiveness and resourcefulness of selected commanders such as Lords Roberts and Napier and General Wolseley. Their exploits in, for instance, the Afghan (1878–80) and Ashanti (1874–5) campaigns achieved legendary status in Victorian England, but concealed the inappropriateness of their methodology for any concept of a modern continental-style war. Until the late 1890s, army manoeuvres were still recreating the traditional square formations as practised at the battle of Waterloo in 1815! The limited role and size of the army also reflected its low priority in terms of government expenditure, and it was not an institution which enjoyed high social esteem during the late eighteenth and early nineteenth centuries. The army's anarchic role in the containment of the 1780 anti-Catholic 'Gordon Riots', for example, prompted the often-quoted remark by the Whig politician Charles James Fox that he would 'much rather be governed by a mob than a standing army'! Despite great victories such as at Waterloo (1815), the reputation of the British military at home was further tarnished by the heavy-handed policing actions conducted by both local militia and regular forces during the post-Napoleonic war disturbances and the Chartist disorders of the 1840s. Of these, the 1819 'Peterloo Massacre', when a dozen men and women were cut down by the sabres of an ill-disciplined local militia and contingents of regular Hussars, left a legacy of hatred in working-class areas of Lancashire which lingered on for decades.[2]

The army's relatively poor image reflected, to a large extent, the appalling conditions of service and consequent problems of recruitment. Most rank-and-file soldiers were recruited from the lowest levels of Victorian urban and rural society, often petty criminals or destitute farm labourers. Before 1870, many recruits had been drawn from Ireland – particularly after the 1840s potato famines – but the great trade depression of the 1870s brought a new influx of urban and rural poor from mainland Britain. By the mid-nineteenth century, service conditions could be brutal, dull and uncompromising, and men were expected to sign on for exceptionally long periods. Up to 1847, men enlisted for life, and after that date, for ten years with the option of continuing for twenty-one years to qualify for a pension. Private living space in barracks was often less than that afforded to prison convicts, and mortality rates were often double those of civilians. On meagre unvarying rations of bread, bully beef and biscuits, the Victorian soldier eked out an extremely hard existence. Military life consisted of parades and fatigues, with training hardly going beyond eternal drill and sporadic gymnastic exercises. In the late Victorian period, out of a gross pay of around seven shillings a week, half would be deducted for food over and above basic rations, and over a tenth of a soldier's pay for laundry services etc. Week-long field training exercises were confined to six or seven occasions a year, and recreational activity devolved upon regimental canteens and local brothels. In India, the regimental authorities were even forced to set up official brothels to reduce the prevalence of sexually transmitted diseases amongst the ranks. Acts of indiscipline such as inter-regimental fights and petty theft faced swift and harsh penalties, with many small offences punishable by flogging.

While the serving conditions for officers were significantly better than the private soldier, their military capabilities were often suspect. With indifferent pay, most officer recruits came from the lower middle classes, often second and third sons of the landed gentry who were excluded from inheritance by the primogeniture system. Class clearly did not ensure quality! Until as recently as 1872, the peculiar anachronistic system of 'purchase of commission' allowed posts to be bought and sold, often for as much as several thousand pounds, a system which, devoid of any meritocratic base, could result in high levels of incompetence at senior officer level.

Between 1856 and 1879, however, a number of significant reforms had improved the overall quality of army life and provided it with a more professional base. The graphic dispatches of *Times* reporter William Russell from the Crimea, which detailed horrific service conditions, had exposed many shortcomings in army administration, as did reports of the stirring medical work undertaken by Florence Nightingale. The great Cardwell reforms of 1872 created a much more professional army. The 'purchase of commission' system was abolished, as were more brutal army practices (although flogging was retained for wartime service). Closer community ties were encouraged through the 'linked battalion' system at town and county level (fully implemented in 1881). The length of service for men in the ranks was changed, and men could serve six years with the colours and six with the reserve. In the 1870s, significant numbers of new barracks were built and the provision of cookhouses soon followed. With educational reforms, the literacy levels of both private soldiers and NCOs significantly improved and this was reflected in the higher quality of, for instance, soldiers' letter-writing.[3]

Equipment had also improved in the decade preceding the Anglo-Zulu War.[4] In 1871, the army replaced the Enfield percussion rifle (maximum range 1,000 yards) with the new, much more effective, single-shot Martini-Henry breech-loading rifle. Dispatching a heavy .450 calibre lead bullet, the rifle was sighted up to 1,500 yards, although most accurate at a distance of between 300 and 500 yards. The bullet was literally a 'man-stopper' and, at close range, could have a terrible effect on the human body, with the potential to rip both cartilage and bone apart. The rifle action was also much easier. When the lever between the trigger guard was depressed, the breech opened. A used round was then extracted and a fresh round inserted in the chamber, and raising the lever closed the breech for firing. The only disadvantage was that the heavy recoil could bruise shoulders and make firing uncomfortable after half an hour or so, while excessive firing could also cause the barrel to overheat, both melting the brass base of the cartridge and sometimes jamming the firing action. As we shall see, these problems did emerge during both the battles at Rorke's Drift and, earlier, at Isandlwana. More seasoned troops, however, learnt to counteract overheating by sewing cowhide around the barrel and stock of the Martini-Henry. The 'lunger' socket bayonet carried by most of the line regiments in 1879 dated from the 1850s and was around twenty-one inches long and, combined with the four-foot rifle length, gave a stabbing reach of over six feet. As we shall see, this proved to be a distinct advantage during close-quarter combat with the Zulu at Rorke's Drift. In addition to the rifle and bayonet, each soldier was issued with the standard seventy rounds when going into action. By contrast, officers were equipped with a variety of swords and revolvers (many with six-cylinder mechanism Navy Colts, purchased in large numbers by the War Office in the 1860s and 1870s and noted for their reliability and rapid firing). Other variations on equipment included sword-bayonets carried by sergeants and short swords carried by drummers.

The 1871 valise Pattern Equipment proved to be reasonably efficient field dress. It included two white calf-leather pouches on each side of the waist-belt, and a black leather 'expense pouch' positioned usually at the back of the belt. Other essential items for the imperial infantry of the 1870s included a wooden water bottle, mess tin, greatcoat and haversack. The uniform was, by contrast, somewhat less practical. The traditional red tunic with facing regimental colours on cuff and collar and secured by regimental buttons was retained, while the blue serge trousers and often poor-quality leather boots completed the infantry field dress. As in India, the only real concession to the African heat was the white 'foreign service' helmet displaying the regimental shako badge attached to the front. In South Africa, veterans, in order to make themselves less conspicuous to the enemy, darkened these helmets by staining, usually with tea, coffee or mud. After a few weeks campaigning in the African bush, much of this uniform, particularly the jacket and trousers, was reduced to tatters, and often humorous-looking patchwork variations in dress took over, complementing the wild beards sported by many of the veterans!

The 24th Foot, comprising the main units of imperial troops that fought at Isandlwana and Rorke's Drift, were an interesting mixture of veterans and relative novices. Of the two battalions of the 24th Foot, the 1/24th were the most experienced in African warfare, having arrived at the Cape as early as 1875. They had spent four successive years engaged in largely fluid short-lived skirmishes with Xhosa rebels in which the new Martini-Henry rifle had been frequently deployed with maximum destructive effect. From the perspective of both senior military and political observers, their virtually unbroken run of success in the ninth and last Kaffir war augured well for the future. Following the decisive victory by the British and their Fingo allies over Xhosa rebels at the battle of Quintane (Centane), none other than the High Commissioner Sir Bartle Frere himself expressed his delight, not only in regard to the easy success of British field tactics, but also the total domination of the battlefield by the new Martini-Henry rifle:

> They seemed to have had great hopes of crushing (Captain) Upcher by enveloping his position, then of raising the Colony. They came on in four Divisions very steadily, and, in the days of Brown Bess, would certainly have closed, and being eight or ten to one, would possibly have overwhelmed our people. They held on after several shells had burst among their advanced masses but they could not live under the fire of the Martini-Henry. The 24th are old, steady shots and every bullet told, and when they broke, Carringtons Horse followed them up and made the success more decided than in any former action. It had been in many respects, a very instructive action, not only as regards the vastly increased power in our weapons and organisation, but showing the Kaffir persistence in the new tactics of attacking us in the open in masses.[5]

Unfortunately, as we shall see, and as the battle of Isandlwana was to so tragically demonstrate, these disparate rebel African groups could not in any way be compared to the sheer size, organisation and fighting power of the Zulu, the most powerful black army in nineteenth-century sub-Saharan Africa. The potential for both Frere and his Commander-in-Chief, Lord Chelmsford, to underestimate their future Zulu enemy was later tellingly referred to by Chelmsford's successor, General Wolseley, who wrote:

> Chelmsford's easily one success in the old Colony last year was a direct cause of his ruin here as it made him underestimate his

Zulu antagonists. The Kaffirs in the Koi are poor creatures when compared with the Zulus, they never act in masses or dare to attack in the open.[6]

The British regulars were supplemented by numerous colonial irregular units. Local white settler volunteer formations were attached to all five of Chelmsford's columns and as units for defence around the major Natal towns and settlements. Sporting a wide variety of weapons and uniform, contingents such as the Natal Mounted Police and the Buffalo Border Guard comprised a vital adjunct to Chelmsford's regular forces, especially before the arrival of massive reinforcements following the disaster at Isandlwana.

Serving alongside these men were the white-officered African levies known as the Natal Native Contingent (N.N.C.). These African troops were predominantly Zulu-speaking and members of clans closely related to the Zulu, or were refugees or descendants of refugees from Zululand. Some had old scores to settle with Cetshwayo, and most were recruited by their chiefs and headmen to assist the British regular troops and all-white colonial volunteer units. The Contingent consisted of three regiments, the first with three battalions and the second and third with two battalions each. The muster strength of each battalion was around 1,000 men, and each African was issued a blanket and a red cloth headband as a distinguishing mark. Around 100 in each battalion (one in ten) were armed with often poor-quality rifles, the remainder with billhooks or their own assegais and shields. Despite constant drilling, their overall lack of experience and poor equipment ensured that their military value was marginal and, as we shall see, often unpredictable.

The Zulu Army in 1879

The Zulu army,[7] once famously described by Sir Bartle Frere as 'a nation of celibate man-slaying gladiators', owed their allegiance to King Cetshwayo Ka Mpande, who had become the Zulu paramount chief on the death of his father in 1872. On this date, the forty-year-old Cetshwayo became ruler of some 300,000 people, most of whom inhabited the territory between the Thukela (Tugela) and Mzinyathi (Buffalo) rivers and the valley of the Phongola. By 1879, the borders of Zululand had dwindled but its social structure still closely resembled that established by Shaka, the founder and 'father' of the Zulu nation. By the 1820s, Shaka, by uniting a few disparate Nguni tribal groups and introducing new fighting techniques, had, chiefly through wars and enforced integration with neighbouring tribes, created a formidable empire dominating much of south-east Africa.

The core of the military system originated by Shaka rested upon the age-set units known as *amabutho* (singular *ibutho*). Under this system, teenage Zulu boys, generally aged between fourteen and eighteen, would firstly be assembled and concentrated at military kraals called *amakhanda* (singular *ikhanda*). Here they would be initiated into basic military and economic skills, including cattle-herding shield and spear techniques. When sufficient numbers were gathered together at various kraals, all would be brought before the king and formally adopted into a regiment or *ibutho*, with orders to built a new *ikhanda*. Those who in this way gave their political allegiance to the king were then given the right to occupy and work his land and even retain part of the fruits of their labour. By 1879, there were twenty-seven *amakhanda* in Zululand and thirteen based on the Mahlabathini Plain surrounding Cetshwayo's capital, Ulundi or Ondini. The *amabutho* would perform a number of functions or services for the king, aside from military service in major wars. These could include raiding and policing operations, such as collecting fines from offenders. By 1879, as Guy has pointed out, the scope of some of these activities, such as raiding, had been severely restricted by the extension of colonial authority to the very borders of Zululand.[8] Thus, unlike the British army, the Zulu army was a fully integrated part of Zulu society as a whole.

The *ibutho* were each commanded by an *induna* or commanding officer with 'one second in Command and two Wing Officers' who commanded the right and left wings. The standard section or *amaviyo* of each *amabutho* usually comprised men of the same age group and location (this reinforced morale and cohesiveness) and were commanded by junior officers 'all of whom were of the same age as the men they commanded'.[9]

In Zulu society, women and girls played a politically subservient but vitally important socio-economic role, particularly as agricultural workers and producers of food for the military. Like their male counterparts, Zulu girls were organised into *amabutho* and only with the king's strict permission could they marry into the male *amabutho*, the latter often having to wait until at least thirty-five years of age before being permitted to marry. In a society where cattle-raising was central to the economy, the bride price or *ilobolo* paid by the male suitor usually consisted of a few cattle. As we have seen earlier in the context of the brutal killing of several Zulu maidens in 1876,[10] the penalties for breaking the marriage laws were severe and uncompromising.

Individual Zulu regiments were mainly distinguished by their shield colouring, although some regimental differentiation had apparently been significantly diluted by the time of Cetshwayo's reign. One 'great distinction' remained, however – that between the married and unmarried regiments:

> the former… obliged to shave the crown of the head and to wear a ring made of hemp and coated with a hardened paste of gum and grease; they also carried white shields while the unmarried regiments wore their hair naturally and had coloured shields [black or reddish].[11]

For battle, Zulu warriors usually wore minimal clothing, consisting of a small loincloth or, less frequently, some minimal ostrich-feather headdress or other ornamentation.

Mobilisation for war was rapid, the king informing the various *indunas* by runners, who then called up the *amabutho* from their specific *amakhanda*. From there, the regiments would converge and congregate at the king's kraal at Ondini. Chelmsford's Intelligence Branch estimated the total number of Zulu regiments in 1879 as thirty-four, of whom eighteen were married and sixteen unmarried. Some of the former consisted of men over sixty years of age, so that:

for practical purposes there were only 27 regiments fit to take the field whose numbers were estimated at 41,900... Of these 17,000 were between 20 and 30 years of age, 14,500 between 30 and 40, 5,900 between 40 and 50, 4,500 between 50 and 60.[12]

Important ceremonies preceded deployment for war, the regiments performing certain rituals in front of the king lasting up to two or three days. These 'superstitious practices' included ritual washing in the river, the consumption of doctored bull flesh and even ritual vomiting. On the third day the warriors were 'sprinkled' with medicine by their doctors.[13]

Zulu weaponry was basic but deadly in terms of close-quarter fighting. By Cetshwayo's time, each warrior still carried the short, extremely sharp, broad-bladed stabbing spear (*ikilwa*), ostensibly introduced by Shaka. In more recent years, this standard weapon had been supplemented by a number of throwing spears (*izijula*). Chelmsford's Intelligence Branch thus observed how

four or five assegais were usually carried by each man. One short and heavy bladed one was used solely for stabbing and was never parted with; the others were lighter and sometimes thrown.[14]

Spears, assegais and cowhide for shields (*isihlangu*) were provided by the king. The spears were constructed by highly skilled Zulu blacksmiths of the Nkandla forest, or at the place of Mlaba's people in the bush country at the Umfolozi.[15] Zulu battle practices were ruthless and uncompromising. Male prisoners were never or rarely taken and women only as booty and the objective, as in Shaka's day, was to totally annihilate the opposing enemy forces. The prevailing Zulu tactic for close-quarter battle, originally perfected by Shaka, was to hook the opponent's shield to the left and deliver the assegai thrust to the exposed belly. Those Zulu warriors who had killed in battle were subsequently isolated in order to carry out further rituals, including the disposal of their own clothes and the wearing of the clothes of the deceased enemy (hence, as we shall see, the Zulu proclivity for acquiring the red jackets of deceased British soldiers at Isandlwana). A further essential part of this ritual was the disembowelment and evisceration of the enemy dead, a practice which horrified and enraged the British, but which was considered by the Zulu essential to prevent retribution by the enemy's spirit or future misfortune. Deserters and cowards faced the death penalty.

The Zulu armoury was supplemented by significant numbers of mostly obsolete European firearms, such as muzzle-loading Enfield 'Tower' muskets. These were acquired mainly from Portuguese traders in the Delagoa Bay area, fuelling Sir Bartle Frere's fears of conspiratorial links between the Zulu and rival European powers. Ingenious methods were deployed to compensate for the frequent lack of modern ammunition. Thus H.L. Hall, a veteran of the Sekukuni campaign in the Transvaal, described the unnerving experience of being under fire from such weapons:

> The natives were armed with muzzle-loaders and flint-lock guns of very ancient makes purchased in Lourenco Marques or from traders who roamed those parts and did very good business. Their bullets were curiosities. They were very short of lead, and to spin it out they would put a stone or a bit of iron pot-leg into the bullet mould and pour the lead in. This accounted for the whizzing noise that we heard after seeing the puff of smoke. You could hear them approaching and wondered who would be hit. They were very poor shots and generally missed us, even at close range. Sometimes they were lucky, however, and that 'pot-leg ammunition', as we called it, sounded very alarming.[16]

Zulu battle tactics, again based on the innovative ideas of the Zulu military genius, Shaka, hinged upon the rapid encircling and enveloping formation known as *impondo zankomo* ('beast's horns'). The Zulu regiments or *impis*, generally comprising the young and more able-bodied *amabutho*, occupied the two fast-moving left and right wings, 'horns' or 'claws' of the crescent-shaped mass, with the aim of rapidly surrounding the enemy on each flank. Meanwhile, a powerful body of the more experienced *amabutho*, comprising the 'chest' of the 'beast', would attack and distract the enemy head-on, with a reserve or 'loins' deployed behind as reinforcements. Strict discipline was paramount: the 'loins' were often kept seated with their backs to the action to discourage premature intervention. Sometimes groups of very young, raw and easily excitable warriors would be deployed even further back and restricted to mopping-up operations only. Chelmsford's Intelligence Branch thus stressed how speed and duplicity were key features of this ingenious battle tactic:

> The Zulus advance in a long thick line which break up and approach the enemy in apparent confusion. The flanks move off rapidly to the right and left and circling round when out of sight, formed the horns or claws which gripped the enemy while the centre attacks in front from the chest.[17]

It was a formidable killing machine, especially when deployed against a demoralised, ill-disciplined or, as we shall see at Isandlwana, complacent enemy. Zulu intelligence, transport and logistics were (like their dress, weapons and tactics) simple but extremely effective in a country comprising extremely rough terrain and intrinsically hostile to any form of wheeled transport. As a rule, the Zulu *impis* marched at the double, covering up to fifty miles on a specific campaign march. Speed and mobility were enormously enhanced by the minimal supply lines required. Chelmsford's intelligence officers were acutely aware of their efficacy:

> The Zulu army required little Commissariat or transport. Three or four days provisions in the shape of maize or millet, and a herd of cattle proportional to the distance to be traversed, accompanied each regiment. The provisions and camp equipage which consisted of sleeping mats and blankets were carried by lads who followed each regiment and also assisted in driving the cattle.[18]

Zulu girls would also often accompany columns for short distances until the food they carried ran out. When away from the *amakhlanda*, Zulu foraging parties would sometimes requisition and thereby prejudice local food supplies. Thus one Zulu boy recollected how his *umuzi* was 'visited' by one such party in early January 1879, at the start of the Isandlwana campaign. As Usutus (generic name for the people of Cetshwayo) appeared through the fog:

> they saw the many sheep belonging to our father and other people... and said, 'a bit of food for us, this, master'. They stabbed some of the sheep; they drained our calabashes, they took the [dead] sheep away with them. Suddenly one of the warriors espied an essessively fine kid. He seized it. Our father [uncle] seized it and the warriors seized it too. The next moment up came the indunas [officers] and scolded the regiment.

The need for long-term food supplies was a glaring weakness in the Zulu military system, as regiments needed to periodically disperse in order to harvest their crops. It was a weakness fully exploited by Chelmsford's commanders later in the war.[19] The rolling hills, deep ravines or 'dongas' and even the larger rivers presented little obstacle to these highly mobile war *impis*. Thus one source described the ingenious Zulu method of crossing swollen rivers:

> When they come to a stream in flood which is out of their depth and does not exceed from ten to fifteen yards in breadth, they plunge into it in a dense mass, holding on to one another, those below forcing the others forward and thus they succeed in crossing with a loss of only a few of their number.[20]

Chelmsford's Campaign Plans

The initial campaign plans[21] of Lord Chelmsford, Commander-in-Chief of the British invasion forces in January 1879, were simple. Aware of Zulu mobility, the overriding main strategic aim was to force the Zulu army to battle by striking decisively at the enemy's centre of gravity, the Zulu capital of Ulundi (or, more specifically, Cetshwayo's Royal Kraal or personal home at Ondini). In such a battle, superior British volley fire would, it was believed, as at Centane, irrevocably smash the exposed Zulu *impis* in the open field. For this purpose, Chelmsford divided his force into five columns, each mixing British regular infantry with other colonial units. Three of these would advance from widely separated points on the Zululand border with Natal, with two columns held in reserve along the border to protect local white settlers against any Zulu breakthrough. These three attacking columns, in a strange replication of Zulu tactics, would be deployed in a slowly enveloping pincer movement aimed towards the Zulu capital. No.4 Column, the northernmost on Chelmsford's left, was commanded by Colonel Evelyn Wood and comprised 2,250 men, while No.1 Column on the right was led by Colonel Charles Pearson and comprised nearly 5,000 men. The main thrust of the invasion centred on No.3 Column, led by Colonel Richard Glyn, comprising just under 4,700 men. This column was accompanied by Chelmsford himself.

An early decisive blow by any of these three columns was considered essential. As Chelmsford informed the Secretary of State for War:

> In conducting operations against an enemy like… the Zulu the first blow struck should be a heavy one and I am satisfied that no greater mistake can be made than to conquer him with insufficient means. He has the advantage of being able to march in one day at least three times as far as the British soldier and he has no Commissariat train to help him… unless his country… is attacked by several columns and each strong enough to hold its own, moving in from different directions he has always the power to evade the blow and to prolong the war to an indefinite time.[22]

Already confident of his military superiority in open battle, much of Chelmsford's pre-invasion preparations were focused on the immense logistical and transport problems presented by such a difficult country, lacking in any form of road. In a letter to the Surveyor General of Ordnance, despatched as early as August 1878, Chelmsford had painted an exceedingly bleak picture:

Transport will be our greatest difficulty and source of expenditure – it will cost more than double the rates paid on the Eastern frontier and, at present, I see no remedy. Even advertisements for transport have failed to produce any reductions in cost.[23]

A rare memoir by H.L. Hall, a Transport Conductor earning the princely sum of ten shillings a day, reveals the extent of the transport crisis, describing a frantic search for bullocks, horses and even mules, with huge purchase sums offered. After initially seeing his mule teams commandeered by no less a man than Colonel Buller because 'they were urgently needed for military purposes', he continued:

> The military authorities in Maritzburg did not want me to leave so offered me one pound a day to stay on in charge of the mule camp in Maritzburg where they had over two hundred mules with harness and wagons and no responsible head… orders for wagons and teams arrived each day and soon there were very few of the original two hundred left but more were constantly arriving.[24]

Conductor Hall was not only a prosperous man but a lucky one. At the last minute, a prestigious assignment to conduct Chelmsford's own wagon and spring cart into Zululand was cancelled and taken over by a young, unnamed lieutenant on the departure day, who was later 'killed at Isandlwana'.[25] Transport was a Herculean, almost nightmarish task. Chelmsford had to shift 1,500 tons of tents, cooking utensils, food, rifle and artillery ammunition and medical stores via eighteen-foot ox wagons hauled by eighteen to twenty strong oxen or mule teams, all of which were highly susceptible to sickness or accident. Thus, Lieutenant Smith-Dorrien recorded the impact of one terrible thunderstorm on his team of oxen:

> Hail was descending as big as pigeon's eggs, the thunder was deafening and the lightning blinding. On the road in front of the store stood a wagon with sixteen oxen. The trek-tow or rope, to which their yokes were attached, was a steel hawser. Suddenly there was a

blinding flash, and when it cleared, low and behold! sixteen oxen
stretched and lying like dead, and six of them were dead.[26]

In such broken country it was rare for oxen or mules to cover
more than five miles a day, with extensive rests needed if they
were deployed for more than eight hours a day. To find oxen for
the 600 to 700 wagons needed for the three columns, Chelmsford
was eventually forced to buy, borrow or hire two-thirds of all
Cape Colony's wagon teams. There was consequently massive
price inflation matched by a mounting death toll amongst the
oxen, who were confined to disease-ridden pasturage during the
weeks it took to build up supplies. Even as late as January 1879,
as the campaign started, one-third of the animal transport was
being lost monthly and Chelmsford had, in desperation, turned
to mule transport.

Rorke's Drift and the Crossing of the Buffalo River

Despite all these difficulties, Colonel Glyn's No. 3 Column crossed
the Buffalo river at Rorke's Drift on 11 January 1879, but with
its commanders still possessing little or no knowledge of the
whereabouts of the main Zulu army. By contrast, long before
the invasion began, Cetshwayo's spies had infiltrated Natal and
obtained accurate information on the strength and deployment
of all three of Chelmsford's attacking columns.

For the tiny garrison of Rorke's Drift, the preparations for invasion had constituted an extremely busy time, with the continual
hustle and bustle of military preparations. The Rorke's Drift station was known to the Zulu as 'Kwa Jim' (the house of Jim). Jim
Rorke, a former border agent and trader, had originally erected
the buildings and, after Rorke's death in 1875, they were finally
purchased by the Reverend Otto Witt on behalf of the Swedish
Church and for the express purpose of establishing a Zulu mission. The main house of De Witt's was located about half a mile
back from the river crossing. The sizeable hill to its immediate
rear known to local Zulu as Shiyane (or 'eyebrow') was named
Oskarberg, in tribute to the king of Sweden. A few yards to the

front of the buildings, in the words of an eyewitness, the main house

> stood within a few feet of the rocky terrace overlooking a wide enclosed garden of two or three acres in extent, planted with standard grape vines, and many fine orange, apricot, apple, peach, quince, fig, pomegranate and other fruit trees. There was a road running parallel with the front of the house, between the garden and the terrace with a strong wall along the terrace side; while the sloping ground between the wall and the summit of the terrace was occupied by a grove of fine Cape poplars, some large gum trees and a luxuriant growth of bushes and shrubs of various kinds.[27]

The main dwelling house was about eighty feet long, the sole wall on the left running back nearly sixty feet. This building had been converted by the Army Medical Authorities into a base hospital for the column. Nearly all the rooms, as well as the large-spaced veranda in front (which was carefully screened by blankets), were occupied by thirty-odd patients.

Forty paces to the left, but with its frontage line of eighty feet running parallel with the extreme back wall of the dwelling house, was another block of buildings comprising store rooms. This extended back fifty-two feet. About parallel with the extreme wall of the block of buildings, with only a space of ten or twelve feet intervening, a stone wall extended to the edge of the ledge of rocks, forming the right wall of a well-built kraal some fifty feet square, which was divided in half by another similar and parallel wall.[28] These buildings were also commandeered by the Commissariat Department and stocked full of all kinds of army provisions, including heavy biscuit boxes, sacks of mealie meal (corn), meat boxes and even barrels of spirits etc.

The post was under the overall command of Major Henry Spalding, 104th Regiment, with the tents of the main regular unit of the garrison and the eighty-odd men of B Company 2/24th Regiment, commanded by Lieutenant Gonville Bromhead, being pitched in the space between the storeroom and the kraal. Other units left behind by the column included a tiny unit of the Army Hospital Corps commanded by Surgeon Major Reynolds, a small Commissariat group commanded by Senior Commissariat Officer Walter Dunne, half a dozen Royal Engineers commanded by Lieutenant Merriot Chard and 200–300 men of the Native Natal Contingent, with their accompanying European officers.[29] In less than a fortnight, from within this disparate group of men was to emerge a score of heroes, a dozen of whom were to be awarded the ultimate accolade, the Victoria Cross.[30] The senior officers were a seasoned group, several with active campaign experience.

Lieutenants Bromhead 2/24th and Chard, RE, the two men destined to command the post in this epic battle, were typical products of the late-Victorian officer class. Bromhead was born at Versailles on 29 August 1845, the third son of Edmund de Granville Bromhead, 3rd Baronet, a wealthy landowner. He entered the 24th Regiment on 20 April 1867 as an ensign by purchase, and while stationed at Croydon became the champion at boxing, wrestling and singlestick. At 5ft 10in tall, his unusually large, broad frame was undoubtedly to prove an advantage in the close-quarter fighting that was to occur at Rorke's Drift. He was also experienced for a relatively young officer, having served throughout the 9th Frontier War.

Lieutenant Chard, fated to assume overall command of the garrison, was thirty-two years old and born at Boxhill near Plymouth. The second son of William Chard, John Rouse Merriott Chard was educated at Plymouth New Grammar School and Cheltenham College and was commissioned through the Royal Military Academy, Woolwich as a Lieutenant in the Royal Engineers on 15 July 1865. After serving in Bermuda, Malta and southern England, he arrived at the Cape on 4 January 1879.

Surgeon James Henry Reynolds was born in February 1844 at Dun Laoghaire, County Dublin (then called Kingstown). Educated at Castle Knock and Trinity College, Dublin, he graduated with a BA MB ChB in 1867. In March 1868 he entered the Medical Staff Corps as an assistant surgeon. For his efficient service as Medical Officer with the 36th (Hereford) Regiment during a cholera outbreak in India, he was promoted to surgeon in 1873.

James Walter Dunne was the senior Commissariat Officer at Rorke's Drift, responsible for the tons of tores crammed inside and outside the garrison buildings. Born in Ireland in 1853, his father was a procurement merchant and shipowner and he served in Dublin from 1873–7 before being posted to South Africa. A tall, handsome man, he had already gained experience on the Cape Frontier and in the war against the Pedi in the Transvaal. His subordinate, Acting Assistant Commissary Officer James Langley Dalton, later perceived by many as the outstanding hero of the Rorke's Drift action, was born in St Andrews in London. He enlisted in the 85th Regiment in London in November 1849 as a seventeen-year-old. After service in Ireland and Mauritius he then left as a sergeant for the Cape and participated in the 8th Frontier or 'Kaffir' War. After returning to England he transferred to the Commissariat Staff Corps in 1862, becoming Colour-Sergeant in 1863. After service in Canada (1868–71) he went to South Africa as Acting Assistant Commissary in December 1877.

The crossing of the Buffalo river was, by all accounts, a most dramatic and stirring sight. In the early morning fog the red-coated imperial infantry were slowly ferried across on the two Rorke's Drift ponts (floating bridges), the imperial cavalry crossing in the shallows. The Natal Native Contingent presented one of the more spectacular sights. A 'truly unforgettable scene' was witnessed by Lieutenant Harford, as his NNC unit crossed 'Zulu style':

> the leading company formed a double chain right across the river, leaving a pathway for the remainder to pass through. The men forming the chain clasped hands and at the moment they entered the water, started to hum a kind of war-chant which was taken up by every Company as they passed over. The sound that this produced was like a gigantic swarm of bees buzzing about us and sufficient to scare crocodiles or anything else away… it was both a curious and a grand sight.[31]

Another eyewitness, Lieutenant Coghill, was similarly fascinated by the NNC methods, describing them:

entering the cold water which must have reached up as far as
their waists and without the shouting which usually accompanies
them... but with a low kind of whistle as they felt the cold water
rising up their naked bodies the further they advanced into the
stream.[32]

As soon as the cavalry and 24th regulars were across and had
'crowned' the ridge on the Zulu side, the remainder of the
column wagon train commenced their crossing. It was a foretaste of the logistical problems to come. Captain Hallam Parr
recalled this as

weary work... wagons had to be brought down as near the pont
as possible, the oxen outspanned and driven round to the shallows
to wade and swim across while the wagon was pushed on to the
pont by hand.[33]

As the fog lifted on the Zulu side:

a very pretty sight presented itself as the troops were dotted about
over the rolling hills in 'Receive Cavalry' square formation showing up distinctly in the clear atmosphere.

Horsemen galloped through and amongst them, linking up to
form scouting and looting parties. In the words of the *Natal Times*,
the 'despoiling of the Egyptians had begun' – herds of cattle and
sheep were rapidly rounded up and 'I do not doubt that two
thirds of the fine imposed on the Zulu King were captured by
the Frontier Light Horse who are adept at stripping the country
of cattle'.[34] The crossing was unopposed – its seem to augur well
for the future. Very few Zulu were to be seen.

Skirmish at Sihayo's Kraal (12 January 1879)

Within twenty-four hours of the crossing, Chelmsford's No.3
Column tasted its first blood. Four miles from the river in the
Bashee valley, a reconnaissance force under Major Dartnell

located Chief Sihayo's kraal, Sokhexe, situated deep in the rocky fastness. It was an appropriate target, in view of the earlier border incursions by the chief's sons that had helped precipitate the war. Here, for the first time, the column experienced determined Zulu resistance and defiance, as from the surrounding rocks and caves sporadic shots were fired, accompanied by taunts such as 'what were we doing riding down along here' and 'we had better try and come up'.[36]

It was a brief but bitter skirmish, the first ragged Zulu volley killing or wounding several NNC attackers. As the Imperial Cavalry charged the hill from the east, the veteran 1st/24th Regulars closed in for the kill. Once again, as at Centane, the volley fire of the new Martini-Henry rifle proved decisive. Thus Lieutenant Harford, heroically involved in close-quarter fighting from rock to rock, testified to its deadly effects. He saw 'several dead Zulus' hanging from the main cave:

> caught in the monkey-rope creepers and bits of bush... later on I learnt that a Company of the 24th Regiment had been firing at this particular cave for some time.[37]

Chief Sihayo was significantly absent, away at Ulundi, but one of the first Zulu to be shot dead was one of his sons. Once the 24th Regulars had secured a position overlooking the main cave the stronghold was quickly and successfully stormed – by 9a.m. the fighting was over. Hallam Parr recorded losses of two NNC killed (one officer, one NCO) and twelve NNC wounded, compared to up to forty dead Zulu. It was an easy victory for No.3 column, considerably sweetened by the capture of over 300 head of cattle, twenty horses and many goats and sheep.

According to at least two contemporary eyewitnesses, this Zulu humiliation and small but decisive British victory had major impli-cations for Cetshwayo's future strategy and for the subsequent battles at Isandlwana and Rorke's Drift ten days later. Until the Sihayo skirmish on 12 January 1879, Cetshwayo's strategy had certainly been relatively passive, one of limited but active defence accompanied by attempts at conciliation (including the sending of some cattle as compensation for Sihayo's alleged border violations). It was a policy merely of hit-and-run tactics, with the preferred aim of picking off isolated columns and hopefully inflicting severe enough casualties to encourage a British withdrawal. The humiliation of his close ally Chief Sihayo, however, was apparently a watershed event for Cetshwayo, encouraging a much more belligerent posture. Thus Coghill's last letter, written on 18 January, reported receiving

> information that as soon as Cetshwayo heard that we had burnt Sihayo's kraal that he despatched four regiments to wipe out the disgrace... According to tradition Zulu tactics are to attack in 'the horns of the morning' ie when the tops of the horns of the cattle in the kraals are just discernible from the general mass against the sky. [38]

His evidence is heavily corroborated by Hallam Parr. After interviewing a Zulu of the uNokhenke regiment, present at the king's final pre-war gathering, he gave evidence that the Sihayo engagement had 'greatly enraged the Zulu King', who

> immediately on receiving news of destruction of the kraal of one of his favourite captains, gave orders for the formation of the forces which were to eat up the English columns.

According to custom, the king reviewed them before they left, so that they might hear his last words:

> I am sending you against the white man, the white man who has invaded Zululand and driven away your cattle. You are to go against the column at Ishyane [Rorke's Drift] and drive it back into Natal, and if the river will allow, follow it into Natal and go on up the Drakensburg. [39]

Such evidence accorded with Chelmsford's own intelligence reports. In one memo written on 8 January 1879, Chelmsford wrote: 'all the reports which reach me tend to show that the

Zulus intend, if possible, to make raids into Natal when the several columns move forward'.[40]

The Doomed Isandlwana Camp Site – 20–22 January 1879

Amidst these ominous intelligence reports, the column pushed on further into Zululand. Within only a mile or two, the transport situation had become critical. It was a tortuous journey – taking over a week to cover the ten miles by wagon track to the next camp site at Isandlwana. The whole column, and in particular the 24th, were 'worked hard', the worst obstacle being 'low lying bits of track on soft soil made swampy by springs and wet weather into which the heavy wagons sank axle deep'.[41] The threat of bad weather was ever present. Earlier, Lieutenant Coghill had written:

I may give you a notion how the mountain streams come down. A bullock-wagon was crossing a small spruit or stream with enough water to cover the soles of your boot but with steep banks. Two teams of 32 oxen were vainly struggling to drag the heavy wagon out, the wheel having stuck – when down came the river. They had *just* time to cut loose the oxen, and the wagon and everything on it was swept away into the Tugela and thence to the sea.[42]

Captain Clery, one of Chelmsford's staff officers, was later highly critical of the General's transport arrangements. Acknowledging that he would have a 'lot to say about many things that were far from perfect with this column', he stressed that the

most unfortunate was the utter break down of the transport branch of the Commissariat… as our transport was utterly deficient we had to wait till the 20th before we could advance.[43]

The arrangement of the centre column's camp beneath the ominous sphinx-like crag of Isandlwana on 20 January 1879, one of several designated staging posts on the road to Ulundi, immediately revealed a number of defensive vulnerabilities. While it was located close by wood and water supplies, Chelmsford chose neither to entrench the camp or laager (form a defensive circle) for his 100-odd wagons. At the subsequent Court of Inquiry into the Isandlwana disaster, it was pointed out that the predominantly rocky ground was unsuited for digging and the wagons had to be kept unharnessed and mobile in order to sustain the essential twenty-mile circuitous return journey between the camp site and the main supply base at Rorke's Drift. Thus logistical imperatives had already severely compromised the defensive capabilities of the Isandlwana garrison. Moreover, it was argued that neither laagering and entrenchment were justified by the temporary nature of the camp site. The situation was not helped by the scattered and sprawling nature of the camp site. The camp fronted nearly east and was partly pitched on the Nek, or Saddle, between two small hills (the hill on the left or north being the higher, and inaccessible), and partly on the slopes below the inaccessible hill. It was organised as follows: the 1/24th camp was situated on the right of the wagon track, while on the other side of the track was the mainly colonial mounted infantry and volunteer horse. Next in line was the 'N' Battery of the Royal Artillery camp; above and a little to the south of the Nek were the tents of Glyn and the column staff. Further to the left was the camp of the 2nd Battalion 24th Regiment and on the extreme left was the camp of the 1st/2nd Battalion, 3rd Regiment of the Natal Native Contingent. Lieutenant Harford, an NNC commander, observed the setting-up of his camp:

> Our camp was on the extreme left… just below Isandlwana hill itself… plenty of wood being close at hand below the hill. The natives soon set to work to run up shelters for themselves… a queer-looking place they made of it, being packed like sardines, the space allotted to them being very limited.[44]

The whole camp extended to about a one-mile frontage, protected only to the rear by the mountain and lacking any physical defensive barriers to the front or flank. It was a potential defensive nightmare, with the two battalions' ammunition wagons positioned as much as half a mile apart. The camp was also severely compromised by the restricted use of vedettes (mounted sentries) and cavalry in general who, until the fateful 22 January, were not deployed beyond the lip of the Nqutu Plateau and were therefore unable to detect the arrival and concealment of the main Zulu army. Some of Chelmsford's officers were aware of these defensive problems. Colonel Glyn's suggestion that the camp be laagered was rejected on the grounds of the time delay and, again, the need to keep the wagons mobile for supply purposes. An officer of the 24th Foot, Lieutenant Melvill, also expressed unease over the vulnerable deployment of the camp, as did several Boer scouts. Thus Melvill addressed a staff officer:

> I know what you are thinking by your face Sir, you are abusing the camp and you are quite right. These Zulus will charge home and with our small numbers we ought to be in laager or at any rate be prepared to stand shoulder to shoulder.[45]

To Chelmsford, the main problem remained – how to locate and bring to battle the main Zulu army, now reliably reported as having departed from the Zulu capital several days earlier. It was in trying to solve this problem that a second tactical error was committed.

On 21 January, a force of mounted men and two companies of the third Natal Native Contingent commanded by Major Dartnell and Commandant Lonsdale were sent out to the Malakata and Hlazakazi hills, both to scout for enemy activity and examine the country surrounding the kraal of Maylan, 'a Chief whose stronghold some ten miles away from Isandlwana hill was supposed to be of importance'.[46] Lieutenant Harford was one of those officers seconded to this reconnoitring force. Hearing the news in Lieutenant Pope's tent while 'looking at some of his sketches and he at mine', and not anticipating the disaster that would follow, he 'very stupidly' took 'but a few biscuits thinking we shall be back in camp before nightfall'. In fact, it was to be 'some 56 hours or a little over two days before we got food of any sort'. During these last fateful hours, the lives of at least two of his fellow European NNC officers were saved, as, 'terribly disappointed at losing the

chance to fight', they were substituted by their unfortunate colleagues as they departed. Harford vividly recalled his last sight of
the doomed camp on the morning of 21 January:

> As the sun rose that morning there was a very wonderful sky scene.
> Overhanging Isandlwana and the camp was a long, tortuous, more
> or less low-lying dark cloud based on the horizon, much in the
> same form as a trail of smoke from the funnel of a steamer and
> ending immediately above Isandlwana hill, which, as the sun got
> higher, was first tinted almost blood red, then passing into ashy-
> brown with broad golden edges, assuming a marvellous variety
> of tints under the rise of the sun. And there it hung for the best
> part of the morning, frowning as it were over the ill fated camp.
> I have never forgotten it.[47]

That evening, having covered at least fifteen miles from the camp,
Dartnell and Lonsdale spotted 'a regular swarm of Zulus... estimated to be over 1,000 men who swept down... in their horn
formation', and which threatened to surround their small contingent. Consequently, an urgent message for help was sent to
Chelmsford via Lieutenant Walsh, accompanied by three mounted
infantry men.

It was almost certainly the start of a Zulu deception plan and
Dartnell and his subordinates, Lonsdale and Harford, had been
duly and utterly deceived. As Harford later ruefully recalled: 'it
had seemed evident... that we were opposed by a very large *impi*
if not the whole Zulu army'.[48] In fact, the main Zulu army had
already arrived, but several miles to the north, only five miles
from the camp, and lay concealed in the Mbaso valley. It was
led by two of Cetshwayo's best tacticians, the Zulu commanders
Ntshingwayo and Mvengwana.

In hindsight, Major Clery's memo of 17 February confirmed
his misgivings about the Dartnell expedition. He had

> felt from the very first very much averse to this movement of send-
> ing out irregulars under commands of irregular officers amounting
> to half the force on a roving commission of this sort. When word

came in that they were going to bivouack out, I could not help speaking strongly to Colonel Glyn on the problems of this sort of thing, dragging the rest of the force into any sort of compromising enterprise that these people may get messed up in.[49]

On the arrival of Dartnell's messengers, it was in fact Major Clery who was tasked by Colonel Glyn to take the fateful pencilled message to the General. He recalled,

the General's tent was close by so I roused him up. Lying on my face and hands close to his camp bed I can still remember how I read out from that crumpled piece of notepaper, written across in pencil, word after word what I just previously had such difficulty in deciphering in my own tent. The General did not hesitate much. He said, 'order the 2nd 24th 4 guns and all the mounted troops remaining, to get ready to start at daybreak'. He also added 'order up Colonel Durnford with the troops he has to reinforce the Camp'.

Clery then 'went direct to each of the Commanders and gave the General's orders'. Clery's last official duty acting on behalf of Colonel Glyn was to write to 'poor Colonel Pulleine', who commanded the 1st/24th, officially as follows:

you will be in command of the camp in the absence of Colonel Glyn – draw in your line of defence while the force with the General is out of the Camp – draw in your infantry out of line first, in conformity. Keep cavalry vedettes still well to the front – act strictly on the defensive. Keep a wagon loaded with ammunition ready to start at once should the General's force be in need of it. Colonel Durnford has been ordered up for Rorke's Drift to reinforce the camp.

I sent this to Colonel Pulleine by my own servant, and just before leaving the camp I went myself to his tent to ensure that he had got it. I saw him and again verbally repeated what he had received in writing, laying stress on the point that his mission was simply to hold and keep the camp.[50]

Dartnell's message had reached Chelmsford at around 2.30a.m. on 22 January, and he now made what turned out to be his third fatal error, which effectively split his forces even further. It was a similar tactical error to that made barely three years earlier by one General Custer at the battle of the Little Big Horn, in July 1876. At around 4a.m. on 22 January, Chelmsford led over half his force, six companies of the 2nd/24th and four out of the six seven-pounder guns, on what proved to be a fruitless mission to reinforce the beleaguered Dartnell. Only six companies, five of the 1/24th and one of the 2/24th, supported by several mounted colonial units and African NNC contingents, were left in camp under command of forty-one-year-old Lieutenant-Colonel Henry Pulleine. Again, as with Lieutenant Harford's earlier departure, it was to prove to be a most poignant farewell. Years later, Captain Hallam-Parr, like Lieutenant Harford, remained traumatised by the memories of what turned out to be their last farewells to doomed comrades on that tragic 'Black Wednesday', 22 January 1879:

> On looking back to that Wednesday morning how every detail seems to stand out in relief! The hurried and careless farewell to the comrades in my tent... my servant who was to leave for Natal that very morning saying when he brought my horse, 'I shall be here, Sir, when you are back; the wagons are not to start today now this force is going out'. The half laughing condolences to the 1/24th as they watched the troops move out of the camp; the men not for duty turning out for the routine work of the camp; the position of the tents and wagons serve to make striking the contrast between the departure and the return to the ill-fated camp.[51]

3

The Isandlwana Massacre:
Day of the Aasvogels

Not even on the recent battlefields of Europe, although hundreds were lying where now I only saw tens, was there a more sickening or heartrending sight. The corpses of our poor soldiers, whites and natives, lay thick upon the ground in clusters, together with the fragments of our commissariat wagons, broken and wrecked, and rifled of their contents, such as flour, sugar, tea, biscuits mealies, oats etc. The dead bodies of the men lay as they had fallen but mostly with their boots and shirts on, or, perhaps, a pair of trousers or remnants of a coat... in many instances they lay with sixty or seventy cartridges surrounding them, thus showing they had fought to the very last.

C.L. Norris-Newman, In Zululand with the British throughout
the war of 1879, *pp. 62-3*

On Tuesday morning, 11 February 1879, Britain's newspapers brought terrible tidings from Zululand, South Africa. Barely three weeks earlier, Chelmsford's No. 3 centre column camp at Isandlwana had been overrun and virtually annihilated by a massive Zulu *impi*. Stunned disbelief greeted this terrible news and a profound sense of horror pervaded the normally genteel breakfast-time of countless Victorian parlours. Major-General

W.C.F Molyneux of the 22nd Foot was one of many who vividly recalled the devastating news of that morning:

> Early on that morning my man (Private Noot of the 2nd Battalion 24th) rushed into my room with *The Times*, 'Oh sir, the Regiment has been cut up by the Zulus and Mr Pope (who commanded Noot's company) and a lot of officers killed... the man was mad with rage. I read the account, ordered breakfast to be ready at once that I might be in Pall Mall as soon as possible. 'We will see if we can't go out together, I added and, at this, the good fellow began to look less mournful.[1]

Similarly, as news reached a regimental dinner held at Hay Castle, shocked fellow officers watched as Colonel Thomas, who knew the 24th officers intimately, staggered from the room overcome with grief.[2]

As the scale of the tragedy unfolded over the next few weeks, it soon became clear that this battle constituted one of the greatest single disasters of Queen Victoria's reign – it was a major blow to Britain's military self-confidence. Over 1,300 men of the 1,700-strong garrison left by Chelmsford to guard the camp had been massacred, including around 600 seasoned imperial regulars of the 1st and 2nd Battalions 24th Regiment of Foot. Fifty-two regular and colonial officers had died in this debâcle, more than at the battle of Waterloo over six decades earlier. Barely fifty Europeans had escaped, mostly on horseback. Only the earlier disaster at Kabul in January 1842 in any way compared with the scale of losses sustained (over 75 per cent casualties), when a 16,000-strong Anglo-Indian army perished in a desperate retreat through the snow-covered Afghan passes (including over 400 regulars of the 44th Foot).

Three weeks earlier, for the sleepy garrison left behind at Isandlwana camp, so abruptly roused by the morning 'reveille bugle' on Wednesday 22 January 1879, the prospect of such a major defeat had been unthinkable. As Chelmsford's column trudged away into the night gloom there seemed to be sufficient men and modern guns (including nearly half a million rounds of

ammunition) to comfortably defend the camp against any con-
certed Zulu attack. The forces remaining behind on that fate-
ful day included five companies of the 1st Battalion 24th Foot
(Warwickshire Regiment);A Company commanded by Lieutenant
Francis Porteous, C Company commanded by Captain Reginald
Younghusband, E Company commanded by Lieutenant Charles
Cavaye, F Company commanded by Captain William Mostyn
and H Company commanded by Captain George Wardell. The
sixth company of regulars, G Company under Lieutenant Charles
Pope, was the lone company from the 2nd Battalion 24th Foot.
F.W.D. Jackson suggests there may even have been an additional
weaker 'composite company' of eighty-odd men of the 2nd/24th
left behind by Chelmsford.[3] Other major contingents and units
which made up the approximate 1,700-man garrison included
around seventy Royal Artillery men (operating the two seven-
pounder guns), five companies of white-officered Natal Native
Contingent (NNC) infantry, and several mounted African and
European colonial units e.g. the Newcastle Mounted Rifles and
the Edendale contingent. These were supplemented by over 100
camp 'casuals' (grooms, servants, cooks, drivers etc).

In order to understand this potentially complex battle, it can
be conveniently divided into three stages: the opening salvos from
8a.m. to 12 noon approximately, the main battle from midday to
1p.m., and thirdly the climax and final moments of the battle
between 1p.m. and 1.15p.m.

First Contacts and Opening Salvos
(8a.m. to 12 noon approximately)

After the departure of Chelmsford's column and the early-morning
awakening, the garrison at Isandlwana had slowly settled down to
normal routine. Breakfast was prepared, the oxen and horses were
fed, the night pickets were slowly relieved and work recommenced
on the road. With the prospect of another restful day in camp,
morale was undoubtedly high. The only hint of danger arrived in
the form of an African vedette who reported a Zulu presence to
the north-east of the camp. The ever-cautious and administratively

thorough Lieutenant-Colonel Pulleine immediately dispatched a scribbled note reading 'Report just come in that the Zulus are advancing in force from the left front of the camp, 8.05am'.[4] The slow descent into one of the most tragic episodes in British military history had begun. All was still very calm in the camp area. Private Wilson of the 1st/24th recalled the routine reaction to this first sighting of the Zulu army:

> The regiment fell in about 8am the 'fall-in' going while we were at breakfast and marched to the camp of the 2nd/24th Regiment. The bandsmen were told off as bearers, ammunition carriers and cooks. I was one of the stretcher party which fell-in with the regiment, the remainder remaining in camp. The regiment remained under arms up to 10.30 or 11am when Colonel Durnford's party came in.[5]

Another survivor, Private J. Bickley, also of the 1st/24th Regiment, recorded the scene in more detail:

> At about 7.45am on 22nd January, 1879, one of the Volunteers who had been away from camp on picket duty came in and made a report to the Commanding Officer; immediately after this I heard Mr Melvill give the order to the Bugler to sound the 'Fall-in' and add 'Sound the column call'. Each corps fell-in front of its own camp and the picquets were then brought in, consisting of a company of each battalion of the 24th Regiment. The infantry formed up in front of an open space between the camps of the 2nd/24th Regiment and the Royal Artillery. At this time I was posted as a picquet sentry at the Officers' Mess, all the Service having fallen in with their companies. About half an hour after the column had fallen in Colonel Durnford's column marched in…[6]

The stage was now set for a fateful meeting between Colonel Durnford of the Royal Engineers, earlier ordered up from Rorke's Drift by direct orders of Lord Chelmsford, with his 500-strong mounted African colonial contingents, and Pulleine, the camp commander. Most sources agree that Colonel Durnford, four years senior to Pulleine, took control of the camp on his arrival, Lieutenant Essex and other officers confirming that he immediately 'assumed command'.[7] Nevertheless, one eyewitness, Lieutenant Stafford, who admittedly wrote his memoirs over sixty years later, and who had accompanied Durnford to Pulleine's tent, postulated 'from what I could hear an argument was taking place between Durnford and Pulleine as to who was the senior. Colonel Pulleine agreed to give way…'.[8] In any event, it was Durnford's subsequent decision-making which was to play a crucial role in the fatal compromise of the garrison's tactical position. Following further reports of Zulu activity on the plateau, Durnford, after a hasty lunch with Pulleine, proposed a foray onto the Nqutu Plateau, to be accompanied by a contingent from the imperial infantry. This request clearly compromised Pulleine's earlier firm orders from Glyn via Clery to 'draw in and defend the camp' – the departure of even two companies, one-third of the imperial company strength, would clearly compromise this order and the overall integrity of the camp's defences. It must have been an uneasy conversation between a cautious Lieutenant-Colonel Pulleine with no combat experience and Durnford, the more cavalier, colourful and adventurous Royal Engineer officer. Lieutenant Cochrane, a crucial eyewitness to this conversation, while acknowledging that Durnford had taken over command from Colonel Pulleine, who had given him a verbal report on the state of the troops in camp at the time, claimed that Pulleine initially stood his ground on the issue of lending Durnford imperial infantry support. Cochrane reported that Pulleine 'stated the orders he had received viz, to defend the camp, these orders were repeated two or three times in the conversation'.[9]

Pulleine's firm stand undoubtedly reflected the considerable support he received from other 24th Regiment officers, notably Lieutenant Melvill, who remonstrated with Durnford: 'Colonel I really do not think Colonel Pulleine would being doing right to send any men out to the camp when his orders are to defend the camp.' Durnford allegedly replied 'very well, it does not much matter, we will not take them', adding the rider that if he 'got into difficulties he could count on Pulleine to help him out'.[10]

Between 10.30 and 11.30a.m. Durnford left the camp with his
Basuto horsemen, including the Hlubi and Edendale contingents,
in order to follow up the continuing reports of Zulu activity to
the east. He was accompanied by the Rocket Battery under Major
Russell and several contingents of the Natal Native Contingent
(including D Company under Captain Nourse), and passed to
the south of the conical copje (see map, p.105). They were an
ill-armed force for what awaited them on the plateau. Lieutenant
Stafford duly noted that while Durnford 'gave orders that full
ammunition was to be issued, it may be here mentioned that the
Native Contingent were armed with rifles to the extent of one to
every ten men, the remainder carrying assegais and shields'.[11]

Back at camp, soon after Durnford's departure, the imperial
regulars were ordered to fall out for lunch 'with orders not to
take off our accoutrements... to get our dinners as quickly as
possible and be in readiness to fall-in at any moment'.[12] The
diary of Lieutenant Pope of the 1st/24th, discovered on the
battlefield after the massacre, succinctly captures the unfolding
drama of that fateful morning, starting with Chelmsford's departure and abruptly ending minutes before the main Zulu army
attacked:

> 22nd January 1879 – 4am – A, C, D, E, F, H Companies of ours
> – 12-3 NNC – mounted troops and four guns off.
> Great firing
> Relieved by 1-24th
> Alarm
> 3 Columns Zulus and mounted men on hill E
> Turn out
> 7,000 (!!!) *more* E.N.E. 4,000 of whom went round Lion's kop
> Durnford Basutos, arrive and pursue – Rocket battery
> Zulus retire everywhere
> Men fall out for dinner.[13]

Around this time, however, the beginnings of what became a fatal
over-extension of the camp defences had already begun. Between
10.30 and 11a.m., one imperial company, No.5 or E Company

under Lieutenant Charles Cavaye, was suddenly deployed outwards to a position on the spur to the extreme left of the camp, a distance of over 1,500 yards. What prompted this risky deployment, literally 'out of sight of the camp' and in direct defiance of Chelmsford's orders, may never be known, but the requisite orders must have been given by Colonel Pulleine and may have either reflected a limited response to further reports of sightings 'with field glasses' of 'kaffirs on the hills to the left quite distinctly' or a belated desire by Pulleine to give at least some support to Durnford's forces on the Nqutu Plateau. Both Private Bickley's and Private Williams' accounts confirm that 'No. 5 company were sent out to the left in skirmishing order to support some of the native contingent' earlier stationed on this extreme position on the Spur.[14]

Meanwhile, on the Nqutu Plateau the main Zulu *impi* had finally been located, but unfortunately not by Chelmsford. He was now over ten miles away from the ill-fated camp. Thus, several miles to the north of the camp, Lieutenant Raw's patrol, casually cantering across the Nqutu Plateau and half-heartedly chasing some Zulu boy herders and their cattle, stopped to peer over the edge of a concealed ravine (the Ngwebeni valley) and were horrified to discover thousands of Zulu warriors crouched in silence in the valley bottom. The shock and surprise was mutual; the Zulu commanders, Ntshingwayo and Mavumengwana, had indeed not planned to attack Isandlwana until the next day, but once discovered, the lead elements of their *impis* (primarily the Umcijo regiment) impetuously committed themselves to a full-scale attack on the weakened Isandlwana garrison. James Hamer, accompanying Raw and his troop, was one of the few survivors to recall this heart-stopping, indeed eerie, scene:

> after going some little way we tried to capture some cattle. They dropped over a ridge... we saw the Zulus like ants in front of us – in perfect order as quiet as mice and stretched across in even lines. We estimated those we saw at 12,000.[15]

Adopting their traditional 'beast's horn' formation, two horns travelling right and left with their 'chest' and 'loins' bringing up the centre, the regiments raced towards Raw's and Durnford's scattered troops. Lieutenant Raw also vividly recaptured this unnerving spectacle: 'They turned and fell upon us... the whole army shewing [*sic*] itself from below the hill and in front of where they had evidently been waiting'.[16] The mounted men now conducted an amazingly orderly retreat, sporadically stopping to fire volleys at the running *impis*. Lieutenant Stafford was caught up in one of the hastily retreating groups:

> there was a force of some 2,000 Zulus steadily advancing several hundred yards off. My first shot at 800 yards went over the enemy and I distinctly recollect the second shot with my sight at 700 yards to have got on the target.[17]

Frantic riders were simultaneously deployed ahead to warn both the rest of Durnford's forces on the plateau and Pulleine's forces in camp. Lieutenant Scott of the Natal Carbineers, on vedette duty over the left ridge, rode past the slowly retiring mounted troopers shouting: 'get back to the camp immediately or you will be killed. The Zulus are in immense strength and are already encircling the camp.'[18] This frightening spectacle had already been too much for Captain Barry's less mobile supporting NNC infantry, who promptly broke and ran.

In the meantime, Pulleine's forces in the camp area had been further overextended. As Cavaye's E Company commenced heavy firing against the rapidly extending Zulu right horn, cascading over the lip of the escarpment, a second company, F or No. 1 Company under Captain William Mostyn and Lieutenant Edward Dyson, as well as two companies of NNC, had arrived in support. Pulleine had now committed one-third of the imperial garrison to this remote position. Soon afterwards, the depleted camp artillery, comprising the two seven-pounder guns and commanded by Major Stuart Smith, were rapidly deployed onto a knoll several hundred metres to the east of the camp and commenced firing 'on the Zulus as they came down the hills to our left and front left'.[19] It was around 12 noon – the second or main phase of the battle of Isandlwana had begun.

The Main Battle Commences
(12 noon to 1p.m. approximately)

It was the slower-moving Rocket Battery, commanded by Major Russell and struggling to keep up with Durnford's forces, that first bore the brunt of the massed Zulu attack as the left horn surged over the lip of the Nqutu ridge. Perhaps subconsciously criticising Durnford's continuing 'gung-ho' tactics, Captain Nourse of the NNC, escorting the Rocket Battery, later recalled how Durnford 'went too fast and left us some two miles in the rear'.[20] Such was the speed of the Zulu envelopment that the rocket crew had only seconds to fire one missile before being overwhelmed. Soon all the mule drivers and five out of the eight artillery men lay dead and mutilated. The three European survivors, 1st/24th Battalion Privates Grant, Trainer and Johnson, vividly recalled the horror of the moment. Johnson wrote:

> While we were getting into action the Zulus kept coming out of a kloof on our left, which the big guns had been shelling from the camp. We had time to fire our rocket when they came over the hill in masses and commenced to fire on us. As soon as they opened fire the mules carrying the rockets broke away. The Native Contingent, who were in the rear of us, after firing a few shots ran away. I observed that a great number of them were unable to extract the empty cartridge cases after firing and offered to do so for some of them but they would not give me their rifles.[21]

The Battery had been leaderless and highly vulnerable from the very first moment. Both Grant and Trainer confirmed how Major Russell had been killed 'by the first volley', Grant noting that their exposure had been total, 'owing to the bad position we were in at the foot of the hill'.

Elsewhere, on the extreme left, Cavaye's, Mostyn's and Dyson's companies on the Spur continued firing, causing significant losses to the uDudu, isaNgqu and iMbube regiments of the Zulu right horn. They were reinforced by C Company under Captain Reginald Younghusband, which had been hastily ordered in support by Pulleine. Half of the imperial regulars were now placed in a precarious position over a mile from the relative safety of the camp area and the mountain. Captain Edward Essex of the 75th Regiment (one of only five imperial officers who survived the disaster, and who was thereafter appropriately named 'Lucky Essex' by his brother officers), represented the only key European witness to the first signs of crisis on the British left wing and the potentially fatal encirclement by the Zulu. Riding out of camp and passing Mostyn's advancing company at around noon, he noted Durnford's distant retreat from the escarpment 'but did not see the enemy' and 'at the far side of the crest of the hill' found Cavaye's company, with Dyson's section 'being detached about 500 yards to the left front'. All were 'in extended order engaging the enemy who was moving in similar formation towards our left, keeping at about 800 yards from our line'. As Mostyn's company plugged the gaps, the line was further prolonged 'on our right along the crest of the hill by a body of native infantry'. With undoubted misgiving, he further observed that while the enemy had 'little progress' as regards his advance, it 'appeared to be moving at a rapid pace towards our left'. Confirmation of the British overstretch and successful Zulu outflanking on the left wing arrived a mere 'five minutes after the arrival of Captain Mostyn's company', as:

> I was informed by Lieutenant Melvill, Adjutant of the first bat-
> talion of the 24th Regiment, that a fresh body of the enemy was
> appearing in force in our rear and requested me to direct the left
> of the line… to fall back slowly, keeping up the fire. This I did…
> I found, however, that it had already retired.[22]

The situation was only slightly more stable in the central camp area. As Durnford's and Shepstone's riders continually rushed in from the Nqutu Plateau, bearing the increasingly ominous tidings concerning the rapidity of the Zulu advance, an undoubtedly harassed Pulleine completed his deployments of the remaining three imperial companies to the left front of the camp, in order to confront the main Zulu 'chest' (consisting initially of the

UmCijo, Xhapo, and uMbonambi regiments) swarming across the ridge and heading towards the distinctive feature known as the 'Conical Kopje'. The three remaining imperial companies, H Company under Captain Wardell, A Company under Captain Francis Porteous and G Company 2/24th under Lieutenant Pope, were deployed to reinforce and protect the two artillery pieces with heavy volley fire. The firing line on the left was completed by the arrival of the undoubtedly fatigued detachments of Cavaye, Mostyn and Dyson returning from the Spur. The position to their extreme left was occupied by Captain Younghusband's C Company, arguably weakened by the inter-position of the ill-armed Natal Native horse and NNC contingents commanded by Captain Erskine, Stafford and possibly returned sections of Barry's already demoralised companies. One NNC company, No.6 Company under Captain Krohn, was kept in reserve. In these final, fixed positions the battle temporarily stabilised, with the various Zulu regiments packed into their distinctive, menacing crescent formation. All six imperial companies had now assumed the classic battle formation for defending against a hostile attack from a colonial enemy, tactics constantly drilled into the minds of every imperial officer and soldier at Sandhurst, Aldershot and Brecon. With the arrival of Durnford's force of roughly 200 men on the right flank, the combined volley fire from up to 1,000 Martini-Henry rifles and carbines, reinforced by shells and, ultimately, case shot from the two seven-pounder guns, ensured that most Zulu casualties occurred at this point. For a brief while it must have seemed that Chelmsford's and Pulleine's battle plans might yet come to fruition. Another survivor, Lieutenant Horace Smith-Dorrien (later to achieve fame as a commander in the British Expeditionary Force in 1914), testified to the initial steadiness of the imperial lines:

> The Zulu army... moved steadily on to the where the five companies of the 24th were lying down covering the camp. They were giving vent to no loud war-cries but to a low musical murmuring noise which gave the impression of bees getting nearer and nearer. Here was a more serious matter for these brave warriors, for the

regiment opposed to them were no boy recruits, but war-worn matured men mostly with beards and fresh from campaigning in the old colony were they had carried everything before them. Possessed of splendid discipline and sure of success, they lay on their position making every round tell, so much that when the Zulu army was 400 yards off it wavered.[23]

As hundreds of Zulu crouched down beneath their shields in desperate and pitiful attempts to evade the merciless tirade, morale remained high amongst the imperial regulars. Other eyewitnesses confirmed this brief imperial domination of the battlefield as a mood of confidence, almost nonchalance, permeated through to the rank and file. James Brickhill, a column interpreter, remarked on 'the increasing gun roll'[24] sustained by the regular infantry, with Lieutenant Essex, now returned from the Spur and positioned near the central firing line, observing the 24th Foot regulars 'laughing, chattering and even joking as they unleashed volley after volley into the dense black masses'.[25]

It was a veritable false sense of security. The imperial forces were still overextended over a two-mile front and, in the words of D.R. Morris, defending a great deal of 'unnecessary real estate'.[26] Behind the lines detached officers such as Lieutenant Horace Smith-Dorrien of the 95th Regiment had rounded up camp casuals to break open ammunition boxes 'as fast as we could'. There were other ominous signs. The artillery fire sustained by 'N' Battery Royal Artillery was, for instance, not as effective as it could have been. After initially firing 'with great effect', destroying at least one kraal and twenty-odd Zulu hidden within it, fire control and direction became less co-ordinated, one gun firing

on to the Zulus coming down the ridge on our left flank and the other onto those advancing on Colonel Durnford's party to our left front.[27]

Lieutenant Stafford volunteered other reasons for the comparative ineffectiveness of the artillery fire. He described it as:

erratic, owing to the fact that the guns had not been unlimbered and were on carriages to which the horses were harnessed – the horses were naturally excited and became unmanageable.

He even claimed a 'blue on blue' instance, when a group of colonial volunteers led by Lieutenant Roberts of Pinetown had retreated into a kraal on the ledge of the ridge only to be 'shelled by our artillery' and even that Roberts met his death 'as a result of this blunder'.[28] An African observer named Malindi of the 2nd/3rd NNC also confirmed: 'I did not think the shells did much execution except one which burst in a group of Zulus'.[29] Zulu tactics may also have undermined the effectiveness of the guns. Many, observing the gunners springing back before the lanyards were pulled, apparently threw themselves down at the signal screaming 'Umoya' ('only wind'), reducing the casualties as the shells whistled harmlessly over their heads.[30] In any event, it was perhaps too much to expect a mere two artillery pieces to have a major impact on a rapidly advancing enemy front, thousands of yards in extent.

The Climax and Final Moments of the Battle *(1p.m.–1.15p.m. approximately)*

In any event, the isolated guns could not operate without sustained infantry support, and abruptly and inexplicably at one momentous point, sometime between 1 and 1.15p.m., the imperial volley fire slackened and in some cases stopped, as the six companies were rapidly recalled (allegedly by a last bugle call) to the tented areas. Hamer remembered this decisive watershed in the battle. After returning from the Plateau, he had 'then joined some soldiers in front of the camp and fired away as far as possible but we had to run as the Zulus came at us like ants on all sides'.[31] With the imperial lines irrevocably broken and outflanked, organised resistance soon ceased. The final moments, amounting to minutes in some cases, can only be loosely pieced together from the accounts of survivors and a few Zulu eyewitnesses. For the less mobile imperial infantrymen the one certainty was death at the hands of an enemy who traditionally took no prisoners. In the words of one Zulu, Kumbeka Gwabe, an UmCijo veteran: 'we spared no lives and did not ask for any mercy ourselves'.

What is known is that there were at least two catastrophic breaks in this clearly overextended British line. One certainly occurred on the extreme right flank, as Colonel Durnford and his men retreated from what had been a brief but successful defence based on either the Mpofane or Nyonga donga or gully (see map, p.105). A second break, as we shall see, possibly occurred on the exposed left wing, due either to the collapse of the ill-armed NNC position or ammunition failure or both.

It is probable that Mostyn's, Cavaye's and Dyson's men were some of the first to be overrun and annihilated, possibly with not even time to fix bayonets. In the dramatic words of D.R. Morris: 'there was a brief flurry and A and F Companies were blotted; not a man survived'.[32] A rare Zulu eyewitness account suggests their early and complete demise:

> The soldiers were at this time in the camp having come back from the front all but two companies which went on the hill and never returned – they were everyone of them killed.[33]

As the isolated groups of imperial infantry fought on, a confused panicking mob of whites and blacks hopelessly entangled together rolled back into the tented area and the wagon park on the Saddle. The hundred or so 'casuals' – grooms, cooks, Vorloopers (drivers) etc – were hacked down without mercy. As non-combatants, their fate was in a sense more tragic than their military colleagues. Lieutenant Stafford witnessed nightmarish scenes, as

> a great many of these unfortunate men were cut up by the encircling movement of the right horn which had commenced to work round to our rear and cut off any retreat by the main road of Isandlwana.[34]

Hamer also recalled the terrible panic: 'the scenes at the top of the camp baffled description, Oxen, yoked to wagons, mules, sheep, horses and men in the greatest confusion and wildly trying to escape'.[35]

The remaining four imperial companies by all accounts survived longer than their counterparts in A and F Companies. Captain Younghusband's less-exposed C Company undoubtedly survived the longest, as its rear and left flank was partly protected by the slopes of Isandlwana Mountain. A last stand by his company consisting of around sixty men was made on the terrace or shelf overlooking the struggling mass in the camp. Probably because of his impressive stature, details of Younghusband's final moments were remembered by both sides. After being forced off the mountain into the wagon park, a Zulu observed his last heroic struggle:

> There was a tall man who came out of a wagon and made a stout defence, holding out for some time when we thought all the white people had been driven out of the camp. He fired in every direction and so quickly as to drive the Zulus, some in one way, some in another. At first some of the Zulus took no notice but, at last, he commanded our attention by the plucky way in which he fought and because he had killed so many. He was at last shot. All those who tried to stab him were knocked over at once, or bayoneted... when I came up he had been stripped of his upper garments. As a rule we took off the upper garment but left the trousers, but if we saw blood upon the garments we did not bother. I think this man was an officer; he had gaiters on but I did not see his coat. His chin was shaved he was killed under Isandlwana hill.[36]

A second Zulu eyewitness from the uNokenke regiment (carrying black shields) recalls the (Younghusband's Company) survivors giving a shout and charging down from the ledge. There was, he observed, an *induna* (officer):

> in front of them with a long flashing sword which he whirled around his head as he ran, it must have been made of fire Whough!

(here the narrator made an expressive gesture of shading his eyes). They killed themselves by running down for our people got above them and quite surrounded them, these and a group of white men on the Nek were the last to fall.[37]

The 'group of white men on the Nek' was in fact a mixed group of imperial regulars and colonial volunteers, who Durnford had managed to extricate from the carnage in the camp and rally together in a last desperate attempt to both stem the Zulu advance and prevent their right and left horns converging. Their gallant last fight was again witnessed by the Zulu veteran Methlokazulu:

> When we had closed in we came on to a mixed party of volunteers and infantry men who had evidently been stopped by the end of our horn: they numbered about 100. They made a desperate resistance, some firing with pistols and others using swords. I repeatedly heard the word 'fire' given by someone, but we proved too many for them and killed them all where they stood. When all was over I had a look at these men and saw an officer with his arm in a sling and with a big moustache [an unmistakable description of Durnford himself] surrounded by Carbineers, soldiers and other men that I didn't know. [38]

The remaining three imperial companies, under Captain Wardell and Lieutenants Porteous and Pope, occupying the centre and centre right of the British lines, faced the full impact of the Zulu 'chest', comprising mainly the UmCijo, the Xapho and possibly elements of the uMbonambi regiments, undoubtedly already incensed by their substantial losses to the early imperial volley fire. Nevertheless, they fought and died well and remnants were able either to link up with Durnford for the last stand on the Saddle or, as some accounts suggest, from a small cohesive defence to the rear of the 1st/24th tents (a possible third and final stand). Another Zulu recorded their final moments, bayonets fixed and fighting back to back:

Some Zulu threw assegais at them others shot at them; but they did not get close – they avoided the bayonet, for any man who went up to stab a soldier was fixed through his throat or stomach and at once fell. Occasionally, when a Zulu was engaged in front with an assegai, another Zulu killed him from behind.[39]

The sense of impending doom must have been heightened by a partial eclipse of the sun which occurred at the height of the battle. A warrior of the uMbonambi regiment (black shields with white patches) recalled that 'the tumult and the firing was wonderful, every warrior shouted "Usutu!" as he killed anyone, and the sun got very dark like night'.[40] Another confirmed that:

the sun turned black in the middle of the battle: we could still see it over us, or we should have thought we had been fighting till evening. Then we got into the camp, and there was a great deal of smoke and firing. Afterwards the sun came out bright again.[41]

Captain Hallam Parr, who was attached to Chelmsford's absent column but interviewed survivors after the battle, provided graphic accounts of individual struggles. One tall man, a corporal of the 24th, killed four Zulu with his bayonet, but his weapon jammed in the throat of his last opponent and the Zulu rushed in on him. The only sailor in camp, seconded from HMS *Active,* was seen with 'his back against a wagon wheel, keeping the Zulus at bay with his cutlass', but 'a Zulu crept behind him and stabbed him through the spokes'. One of the Natal volunteers, sick in hospital, was 'found with his back against a stone near the hospital tent' with 'nearly a 100 fired cartridges around him, his revolver empty and his bowie knife clutched in his hand'.[42]

Others chose more desperate strategies to evade the stabbing assegais. Captain Harford later

found the dead bodies of our two drivers, their faces blackened and it struck me at the time that they must have done this themselves in the hope of being able to escape.[43]

Few will forget the descriptions of a fleeing Band Sergeant Gamble of the 1st/24th desperately importuning escaping riders for a mount as the Zulu closed in.[44] Others may have survived by sheer luck. To his dying day, Lieutenant Smith-Dorrien was convinced that he and four fellow imperial officers only survived because they were wearing blue patrol jackets, and Cetshwayo had reputedly ordered that only those clad in red should be killed.

The fate of Lieutenant-Colonel Pulleine, the camp commander, remains a mystery. One account places him amongst the dead at Durnford's last stand, another shot or assegaied near or in his tent as he wrote a last letter or order. A third account has him falling with forty-odd survivors, 800 yards to the rear of the Nek by the Manzinyama river. One of his last acts, however, was to entrust the safety of the Queen's Colour of the 1st Battalion to Lieutenant Melvill, who with Lieutenant Coghill fought his way out of the camp. Similarly, a brave but futile attempt was made to rescue the guns. As the lines broke they were hastily limbered up but many of the gunners were assegaied as they careered across the camp in front of the mountain and over the Saddle of Isandlwana. Lieutenant Curling of the Royal Artillery provided the main eyewitness account of their fate:

> The enemy advanced slowly without halting; when they were 400 yards off the 1st battalion of the 24th Regiment advanced about 30 yards. We remained in the same position. Major Smith returned at this time with his gun and came into action beside mine. The enemy advancing still, we began firing case, but almost immediately the infantry were ordered to retire. Before we could get away the enemy were by the guns; and I saw one gunner stabbed as he was mounting on to the axle-tree box. The limber gunners did not mount, but ran after the guns. We went straight through the camp, but found the enemy in position. The gunners were all stabbed going through the camp with the exception of one or two. One of the two sergeants was also killed at this time. When we got on to the road to Rorke's Drift it was completely blocked up by the Zulus.[45]

As the bloodied and exultant Zulu commenced a systematic sacking and looting of the camp, finishing off the last groups of resistance by around 2p.m., Chelmsford's force, bivouacked up to twelve miles away to the south-east, remained blissfully unaware of the terrible events that had unfolded in the camp that morning. Chelmsford's response to Pulleine's first message at 8.05a.m., reporting 'Zulus advancing in force for the left front of the camp', again demonstrated both his dangerous complacency and overall underestimation of his Zulu enemy. He had returned the note to his senior staff officer, Major Clery, without a word. When Clery asked him 'what is to be done on this report?', Chelmsford allegedly replied, 'there is nothing to be done on that'.[46] The failure of his naval aide, Lieutenant Berkeley Milne, to discern through his field glasses any major hostile activity in the camp area from the nearby hill only served to enhance Chelmsford's continuing over-confidence. Colour-Sergeant James Gittins provided a rare account from the ranks of the Columns, revealing their overall ignorance of the terrible events occurring at Isandlwana camp that morning and the elusiveness of their Zulu enemy:

We were off before daylight and before 5 o'clock we had got to the place were we expected to find the enemy, but they had been too quick for us and had gone. We marched many miles but could not get in touch with them. The general decided to camp for the night and sent my own and 'F' company with four guns to select a suitable site, and meant to send back to the camp for the troops remaining behind to bring out the camp to us. We were at this time about twelve miles from Isandlwana and could see it distinctly, each lot of tents looking like great patches of snow; we were about three miles from where we had left the general. Our attention was attracted by distant firing and looking towards Isandlwana we could see the two guns firing rapidly and the smoke of musketry. I borrowed a pair of field glasses and could see masses of Zulus attacking the camp. When the firing ceased we thought, of course, that our people had driven them off. [47]

It wasn't until dusk, around five hours after the last survivor had escaped the camp, that Chelmsford's stunned, exhausted and dispirited force stumbled into the desolate and wrecked camp. Despite receiving other vague reports of action in the camp area, Chelmsford and his staff had only received a definitive eyewitness report of the disaster early in the afternoon, when all fighting had ceased. This eyewitness, Commandant Lonsdale of the 3/9th NNC, had himself only escaped death by inches. Half asleep in the heat of the early afternoon sun, riding a 'broken-kneed old crock' called 'Dot', he had returned by himself to the now occupied camp. Thirty-two years later Lonsdale still vividly recalled the horrific scenes that greeted him:

I was very short of sleep, and awfully tired. When we were within a few miles of the camp Isandlana [*sic*] mountain, I asked the general [Lord Chelmsford] if I might ride on ahead, get back to camp and get a rest. This was granted, and I rode on my way. I was shot at by a couple of natives as I went on, but I thought nothing of it, as I imagined they were two of my own Swazis who had made a mistake, and I did not discover they were Zulus until later. I approached the camp we had so lately left, but being three quarters asleep did not notice anything was amiss until I was well inside it. The first thing that woke me up and put me on the *Qui vive* was a Zulu coming for me with a stabbing assegai, already red with blood in his hand. I was wide awake enough then, and on the alert in a moment. I glanced around me and became fully alive to what had taken place, and that the camp had been captured by the Zulus. I saw in a flash dead bodies of both soldiers and Zulus all over the place, tents rent in fragments, bags of flour cut open and the contents strewn about, boxes of ammunition broken, everything, in fact, smashed and done for. Last but not least, Zulus with assegais still reeking with blood sitting and wandering about in all this indescribable chaos. I saw it all in a flash, turned and fled. My horse was as tired as I was. Many Zulus, becoming alive to the fact that an enemy and a white man was among them, rushed after me yelling and firing at me. It was the most deadly, awful moment I have ever had in my life… I could only screw a very moderate canter out of my poor gee… Kafirs are uncommonly fleet of foot. It was two or three minutes before I was clear of those howling devils. It seemed to me like two or three hours. At length they all gave up the chase and I went on my way to rejoin the column… When I rode up to the General and reported what I had seen I believe he thought I was mad… I don't think I shall ever close my eyes in sleep again without seeing that yelling horde of Zulus rushing after me, brandishing their bloody spears and wondering whether my poor horse had steam enough left in him to carry me out of their reach.[48]

Arriving at the camp just before sunset and departing before dawn the next day, the relief force were spared the full horror of seeing the putrefying corpses of their mutilated comrades. Colour-Sergeant Gittins again recalled the organised but fearful return to the camp, many of the 24th still desperately hoping that at least some of their comrades would have survived:

We… had got within three miles of the camp when the General [Lord Chelmsford] halted us and spoke to us. I will endeavour to give you his exact words. He said, 'Now then 24th Regiment, I am sorry to say that during our absence today the enemy has turned our flank, attacked and taken our camp, stores and ammunition and are in possession. Our only course now is to take it back. I know you 24th and can depend on you. Mind you, it means hard fighting at the point of the bayonet. We must get to Rorke's Drift and we cannot get there without retaking the camp'… We were simply thunderstruck. None of us had any idea that such a thing had happened but as soon as he had finished speaking we gave three hearty British cheers which meant every man meant to do or die. It was now nearly dark. The General formed us up in fighting order and the command was given to advance and on we went. The Left party (in which I was) continued their advance and the right was halted and with them in the centre the four guns fired rapidly to cover our advance. Our orders were to fire a volley and then charge when we had got sufficiently near the enemy, but thank God there was no occasion for it, as the enemy had gone.

The right party had also advanced and when we arrived at the top of the hill we again gave three cheers, as we knew that as there were plenty of large stones we could make breast works and were as safe as long as our ammunition lasted. We occupied that hill, afterwards Blacks Kopje, having that day marched over 40 miles with belts and accoutrements and seventy rounds of ammunition. We were thoroughly tired out. We were nearly starved to death. It was as cold as night as ever I felt, so you can imagine we were not very comfortable expecting thousands of Zulus at any minute. We started off from this Kopje, below which had been our camp about daybreak, and the sight that met us was truly awful. The ground was covered for about two miles with dead men, black and white, and as we formed up at the bottom we had to move them to make standing room for the company. The Zulus had not been content with killing our men but had ripped them up from the bottom of the stomach to the throat. The sight was truly shocking. We could do nothing. We had lost food, blankets, tents, greatcoats, ammunition in fact we had nothing but what we stood up in.[49]

For senior officers, the eerie sight that greeted them in the camp proved equally devastating. Chelmsford's military secretary, Lieutenant-Colonel Crealock, in a dispatch to the *Illustrated London News*, also dramatically recorded the dismal scene, providing a fitting epitaph to one of the darkest days in Britain's military history:

Day waned and the night hung over the hill as we reached the last ridge beyond which had been our camp – to the little hill on the left we sent Major Black and three companies of the 2nd 24th to seize it, for the nek between and the hill we must gain at all hazards – in silence we marched down into the gloom below where lay, shrouded by a merciful pall, the horrors of the past day.[50]

4

Battle Analysis:
The Lessons of the Isandlwana
Disaster

I regret to have to report a very disastrous engagement which took place on the 22nd January, between the Zulus and a portion of No. 3 Column… the Zulus came down in overwhelming numbers but a few of its defenders escaped

Chelmsford to SOS, 10 February 1879, RA Vic/o/33

Overextended Lines

It is appropriate here to discuss the deeper reasons why the Isandlwana garrison had suffered such a catastrophic collapse. Virtually all the problems encountered by Pulleine's force can be traced back to the flaws in Chelmsford's initial battle plan. First of all, the imperial lines were clearly overextended and highly susceptible to any flanking movement. Chelmsford's departing order to defend the camp had committed Pulleine to an impossible defence of what was, in effect, a great deal of unnecessary terrain. Vastly outnumbered, the only hope for Pulleine was to sustain a continuous imperial volley fire. This, in turn, depended on an uninterrupted supply of ammunition, and it was here that Chelmsford's disposition of the campsite played a crucial role in precipitating the disaster. Virtually all sources agree that the excessive distance of mounted colonial forces from the main ammunition supply was almost certainly the key factor in the collapse of the right wing. Jabez Molife, one of the few survivors from Durnford's command, vividly recalled that, after the initial check to the Zulu left horn, 'our cartridges were nearly done',[1] with inexplicable delays in securing fresh ammunition from the camp.

It is possible that the British left wing was also severely compromised by its distance from the two ammunition wagons of the 1st and 2nd 24th Regiments. Captain Henry Hallam Parr confirmed that Cavaye's, Mostyn and Dyson's men, almost certainly fatigued after their rapid return from the Spur and from being longest in the firing line, were

> very short of ammunition, and their initial accoutrement of only seventy rounds apiece was rapidly expended owing to the hot fire that they had been forced to sustain to keep the Zulus from closing upon them while they were retreating on the camp.[2]

Firing an average of three rounds per minute, one source estimates that the imperial infantry alone expended up to 70,000 rounds during the first half-hour of the main battle.

Ammunition Shortages

Ammunition distribution was clearly not helped by the inflexible nature of quartermastering. At least one quartermaster, Edward Bloomfield of the 2nd/24th Foot, was recorded as obdurately refusing the issue of cartridges to 'non battalion' members, culminating in a confrontation between him and Lieutenant Smith-Dorrien, who was still desperately trying to 'feed' the imperial firing lines. Thus Bloomfield said to Smith-Dorrien, in regard to ammunition boxes he was then breaking open, 'For heavens sake don't take that, man, for it belongs to our Battalion', to which Smith-Dorrien scathingly replied 'hang it all man, you don't want a requisition now do you'.[3] Similar scenes elsewhere behind the British firing line give equal credence to supply problems. Captain Barton, NNC Commander, provided telling evidence in an interview with Charles Norris Newman, Special Correspondent for the *London Standard*. He told Newman that his mounted Amangwane men

> really fought well at their first charge, and, until all the ammunition was exhausted; they were then compelled to fall back on the camp, where they sought for a fresh supply of ammunition. Unfortunately this was refused by the officer in charge as it would all be required by the infantry themselves. This was assuredly a fatal error of judgement.[4]

The early recorded death of Bloomfield, possibly due to Zulu rifle fire, must have also greatly exacerbated the command and control situation with regard to the ammunition supply. Unfortunately, the otherwise brave action of the other quartermaster, James Pullen, who controlled supply from the 1st/24th ammunition wagon, undoubtedly added to these recorded breakdowns in ammunition supply as the lines collapsed. Pullen, if Brickhill's account is to be believed, courageously but possibly recklessly decided to abandon his post. Brickhill recorded that:

> above the 1st/24th camp I met my poor tent companion, Quartermaster Pullen, who shouted to the running soldiers, 'come on men rally here follow me. Don't be running away like a parcel of women. Let's try and turn their flank'. Turning to me he said, 'Mr Brickhill, do go to Colonel Pulleine and ask him to send us help, as they are out-flanking us here on the right'. He went away toward the front of the stony Kopje followed by several of the soldiers.[5]

Private Bickley provides crucial further supporting evidence confirming Pullen's abandonment of the 1st/24th ammunition wagons just as the regulars retreated to the camp area:

The Quartermaster then came up and asked me if I could saddle his horse for him… he left the horse tied up by the wagon by the head Stall, but saw no more of the Quartermaster who had gone away in the direction of the officers' latrine. By this time all the idlers were clearing out of the Camp, and the skirmishers driven in….[6]

The alleged panic of elements of the NNC, which may have caused the first gaps in the left of the British line of defence, remains hotly contested today. But widespread panic on their part was quite understandable as they were poorly equipped and, as we have seen, generally armed with fewer than ten rifles per company. Indeed, it was possibly a collapse of the left which, by creating mass panic and confusion and a 'knock-on effect' on the central administration supply lines, may have fatally damaged the central defensive position far more than Durnford's retreat from the right. Thus Private H. Grant of the 1/24th, having arrived back in camp and escaped the destruction of the Rocket Battery out on the plain, found that the

Companies on the left were completely surrounded by the enemy and everyone was making the best of their way out of the camp.[7]

Private John Williams of the 1/24th recalled the possible effective severance of this logistical lifeline by the panicking NNC contingents, which were rapidly joined by scores of camp casuals:

The men in Camp, Bandsmen and men on guard etc were trying to take ammunition to the companies but the greater part never got there as I saw horses and mules with ammunition on their backs galloping about the camp a short time afterwards.[8]

Clearly, many of the camp stragglers rounded up by Lieutenants Essex and Smith-Dorrien earlier in the battle to help supply the imperial firing lines were now either fleeing their posts or had been swept along by the mass exodus through the camp. Private E. Wilson, a 1st/24th stretcher bearer, recalled the knock-on effect of this panic-stricken flight upon even those hard-pressed military units still supporting the front lines:

> when the idlers and men among the tents were making the best of their way out of the camp the doctor told us that we were no longer likely to be of any use and the band sergeant told us we had better get away as best we could.[9]

It was perhaps this deadly human and logistical chaos reigning within the camp that inspired Pulleine to recall the remaining intact imperial companies, in a last desperate attempt to bypass the collapsing supply lines and conduct an organised defence based solidly upon the ammunition wagons. Private Bickley, a 1st/24th survivor, probably witnessed this critical moment just before the bugler called the retreat:

> The companies out skirmishing were now apparently getting short of ammunition... and the Native Contingent had been driven into the camp and, together, with most of the transport other employed natives were rushing out of the camp towards the road to Rorke's Drift.[10]

Moreover, even where the runners were reaching the rifle companies, demand may well have been exceeding supply. With the leading Zulu formation '100 to 150 yards distant' from the front lines, the rate of fire and ammunition expenditure must have increased immensely. As Private Williams recalled: 'when the natives fell back on the camp we fired 40 to 50 rounds each'. What could only have been a few minutes later – as Zulu appeared not only from the left and right but ultimately from the last escape route at the rear of the Nek – he 'got 40 rounds more ammunition' of which he 'then used 29'.[11] Indeed, it is only a natural human tendency to massively increase your rate of firing when your enemy is within yards of killing you. Lieutenant Mainwaring's sketch map of Isandlwana, prepared on behalf of the Intelligence Branch months after the battle, confirmed the 'signs of heavy fighting' along the 'southern crest line' occupied by

Pope's, Wardell's and Porteous's centre companies, an area 'strewn with empty cartridge cases'.[12]

Moreover, we know that large numbers of men of these three centre-line companies had survived the final retreat into the tented areas. Major Wilsone-Black's subsequent reports on the battlefield confirmed the paucity of bodies in the firing line, and the heaviest concentration of 24th corpses around the 1st/24th tented areas and wagons on the Nek or Saddle.[13] Indeed, Lieutenant Higginson of the NNC recalled the number of men coming in from the out-lying companies searching for ammunition, and that, although the men of the second battalion (NNC) were 'running', the 24th were 'retreating also but very slowly'.[14] At least two companies were seen still intact kneeling and firing even in the camp area.

In the event, effectively deprived of their ammunition supply, these imperial regulars were left to fight for their lives, either individually or in small groups, with possibly one weakly formed square established behind the 1st/24th tented area. They were clearly doomed and most probably died in a matter of minutes. As one Zulu eyewitness recalled, with direct reference to failing ammunition supply:

> Your people, when, as in several instances, only numbering three, would stand back to back and defy us to approach. While the ammunition lasted, we did not attack; but took advantage of them when their powder failed. We allowed none to escape.[15]

Amongst the last stands in and above the camp area, notably Durnford's mixed group of regulars and colonials on the Nek, and Younghusband's sixty-odd men trapped on a ledge of the Isandlwana Crag, there is evidence, however, of last-ditch attempts to rectify what had become a deadly logistical nightmare. One Zulu eye-witness, Uguku, significantly noticed how 'one party of soldiers came out from among the tents and formed up a little above the ammunition wagons'.[16] The last desperate charge of another group 'on the steep slope under the cliff behind the camp' (Younghusband's survivors) may well have been aimed at reaching one of the precious ammunition wagons. A Zulu of the Unokhenke recalled that:

They fought well… and the Zulus could not get at them at all; they were shot and bayoneted as fast as they came up. At last the soldiers gave a shout and charged down upon us… they killed themselves by running down, for our people got above them and quite surrounded them; these and a group of white men on the Nek were the last to fall.[17]

The fate of 'a group of white men on the Nek' (along with Lieutenant Anstey's final stand a couple of miles along 'Fugitives Drift', the last to die) was probably witnessed by a fleeing 'government conductor of wagons'. He provided a fleeting glimpse of a final attempt by elements of Durnford's group to restore the broken ammunition supply line:

When I left the camp Colonel Durnford was still alive as well as a small remnant of the Regulars, but they were so hemmed in that escape was impossible, and their ammunition seemed expended, for artillery men were trying to break open the cases on the wagons to supply them but it was to late.[18]

The Zulu eyewitness Mehlokazulu, attached to the iNgobama-khosi regiment, provided a fitting epitaph to the possible role of ammunition failure in this imperial disaster. Examining the corpses, mainly of the 1st and 2nd 24th after the battle in the camp area, he tellingly observed:

We searched the pouches of the men; some had a few cartridges, most of them had none at all; there were very few found. Some had cartouche boxes, others cartridge belts: the belts were all empty, but a few cartridges were found in a few of the cartouche boxes.[19]

Absence of Defensive Fortifications

While the ammunition supply controversy may never be finally resolved,[20] Chelmsford's (and to a lesser extent Pulleine's and Durnford's) failure to establish a final reserve or bastion of defence also played a major role in the disaster. The absence of any laagering of the wagons, and of entrenchments, meant that the troops, once in retreat, stood no chance of recovering or stabilising their position. Had there been a final redoubt position, possibly in square formations at the base of the Isandlwana mountain, or grouped around the vital ammunition wagons, many more men might have survived. Years later, Captain Stafford recalled that:

> I can never understand to this day why this was not done. The advice to form laager in every camp when campaigning against Zulus, had been told and retold to the British by the Boer advisers over and over again. It was the old, old mistake of underrating an enemy, that has been made by the British before and since the fatal mistake at Isandlwana.... Had a laager been formed at Isandlwana with the wagons, boulders, boxes etc we could have withstood the Zulu armies at any rate until such time as reinforcements arrived.[21]

In the event, devoid of such physical protection and vastly outnumbered, men were left to perish alone or in small vulnerable groups.

Underestimation of the Zulu Enemy

Thirdly, Chelmsford, Durnford, and again to a much lesser extent Pulleine, had clearly totally misjudged not only the mobility but the sheer raw courage, fighting spirit and resilience of the Zulu army. Even at the height of the battle as the uKhandempemvu, uMbonambi and InGobamakhosi regiments in particular were decimated at as little as 150 yards range, there had been no Zulu mass panic and no attempt to retreat. When the imperial lines, starved of ammunition, were fatally outflanked and had finally wavered, the Zulu bravery and overall fighting spirit was graphically symbolised by one brave *induna*, Ndlaka of the uKhandempemvu, who, before being killed by a rifle bullet to the head, exposed himself to the British firing line in order to rally his warriors for the final ferocious charge. Zulu sustained resistance and resilience to the hitherto unchallenged destructive power of the Martini-Henry rifle was, undoubtedly, a major contributory factor to the eventual defeat of Pulleine's force. It was, in essence, a stunning Zulu victory.

Division of Forces

Finally, Chelmsford's fatal decision to divide his force early that morning undoubtedly represented a major tactical error. By 1p.m., at the critical moment of the battle, Chelmsford's force was at least three hours' marching time away and any possibility of rescue and reinforcement was out of the question. In the interim period, after the first message from Pulleine (received at 9.30a.m.), Chelmsford had stubbornly sustained his aloof attitude to the steady procession of reports and rumours of fighting occurring within his camp area.

In mitigation, neither Chelmsford nor his subordinate commanders, in their long military experience, had ever before confronted such a formidable enemy as the Zulu. Nevertheless, the poor initial defence plans and the misjudged decision to divert to the south-east were both negligent acts bordering on recklessness. To the end of his days, even after the subsequent Court of Inquiry, Chelmsford never admitted his direct culpability for this disastrous failure of his battle plans. Much of the blame, as we shall see, was shifted onto the shoulders of the deceased Durnford and, to a much lesser extent, Pulleine, for overextending their lines. In Chelmsford's obdurate view:

> the rear was perfectly secure… I consider never was there a position were a small force could have made a better defensive stand.[22]

But, in other correspondence addressed to both Sir Bartle Frere and to his column commanders, Chelmsford tacitly admitted to his underestimation of the 'heavier numbers of Zulu' attacking his depleted force and, above all, of the 'desperate bravery of the Zulu' which had been the 'subject of much astonishment'.[23] It was a lesson soon understood by the brave defenders of Rorke's Drift.

5

The Flight from Isandlwana:
Prelude to Rorke's Drift

Our flight I shall never forget; no path, no track, boulders every-where. Our way was strewn with shields assegais, blankets, hats, clothing of all descriptions, guns, ammunition belts and saddles which horses had managed to kick off, revolvers and belts and I know not what else. Our stampede was composed of mules – oxen – horses and flying men all strangely inter-mingled man and beast, all apparently impressed with the danger which surrounded us.

Hattersley, Annals of Natal, *pp. 156-7 Brickhill account*

By 2p.m., resistance in the camp had virtually ceased. Those who survived the holocaust in the tented areas made a desperate dash over the Saddle and along a tortuous ten-mile route to the near-est British outpost at Rorke's Drift, or further, to Helpmekaar. Their escape route was, however, almost immediately blocked by the convergence of the two Zulu 'horns' from behind the Saddle, a brilliant culmination of overall Zulu strategy that day. Scores more civilians and soldiers died in further hand-to-hand combat. Lieutenant Stafford recalled the terrible scenes that confronted him as he galloped across the Nek or Saddle and proceeded along the route which later became known as 'Fugitives Drift' or 'Trail':

It was perfect pandemonium. The mules and pack horses and oxen, some with ghastly gashes, were galloping over the veldt at will, some with saddles and others only with blinkers. How sad to think what these noble animals are called upon to suffer in their masters' wars.[1]

The men and horses of the Royal Artillery, dragging both seven-pounder guns behind them and already decimated in numbers during their desperate ride through the camp area, were clearly doomed. Lieutenant Curling again later recalled their horrible demise:

We crossed the road with the crowd, principally consisting of natives, men left in camp and civilians, and went down a steep ravine leading towards the river. The Zulus were in the middle of the crowd stabbing the men as they ran. When we had gone about 400 yards we came to a deep cut, in which the guns stuck. There was, as far as I could see, only one gunner with them at this time, but they were covered with men of different corps clinging to them. The Zulus were on them almost at once and the drivers pulled off their horses...[2]

Nearby, on the reverse slopes of Isandlwana, Captain Shepstone and several of his men were surrounded and annihilated by the Zulu right horn.

In the midst of panic there were moments of calm, indeed courageous self-sacrifice. James Hamer, by his own account one of the last four horsemen to escape the Zulu pincer movement behind the mountain, was forced to 'use our revolvers very freely for the Zulus followed us up quickly', and was placed in a 'jolly predicament' when his already fatigued horse (Dick) collapsed

completely down and would not move a step further... then (thank God) a man of the Rocket Battery galloped up with a led horse and let me have it. I had just taken the saddle off Dick when a bullet struck him dead and the poor fellow who gave me the horse had only ridden three yards when I saw him fall, killed from his horse.

Malindi of the NNH recorded an act of exceptional self-sacrifice and generosity. As the camp defences had started to collapse:

> our Captain now got off his horse and gave it to me, telling me to take it to the ammunition waggons and turning back… he joined the red soldiers who were firing and I never saw him again.[3]

Some lives were lost for less logical reasons. Trooper Charles Montague-Sparks of the Natal Mounted Police, on escaping via the officers' quarters in the camp area, 'found them untenanted' and while hesitating as to what he should do he came across Pearce, another member of the corps 'who was a saddler and over 6'6" high'. As Sparks expressed the opinion that things looked grave, Pearce ejaculated the words 'my oath!' and started off to retrieve his big bit which he said was in his tent. Sparks, seeing the red-coated men of the 24th Regiment running towards the tents with the Zulu in close pursuit, shouting their slogan 'Gwas Umhlongo! Gwas Inglubi!' which means 'stab the white men, stab the pigs', became much alarmed and shrieked after Pearce 'come back man and let's ride off!, we shall both be killed'. Pearce's reply was:

> what a choking off I would get if the Sergeant Major sees me riding with a snaffle instead of the regulation bit.

With this remark he disappeared into the tent, which a moment later was surrounded by Zulu, and 'that was the last of Pearce'.[4]

Of the other several vivid accounts of this nightmarish retreat, those of Lieutenants Erskine and Smith-Dorrien stand out. Following half a mile behind Melvill and Coghill and pursued by hundreds of Zulu, Smith-Dorrien came across a wounded mounted infantryman named Macdonell. Again, in a significant act of gallantry, he applied a tourniquet with a handkerchief to stop the bleeding. Smith-Dorrien then attempted to manhandle the trooper down the gorge and was startled by a desperate shout from the white-faced and bleeding Major Stuart Smith, commander of the ill-fated gun detachment: 'Get on man, the Zulus are on top of us.' But:

in a second we were surrounded and assegais accounted for poor Smith, and my wounded mounted infantry friend and my horse.

Struggling across the raging eighteen-yard torrent of the Buffalo river, Smith-Dorrien commenced a running retreat pursued by around twenty Zulu. However, by wisely husbanding the last few rounds from his revolver, he kept them at bay. It was a miraculous escape. He finally reached Helpmekaar at sundown, having covered a dozen miles on foot in around five hours.[5]

Lieutenant Erskine similarly experienced an amazing escape and one undoubtedly aided by his fortuitous knowledge of the Zulu language. Attached to the 3/4th Natal Native Contingent, he was helplessly carried along by the panicky retreat. Exhausted and overburdened with the ammunition that he had wisely snatched from nearby wagons, Erskine briefly rested, only to witness soldiers all around him being killed, thrown on their backs and disembowelled. With a renewed sense of urgency, he acquired a horse, and after riding about two miles, recalled seeing

a soldier who was running about ten yards from me, when, just as he had passed a bush, a Zulu sprang out and said 'Uya ngapi Umlungu?' (where are you going white man?) and threw a broad bladed assegai which pierced the poor fellow between the shoulders. The poor fellow fell forward on his face and the Zulu ran up to him, calling out 'Usutu', stabbed him to the heart... The same Zulu then threw the assegai at Erskine himself, wounding him in the leg. After shaking it out he proceeded a further 500 yards at which point he saw 'a puff of smoke and a bullet whizzed about an inch from my nose. I shouted out to the Zulu marksman, 'Iya wa utiuya dubula bane na' (who do you think you are shooting).[6]

The predictably astonished Zulu let him pass. He finally negotiated the river, and like Smith-Dorrien, reached Helpmekaar in the early evening.

Melvill and Coghill, escorting the Queen's Colour, were not so fortunate. Struggling across the Buffalo river, they lost their horses. Drifting downstream, weak and exhausted (Coghill had injured a leg prior to the battle), they reached the opposite bank only to be run down and assegaied by around thirty Zulu in front of a large rocky outcrop, barely 100 yards above the river.

With the January rains having swollen the river to peak levels, many men who reached that far were either drowned or exhausted, easily killed by the Zulu waiting on the other side. In the words of Captain Stafford:

> a strange sight greeted us as we got to the edge. Men were strug-
> gling in the water. The various uniforms presented all the colours
> of the rainbow. Half a dozen bodies were washed ashore on the
> bank at the end of the river on our side.[7]

This desperate retreat was not a total disaster. Here and there, and especially around the river bank, small groups of infantry and horsemen did demonstrate great courage and discipline and thereby saved several lives. Erskine recalled the coolness and discipline of the African mounted Edendale contingent. After struggling to the far side of the Buffalo river alongside Lieutenant Cochrane, he met 'the Edendale men', who

> told me to lie flat on my horse's neck, which I did, thinking the
> Zulus were going to fire at me, but was surprised to hear our own
> men firing over my head; they killed about a dozen Zulu. While
> watching this little skirmish I saw one of our Kaffirs brought to
> bay by a Zulu. After some preliminary guarding on the part of
> both, the Zulu stabbed our Kaffir in the shoulder; thereupon our
> Kaffir jumped into the air and struck his assegai to the Zulu's heart.
> Both of them then rolled into the river.[8]

Amidst this carnage behind the Saddle, and the chilling screams of the wounded and dying men and animals, the Undi corps which had been held in reserve belatedly arrived 'fresh and eager for fighting'. It was clearly too late to achieve full battle honours here, but it was patently obvious to their disappointed men and commanders that only the small garrison at Rorke's Drift now stood in the way of a major incursion into Natal Colony. Their forty-year-old commander, Prince Dabulamanzi, Cetshwayo's aggressive half-brother, was an inexperienced commander but a highly intelligent and domineering personality. A keen horseman and excellent shot, his ruthless political manoeuvrings had given him an artificially elevated status in the Royal Council.

An invasion of Natal would suit this deeply ambitious man, and the powerful 4,000-strong Undi Corps, comprising the crack uThulwana regiment and the inDluyengwe, inDlondlo and uDloko *amabutho*, provided ample means to achieve this task. The seriousness of this enterprise was underlined by the actions of one Undabuko, another of the king's brothers, who even called on members of his own already decimated regiment, the uMbonambi, 'to join them but… they declined on the ground that it was necessary to return to the field of battle to attend to their wounded'.

The next morning after 'Black Wednesday', following the departure of the victorious Zulu army and of Chelmsford's demoralised and weary force from the devastated battlefield area, only one living creature appeared to flourish. For days afterwards, in the words of Smith-Dorrien:

> the sky was darkened at times by continuous streams of 'aasvogels' [vultures], heading from all directions to the battlefield marked by that precipitous and conspicuous crag… Isandlwana where nearly 900 British and 2,000 or 3,000 natives, friend and foe, had breathed their last on the fateful 22nd.[9]

Rorke's Drift
(early morning to 3.15p.m. approximately)

Nothing will happen and I shall be back again this evening early.

Major Spalding to Chard, midday, 22 January 1879

Major Spalding's blissful ignorance of the severe threat to his command, emanating from the terrible massacre of Pulleine's garrison less than ten miles away, was shared by everybody within the remote outpost of Rorke's Drift on that fateful morning of

'Black Wednesday'. As the day dawned the scene was peaceful and uneventful: in short, just another routine day. Private Hook, 2nd Battalion 24th Regiment, laconically recalled: 'we were all knocking about and I was making tea for the sick, as I was hospital cook at the time'.[10] Private Hitch was engaged in similar duties, brewing up for his mates in the company area outside the buildings.[11] For many men, there was a profound sense of boredom, even vacuum, as, with Durnford's departure, the hustle and bustle caused by hundreds of men of No.3 Column passing through had abruptly ended. Surgeon James Reynolds was particularly miffed:

> I remember... my feeling of disappointment when Lord Chelmsford marched away with his army and left me with about 100 other men to sit still and bite the bullet of inactivity at Rorke's Drift. There was no fighting for us, no doctoring for me; the army moved away to gain glory and we sat down in what Lord Halsbury would call a sort of base, to envy the other chaps their chances![12]

Private Hook expressed similar emotions:

> everything was perfectly quiet at Rorke's Drift, particularly after the Column (Durnford's force) had left – not a soul suspected that only a dozen miles away the very men we had said 'goodbye' and 'good luck' to were either dead or standing back-to-back in a last fierce fight with the Zulus.[13]

Colour-Sergeant Bourne expressed a palpable sense of frustration and despair:

> One company was left behind at Rorke's Drift to guard the Hospital stores and the pontoons at the Drift on the Buffalo River. This was my company and at the time I was bitterly disappointed. We saw the main column under Lord Chelmsford engage the enemy at once and I watched the action, along with my four Sergeants from a little hill by Rorke's Drift. Then we saw them move on again, and they disappeared.[14]

By contrast, Walter Dunne simply felt isolated:

> our post at Rorke's Drift seemed silent and lonely after they had
> left; but we expected to join them soon and to hear of some fierce
> but successful fight with the enemy.[15]

Two men, Lieutenants Chard and Smith-Dorrien, were at least busy early that morning. Lieutenant Smith-Dorrien had arrived at the Drift just before dawn, bearing the ill-fated message from Lord Chelmsford, ordering Durnford and his 500 African levies to reinforce the camp at Isandlwana. Apparently 'hearing heavy guns over at Isandhlwana', Smith-Dorrien rode the ten miles back to the doomed camp, arriving about 8a.m. Before he left he started the erection of a fifteen-foot-high 'gallows' for making bullock ropes and, anticipating a 'big fight', borrowed eight revolver rounds from Lieutenant 'Gonny' Bromhead.[16] It was to be a very 'big fight' for all three officers that momentous day.

Chard was also busy that morning. The night before he had received an order from No.3 Column HQ, 'to say that the men of the Royal Engineers who had lately arrived were to proceed to the camp at Isandlwana at once' (although he 'had received no orders himself'). With the permission of the commanding officer, Major Spalding, Chard had accordingly put his three RE sappers and their full accoutrements into an empty wagon, but as the wagon slowed up, with the difficult terrain, he rode ahead in advance. On his arrival at the camp, probably at around 10a.m., Chard experienced the first sense of unease. Borrowing a 'very good' field glass from an unnamed 24th Regiment NCO, he observed the Zulu enemy moving on the distant hills 'apparently in great force'. This chilling sight alarmed him sufficiently to postulate that the Zulu might sweep round and 'make a dash at the Ponts'. Chard hurriedly left the camp. A quarter of a mile out of the camp, on the road to Rorke's Drift, he met the doomed Colonel Durnford and his mounted force, with whom he left his three men, now sadly destined to die that afternoon alongside Durnford and his ill-fated force.[17] On his return to Rorke's Drift, Chard was issued with his 'Order for the Day' from his commanding officer, which interestingly survived intact 'from the fact of it being carried in my pocket during the fight'.

Camp Rorke's Drift
22 January 1879: Camp Morning Orders

No.1 The force under Lieutenant Colonel Durnford, RE, having departed, a guard of six privates and one NCO will be furnished by the detachment 2nd/24th Regiment on the Ponts.

A Guard of 50 armed natives will likewise be furnished by Captain Stevenson's detachment at the same spot – the Ponts will be invariably drawn over to the Natal side at night. This duty will cease on the arrival of Captain Rainforth's company, 1st/24th Regiment.

No.2 In accordance with Para 19, Regulations for Field Forces in South Africa, Captain Rainforth's company, 1st/24th Regiment, will entrench itself on the spot assigned to it by Column Orders Para – dated –

H Spalding, Major Commanding[18]

In the event, Rainforth's company failed to arrive and a concerned Chard, aware of the consequent vulnerability of the Ponts, guarded by only seven men and possibly further weakened by the lack of entrenchment, spoke to Spalding. Spalding subsequently decided to track down the missing company himself in the vicinity of Helpmekaar. Just before riding away, he paused to establish with Chard the command situation in his absence:

Which of you is senior, you or Bromhead? I said, 'I don't know' – he went back into his tent, looked at an Army List and coming back said 'I see you are senior, so you will be in charge, although, of course, nothing will happen, and I shall be back again this early evening'.[19]

For some, Major Spalding's absence has been interpreted as at best negligence and at worst desertion of his post. Clearly, however, Spalding, ignorant of the massacre of his colleagues at No.3 Column camp site, could not anticipate in any way an attack on his post by up to one-fifth of that attacking Zulu force.[20]

Clockwise from above:

1 The Earl of Carnarvon, the primary force behind the South African Confederation.
2 Sir Henry Bartle Edward Frere (1815–84), Governor of the Cape and High Commissioner for South Africa from 1877; entrusted with the arduous task of completing Lord Carnarvon's ailing confederation scheme.
3 Sir Michael Hicks Beach, Secretary of State for the colonies.

Clockwise from top left:

4 Chief Cetshwayo Kampande (1832–84) in traditional dress.
5 Lieutenant-General Frederick Augustus Thesiger (Lord Chelmsford),
Commander-in-Chief of the British forces in Zululand.
6 The swotting of a 'Zulu wasp' by the British lion. This 1879 *Punch* cartoon
graphically shows that the Zulu threat was only one of several problems besetting
the hard-pressed Disraeli government.

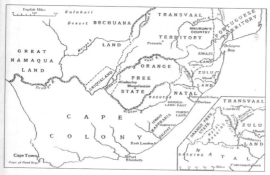

7 Sketch map of South Africa, 1879.

8 Reading the Ultimatum on the banks of the Tugela.

9 & 10 Two close-ups of the Martini-Henry firing mechanism.

11 The formidable 'lunger' socket bayonet, so feared by the Zulu attackers at Rorke's Drift.

12 Officers, NCOs and men of the (1st Battalion?) 24th Regiment, pictured in Zululand in 1879. Note the officer's sphinx cap badge, the young drummer boy/musician and the prevalence of beards among members of the lower ranks.

13 Natal Native Horse, one of several African irregular units.

14 The Edendale Contingent, who later distinguished themselves in the retreat from Isandlwana.

15 Swazi warriors of Wood's irregulars, traditional enemies of the Zulus.

Right and overleaf: 16 & 17 Zulu warrior groups. Zulu boys would be taught basic economic and military skills at military kraals, known as *amakhanda*.

Above left: 18 A classic, accurate engraving of a Zulu charge. Note the deployment of muskets alongside traditional spears and assegais.

Above right: 19 A deceased 24th soldier's buff belt, converted to a bandolier by a victorious Zulu warrior after Isandlwana.

Above left: 20 Colonel R.T. Glyn, Commander of No. 3 Column and heavily criticised in Chelmsford's recently discovered memo of February 1879.

Above right: 21 Colonel Evelyn Wood (1838-1919), Commander of No. 4 Column, pictured in later years after promotion to General.

Above: 22 The perils of campaigning in Zululand, *Punch*, August 1879.

Right: 23 British logistics, ammunition and general supply wagons by the Lower Tugela river, 1879.

Clockwise from above:

24 A rare contemporary view of the Rorke's Drift crossing point on the Mzinyathi (Buffalo) river.

25 Lieutenant Harford, NNC Commander and a key eyewitness to the aftermath of Rorke's Drift and Isandlwana.

26 An informal group photograph of the 24th Foot officers before the outbreak of war (1878).

27 Major Cornelius Clery (1838–1926), Principal Staff Officer to Colonel Glyn and a private critic of Chelmsford.

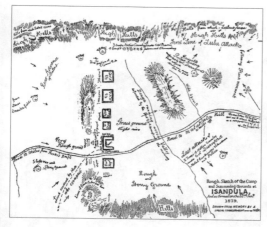

28 A rough sketch of the camp of 'Isandula,' near Rorke's Drift.

29 'A Lesson', from *Punch*, March 1879.

30 Rorke's Drift, the mission station before the attack. Witt's house, which served as a hospital, is on the right; his chapel, used as a storehouse, is on the left.

31 Prince Dabulamanzi, the Zulu commander at Rorke's Drift, with some of his attendants. Note the prevalence of firearms.

Above left: 32 Lieutenant Gonville Bromhead VC, the second-in-command at Rorke's Drift.
Above right: 33 Lieutenant John Merriot Chard VC, Commander of Rorke's Drift.

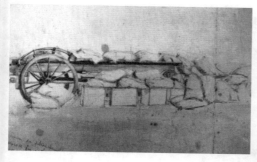

34 Henry Degacher's sketch of one of the wagons built into the back wall at Rorke's Drift.

Above: 35 The Reverend George Smith, who played such a crucial role in sustaining garrison morale at Rorke's Drift, wearing his campaign medals.

Above: 36 Surgeon-Major James Henry Reynolds, MB VC, one of the defenders of Rorke's Drift. *Right:* 37 The famous painting by Alphonse de Neuville, depicting Lieutenants Melvill and Coghill's desperate attempt to save the Colours at Isandlwana.

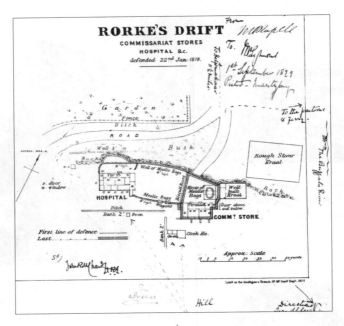

RORKE'S DRIFT
COMMISSARIAT STORES
HOSPITAL &c.
defended 22ⁿᵈ Jan: 1879.

38 Lieutenant Chard's famous drawing of the Rorke's Drift battle, showing the main thrusts of the Zulu attack.

Above left: 39 Colour-Sergeant Frank Bourne, one of the lynchpins of the Rorke's Drift defence.
Above right: 40 Mr W. A. Dunne, Commissariat Department.

Above: 41 The Zulu perspective of the view of Rorke's Drift as they commenced their first assault. *Left*: 42 Prince Dabulamanzi on horseback, with two retainers, facing John Dunn, the famous white trader.

43 The defenders of Rorke's Drift, B Company 24th Regiment after the battle. A good many men were absent after being invalided home. Colour-Sergeant Bourne is on the extreme left and Lieutenant Bromhead is to the left of the front row.

44 A close-up view of the Shiyane or Oskarberg terraces behind Rorke's Drift which provided such excellent cover for the Zulu.

45 View from the front. Only one or two trees have survived the siege. The Oskarberg terraces behind the post proved a fertile ground for scores of Zulu snipers. The depression in the foreground may have been the site of a mass Zulu grave.

46 Close-up view of the front of the storehouse, clearly revealing the formidable loopholed walls added after the battle. The final mealie-bag redoubt would have been positioned in the immediate foreground.

Clockwise from above left:

47 Acting Storekeeper Byrne.
48 Private George Edwards
(alias Orchard), one of the
lesser-known heroes of Rorke's
Drift.
49 This front view of Rorke's
Drift demonstrates how
effectively the Zulu snipers
based on the Oskarberg could
dominate the garrison, especially
the front wall defenders.

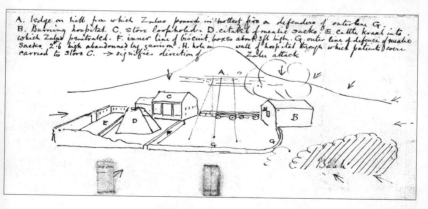

A. ledge on hill from which Zulus poured in hottest fire on defenders of outer line G.
B. Burning hospital. C. Store loopholed. D. citadel of mealie sacks. E. cattle kraal into
which Zulus penetrated. F. inner line of biscuit boxes about 3 ft high. G. outer line of defence of mealie
sacks, 2'6 high abandonned by garrison. H. hole in ——— wall of hospital through which patients were
carried to store C. → signifies direction of Zulu attack

50 A rare contemporary sketch of the siege of Rorke's Drift, clearly showing the
direction of the Zulu assaults and the organisation of the defences.

Above left: 51 Private Hook, VC.
Above: 52 Lieutenant John Rous Merriot Chard, Royal Engineers.
Left: 53 Mr Melton Prior, war correspondent of the *Illustrated London News*, one of several journalists who accompanied Chelmsford's three columns in Zululand in 1879.

54 The Isandlwana massacre site, May 1879. Drury-Lowe's cavalry search the remains of the camp area. Note the scattered wagons and supply and ammunition boxes in the foreground.

Clockwise from above:

Four of the eleven soldiers awarded the Victoria Cross:
55 Corporal William Allen.
56 Private William Jones.
57 Private Frederick Hitch.
58 Private John Williams, RRWM.

Below: 59 Isandlwana after the massacre. A lone
sentry guards a wrecked wagon, surrounded by the
detritus of the battle (May–June 1879).

Above: 60 In this *Punch* cartoon, Lieutenants Chard and Bromhead are saluted for their gallant defence at Rorke's Drift. March 1879

Above: 61 J.N Crealock's original sketch of the Mounted Infantry relieving Rorke's Drift on the morning of 23 January 1879.
Right: 62 Lord Chelmsford, pictured after the Zulu War.

63 The seven VC holders from the 24th Regiment, in Brecon for the unveiling of the Zulu memorial tablet in 1898. Left to right, back row: Ex-Pte R. Jones VC, Sgt H. Hook, Ex-Pte W. Jones VC. Front row, sitting: Ex-Pte D. Bell, Col. E.S. Brown VC, Ex-Pte F. Hitch VC and L/Cpl J. Williams VC.

Above: 64 The Colour Party, 1st Battalion, 24th Regiment, after being presented to Queen Victoria at Osborne House, 1880. The Queen's Colour (on the left) is the colour rescued from Buffalo river after Isandlwana.

Left: 65 A close-up contemporary photograph of a Zulu warrior.

66 A modern reconstruction of a Zulu military kraal, with traditional 'beehive' huts.

67 A collection of British and Zulu weoponry. Note the potential stabbing length of the Martini-Henry rifle once the bayonet is attached. The shorter stabbing assegai is a modern replica.

68 The heads of two Zulu spears/assegais, discovered after the Rorke's Drift battle by Lieutenant-Colonel J. Audley-Lloyd.

69 A depiction of an incident during the Hospital fight, revealing the savagery of the struggle.

At around 12.30p.m., as Chard returned to his tent by the river to both write letters home and indulge in a 'comfortable' lunch, three other members of the garrison – Surgeon Reynolds, Padre Smith and Reverend Witt, the resident missionary – were abruptly alerted by the sound of heavy guns. After a conversation, Reynolds remarked: 'if we can't fight... at least we can look on'. The three men then climbed the Oskarberg Hill, gazed across the Buffalo river, but were disappointed to discover that Isandlwana mountain (five miles away) 'shut our view from the scene of the action'. Nevertheless, the report of three or more big guns was 'distinctly audible' with 'a quarter of an hour's interval between each of them'. The timing of their excursion clearly coincided with the height of the battle for the Isandlwana camp site. Within an hour, a potentially more ominous sight greeted their eyes as 'a large body of natives' 'scrambling about' the slope of Isandlwana 'headed in their direction', which they imagined was 'our own Native Contingent'. It was regretfully to prove a misinterpretation. Soon afterwards, the first hint of danger materialised as three or four horsemen on the Natal side of the river furiously galloped in the direction of the Rorke's Drift post. Again, Reynolds innocently believed that they might be messengers calling for additional medical assistance to the distant battle and hurried down to his hospital.[21] As they neared the post, however, Reynolds' heart must have missed a beat as he observed 'the awfully scared' expression on their faces and the fact that one of them was riding a pony which he recognised belonged to his colleague, Surgeon Major Shepherd[22] (earlier assegaied in the frantic retreat from Isandlwana). The terrible truth soon dawned as they shouted 'the camp at Isandlwana has been taken by the enemy' and 'all our men in it massacred and that no power could stand against the enormous number of Zulus and the only chance for us all was by immediate flight'.[23]

A few hundred yards away, at around 3.15p.m., Chard was himself greeted by identical news from two other panic-stricken riders. This time, Chard guessed 'from their gesticulations and shouts' that 'something was the matter'.[24] After ferrying the men across the river, one of them, Lieutenant Adendorff of Lonsdale's Regiment, the Natal Native Contingent – later to play an enigmatic role in the siege[25] – promptly jumped off his horse, took Chard to one side and told him that the camp was in the hands of the Zulu and the army destroyed. Lord Chelmsford and the rest of the column had probably shared the same fate. Demonstrating coolness and presence of mind, even at this terrifying juncture, Chard, noting his high excitement, expressed some doubt and intimated that he probably had not remained to see what did occur.[26]

Chard's initial incredulity at this news was shared by his men. Private Waters, a special hospital orderly, encountered another desperate survivor, 'Private Evans... without coat or cap on',[27] and he also could hardly believe the news. Private Hook, positioned near Lieutenant Bromhead in the camp area, saw the same horseman and was mortified by the news of his dear comrades 'butchered to a man'. He watched as Bromhead received the fateful confirmation note: 'that the enemy was coming on and that the post was to be held at all costs'. It was the first major test of the garrison's morale and they passed it with flying colours. Private Hook recalled that 'for some time we were all stunned then everything changed from perfect quietness to intense excitement and energy'.[28] There was certainly no energy lacking amongst the officers. Chard's conversation with Adendorff at the river was soon interrupted with an urgent message from Lieutenant Bromhead at the Commissariat stores 'to ask me to come at once'.[29] Before leaving, Chard gave an order to load and inspan the wagon. He then posted a sergeant and six men on high ground above the pont, a strong position on a natural wall of rocks with a view over the river and ground beyond it, with orders to wait until he returned or sent for them. Galloping up to the Commissariat stores, he found the pencilled note from Captain Alan Gardner of No. 3 Column, stating that the enemy were advancing on Rorke's Drift in force. Meanwhile, Bromhead sent an urgent message forward to Helpmekaar via two mounted infantrymen, also escapees from Isandlwana, detailing news of the dire situation now confronting the garrison and the whole region.

Soon Chard's fellow officer, Lieutenant Bromhead, and key assistants Acting Assistant Commissary Dalton and Dr Reynolds, had joined him to discuss the options for survival against what was clearly going to be an overwhelmingly superior Zulu force. With this in mind, Bromhead had already, on his own initiative, given orders to strike the camp and had even loaded up the two garrison wagons. It was at this point that Dalton made his crucial intervention which, in hindsight, probably saved the garrison. Private Hook remembered:

> Mr Dalton of the Commissariat Department came up and said that if we left the Drift every man was certain to be killed.[30]

It was excellent tactical advice. Chased by over 4,000 highly mobile Zulu warriors, such a slow-moving convoy of men and wagons, heavily encumbered by thirty-odd sick men, would have been easily and rapidly overtaken and destroyed in open country. In Reynolds' words:

> removing the sick and wounded would have been embarrassing to our movement and desertion of them was never thought of.[31]

Having wisely accepted Dalton's advice, Chard and Bromhead held a 'short and earnest' conversation, both officers clearly appreciating Dalton's 'energy, intelligence and gallantry – a man of the greatest service to us'.[32] All three then toured the garrison area. As Chard hurriedly left to close down the pont operations on the river, Bromhead, Dalton and the ever-supportive Surgeon Reynolds commenced barricading and loopholing the store building and the hospital, connecting the defence of the two buildings by a wall of mealie bags and two wagons that were on the ground. As Private Hook observed, the heavy-duty stores proved to be a veritable godsend for the rapidly constructed barricades:

> The mealie bags were good, big, heavy things weighing about two hundred pounds each... the biscuit boxes contained ordinary biscuit. They were big, square, wooden boxes, weighing about a hundred weight each. The meat boxes, two, were very heavy, as they

contained tinned meat. They were smaller than the biscuit boxes. Even barrels of rum and lime juice were pressed into service.[33]

On his return to the river, Chard witnessed an incident which provided an excellent foretaste of the incredible courage, resilience and spirit existing within this small group of British soldiery. With the ponts floated in mid-stream and both the hausers and cables sunk, the Pontman Daniells and Sergeant Milne, 3rd Buffs, spontaneously offered to defend the ponts from their position in the middle of the river. Moreover, Sergeant Williams and his small 24th Guard contingent also indicated their willingness to join them.[34] This risky but courageous initiative must have provided a massive boost to Chard's own personal morale, knowing as he did the enormity of the threat now confronting him and his diminutive command.

Back at the post Bromhead, supported by Dalton and all able-bodied men in the area, black and white, had continued building the defences at rapid pace. Colour-Sergeant Bourne in particular recalled the usefulness of the two Boer transport wagons that formed 'excellent barricades' as a means to join up the front of the Commissariat stores with the rear of the hospital (see sketch p. 107). In these early stages at least, the 200–300 men of the Natal Native Contingent under Captain Stephenson proved vital to this frenzied process of extending the post's defences. Dunne gratefully confirmed their initial role:

> It was well for us that we had the help of the three hundred natives at this juncture otherwise the works would not have been accomplished in time.[35]

It was a tribute echoed in Chard's official report of the action which observed that the Native Contingent were 'working hard… with our own men, and the walls were rapidly progressing'.[36]

Lieutenant Bromhead was also proving his worth as a competent line officer, setting up the Vedette and watch positions. Private Hitch was despatched to the top of the house to report any sign of the approaching Zulu *impi*. Responsibility for some of this work was delegated to the NCOs. Thus Sergeant Bourne was detailed to post men as lookouts in the hospital and at the most vulnerable points and to take out and command a line of skirmishers.[37]

Indeed, the NCOs were fast proving to be the backbone of the garrison. Sergeant Windridge exemplified such reliability and steadfastness, which undoubtedly proved to be a key factor in sustaining morale. He was tasked with securing the casks of rum in the store, with further orders to shoot anyone who attempted to force his post, further demonstrating 'great intelligence and energy in arranging the stores for the Commissariat Store forming loop-holes etc'.[38]

For Surgeon Reynolds, it was the energy and ingenuity of Dalton and Bromhead that proved 'invaluable'. Dalton

> without the smallest delay, which would have been so fatal for us,… called upon the men (all eager for doing) to carry the mealie sacks here and there for defences, and it was charming to find in a short time how comparatively protected we had made ourselves.[39]

Chard, arriving as the work was in progress, 'gave many useful orders as regards the line of defence'. His practical engineering mind was everywhere in evidence in the whirl of activity, in which even the walking sick were commandeered. Chard

> approved also of the Hospital being taken in and between the Hospital orderlies, convalescent patients (8 or 10) and myself, we loop-holed the building and made a continuation of the Commissariat defences around it.[40]

Purely in terms of morale, Dalton was perceived as the main symbol of defiance, 'as brave a soldier as ever lived', who

> hearing the terrible news said now we must make a defence! It was his suggestion which decided us to form a breastwork of bags of grain, boxes of biscuits and everything that would help to stop a bullet or keep out a man.[41]

Other preparations included the filling of the station water barrel, which was brought inside the perimeter, as well as the opening of several boxes of ammunition which were placed at strategic points. All these endeavours soon bore fruit, and within two hours a wall about four feet high had been made nearly all round the post, incorporating both the hospital and the store.

Amidst these hurried defensive preparations there was at least one surreal, amusing episode. On returning from a ride, a heart-broken Reverend Witt had been traumatised by the sight of the severe damage caused to his beloved buildings. Nevertheless, as Trooper Lugg recalled, it became a brief, highly comical moment for the already tense, dust-covered and sweating soldiers:

> no-one could help laughing at their gesticulations when they came back on seeing the best parlour paper being pulled down and loop-holes being knocked out, while splendid furniture was scattered about. His first question was, in broken English, 'vot is dish?' Someone replied that the Zulus were almost upon us, upon which he bolted, saying, 'Mein Gott, mein wife and mein children at Umsinga! Oh mein Gott!' [42]

There were, by contrast, some far more unwelcome interruptions. A series of doom-laden Isandlwana survivors continually rode into the post, much to the chagrin of the NCOs, officers and, in particular, Lieutenant Chard – all concerned at the potentially disastrous impact on garrison morale. One fugitive accordingly whispered to the otherwise immutable Colour-Sergeant Bourne: 'not a fighting chance for you, young fellow'.[43] Other survivors insensitively informed a nervous Private Hook that Zulu would be 'up in two or three minutes'.[44] Likewise, a mounted infantry-man and two of his 'excited and breathless' fellow Natal Mounted Police, Troopers Shannon and Doig, approached Trooper Lugg:

> Upon my asking, 'what is it, is it true?' Doig replied, 'You will all be murdered' and he rode off with his comrade. Lugg however steadied his nerves, asserting that 'nothing remains but to fight and that we will do to the bitter end'.[45]

Chard was singularly unimpressed, indeed contemptuous of these men, most of whom refused to stay and help, as well as being angered by the constant distractions they provided from the vital work of building the defences.

> Who they were I do not know but it is scarcely necessary for me to say that there were no officers of Her Majesty's Army among them. They stopped the work very much – it being impossible to prevent the men getting round them in little groups to hear their story. They proved the truth of their belief in what they said by leaving us to our fate and in the state of mind they were in, I think that our little garrison was as well without them. In fact, in the face of all this pressure the morale of the garrison remained high, responding heartily to their officers' rallying cry that 'we were never to say die or surrender'.[46]

It is perhaps useful at this point to assess the soundness of Rorke's Drift as a defensive position. Hallam Parr considered it intrinsically weak, which might be considered a backhanded compliment to the subsequent resourcefulness and bravery of the defenders:

> A worse position could hardly be imagined. Two small thatched buildings about 39 yards apart with their walls commanded by rising ground on the south and west, completely overlooked on the south by a high hill. On the north side an orchard and garden gave access to an enemy up to within a few yards of the houses.[47]

Several of the defenders were conscious of such weaknesses. Surgeon Reynolds observed that, at first sight:

> the Hospital, for instance, occupied a wretched position having a garden and shrubbery close by which often proved so favourable to the enemy [but] compared with that of the Isandlwana affair we felt that the mealie barriers might afford us a moderately fair chance.[48]

Dunne was also very concerned by another glaring shortcoming in the hospital defences. Touring the area just before the battle commenced, he spotted an extremely vulnerable section of the back wall which, in his view, was the

> weakest point, for there was nothing but a plank to close the open-
> ing at one part; but before anything could be done to strengthen
> it a shot was fired outside – the Zulu had arrived.[49]

While it was true that the two thatched buildings were a major disadvantage, prone to being fired (as one subsequently was), they were in fact only about thirty yards apart, making it relatively easy to construct a defensive wall between them. In front of them was a patch of flat ground which dropped away in a rocky ledge about four feet high. With the mealie bag wall placed firmly on top of that ledge reaching around six to seven feet in height, the front of the post did provide a formidable obstacle for a Zulu enemy pri-marily armed with shields, assegais and knobkerries, notwithstand-ing the cover provided by the orchard and shrubbery. Moreover, the buildings, particularly to the rear, had very few doors and windows, and with loopholes knocked through them provided a good potential protection for defenders deployed at these posi-tions. Overall, around the Mission there was little room for the Zulu to manoeuvre *en masse*. The ground in front, with trees and shrubs, was awkward in terms of cover, but there was effectively a killing zone all round the buildings within thirty or forty yards. Nevertheless, the close proximity of the Oskarberg Hill over-looking the garrison was, as all contemporary observers confirmed, a major tactical problem, and many of the garrison's casualties were to be caused by Zulu sniper fire from this dominating position.

6

The First Zulu Assaults

As black as hell and as thick as grass,
  Hall, Natal Mounted Police, Lugg Account, Emery, Red Soldier, *p. 132*

I myself had given up all hopes of escaping,
  Sergeant G Smith, 2/24th Regiment, Holme, Silver Wreath, *p. 61*

Here and there a black body doubled up, and went writhing and bouncing into the dust; but the great host came steadily on, spreading out – spreading out – spreading out till they seemed like a giant pair of nutcrackers opening around the little nut of Rorkes Drift. It was nasty, really nasty, the inevitability of that silent (mass) closing in upon us.

  AMCM, Surgeon Reynolds, How VCs are Won

At around 3.30p.m., an officer of Durnford's ill-fated Horse arrived, accompanied by several score of highly nervous riders. It appeared to be a welcome reinforcement, and a delighted Chard duly requested the officers to observe enemy movement and check their advance as much as possible until forced to fall back. Events now moved rapidly. Although many of the defence works were complete, there were some worrying gaps. Reynolds was relieved to see his two colleagues on the hill, the Reverend Witt and Padre Smith, hurriedly return to safety

inside the laager. They had been convinced 'up to a late moment
that the approaching African force' were 'our own men'.[1] The
men quickly reported that the Zulu, led by two mounted men,
had crossed the river by a drift about a mile away, in a tactical manoeuvre suggesting a possible attack on the rear of the
post. They had watched as the Zulu crossed in three bodies,
and after snuff-taking and other ceremonies had recommenced
their advance.

Around 4.20p.m., the 'sound of firing was heard from behind
the Oskarberg'. The battle for Rorke's Drift had begun. As the
outposts sprinted in, there was barely time for the last non-
combatants to leave. The Reverend Witt now took this last
opportunity to ride away to try and secure the safety of his family
stranded on a local farm at Umsinga. By contrast, Padre Smith
was left trapped 'as his Kaffir groom had bolted and apparently
taken with him the horse'.[2]

Desertion and Defensive Redeployment

Chard was still relatively confident, having more than enough
manpower (up to 400 white officered NNC and white regulars)
to defend almost the complete perimeter. At this critical juncture,
however, as the first Zulu appeared, two potentially catastrophic
events occurred, either of which could have fatally undermined
garrison morale and cohesion. The first blow was delivered when
the 100-odd mounted survivors of Durnford's force suddenly
returned from their vedette positions – not to stay and fight,
but to flee to the next post at Helpmekaar – the officer merely
stopping to report to Chard that the enemy were 'close upon
us and his men will not obey his orders'. It was a bitter blow, as
the Zulu were known to have a mortal terror of cavalry, and this
sizeable force might have played a key role in driving back or
dispersing the attackers.

Worse was to follow. 'At about the same time' (4.20 to 4.30p.
m.), having heard the news of an imminent Zulu arrival and the
first shots, the whole of the Natal Native Contingent 'took up
their assegais' and bolted, following their European mounted

counterparts towards Helpmakaar. In a flash, the garrison of up to 400 fighting effectives was reduced to barely 100. This potentially demoralising spectacle, rather than instigating mass panic, produced a variety of responses from the defenders, ranging from anger to relief and even to pragmatism. Some soldiers of the 2/24th, including Private Hook, were enraged: 'to see them deserting like that was too much for some of us and we fired after them. The sergeant was struck and killed'.[3] There is only one specific record of an African member of the Natal Native Contingent being hit, but more were almost certainly killed if not wounded.[4] Sergeant Bourne was more calm and philosophical. Having later recalled with grim satisfaction how the European NNC officers were arrested some days later, tried and dismissed from the service, he postulated:

> The desertion of this detachment of 200 men appeared, at first sight, to be a special loss with only a 100 of us left, but the feeling afterwards was that we could not have trusted them, and also that our defence was too small to accommodate them anyhow.[5]

Chard, although undoubtedly shocked by the suddenness of this departure and annoyed that the officer had 'deserted us', was more pragmatic. Immediately recognising the need to consolidate the now undermined and overextended defences, he commenced a retrenchment of biscuit boxes, 'so as to get a place were we could fall back upon if we could not hold the whole'.[6] Private Hook recalled with admiration this clever tactical ploy:

> As soon as the Kaffirs bolted, it was seen that the fort as we had first made it was too large to be held so Lieutenant Chard instantly reduced the space by bringing a row of biscuit boxes down across the middle about four feet high. This was our inner retrenchment and proved very valuable.[7]

In an interview recorded just before the twenty-fifth anniversary of the battle, Surgeon-Major Reynolds praised this tactic, but mistakenly gave the credit for this achievement to Lieutenant Bromhead:

> Bromhead at this point, certainly saved the situation by cutting the laager in half by means of biscuit tins. But for that we should have been smashed to pieces – not a doubt of it. He saw the wisdom of concentrating our defence in the nick of time, and accomplished it.[8]

Initial Sightings
(4.20–4.30p.m. approximately)

In fact, it was only a few minutes before the shrunken garrison encountered the first Zulu assault. Private Hitch, from his elevated vantage point on top of the house, first observed the ominous approach of the 4,000-strong *impi*. As soon as he reached the top, he could see the advancing Zulu were already at the other side of the rise and extending for attack. The following brief, almost flippant, conversation with Lieutenant Bromhead occurred as the news was conveyed by Hitch to him and the men in the yard below:

> I told Mr Bromhead… they were extending for the attack. Mr Bromhead asked me how many they were? I told him I thought [they] numbered up to 4-6000. A voice from below – 'is that all, we can manage that lot very well for a few seconds!![9]

Such apparent frivolity belied the huge tension within the garrison defence as, outnumbered by as much as thirty to one, they prepared for a desperate struggle for survival.

Surgeon Reynolds recalled being mesmerised by the awesome initial sighting of the enemy, as

> a swarm of Zulus came round the crook of the mountain at a slow, slinging trot, spreading themselves out in skirmishing order and made straight at us, an innumerable swarm of blacks. They came in perfect silence – no war whoops, no dancing, no shouting, and

holding their fire. Striking–looking figures of great physical beauty, the Martini in one hand the assegai slung across the back – fresh from the massacre of Isandlana, running in perfect silence to wipe out the little body of left behinds at Rorkes Drift.[10]

Assistant Commissary Dunne also remembered the eerie silence of the first Zulu approach, a 'black mass coming on without a sound at a steady trot',[11] while Sergeant Bourne observed them 'driving in my thin red line of skirmishers' to make 'a rush at our south wall'.[12] Corporal Lyons was also struck by the silence of the approach:'The Zulus did not shout, as they generally do, but, after extending and forming a half moon they steadily advanced and kept up a tremendous fire'.[13] Private Waters was more impressed by their discipline – fifty of them 'forming a line in skirmishing order, just as British soldiers would do'.[14]

Opening Shots
(4.30–4.45p.m. approximately)

Private Hitch probably represented the first identifiable target for the approaching Zulu lead elements, as he watched them deploying in front of the Oskarberg and creeping under the rocks with snipers, while taking cover in the caves. A number of shots were in fact fired at him, but, fortunately for him, 'their direction was good but their elevation bad'. Hitch 'fired three shots these being the first that were fired at the Zulus at Rorke's Drift'.[15]

So far, aside from the folly of attacking a defended post, the tactics of Dabulamanzai and his *indunas* (commanders) were relatively sound. He was already testing the weakest line of defence around the hospital, and the posting of snipers on top of the Oskarberg mountain gave him some valuable intelligence regarding the numbers and deployment of the garrison as well as a clearly defined killing ground. Hitch spotted the problem immediately, with a sole Zulu vedette

on the top of the mountain; from the other side he could see us in the laager plain enough to count us.

Private Hitch then tried to pick him off but 'my shot fell short of him'.[16]

The opening shots from the rest of the garrison were, according to Dunne, fired at the relatively extreme range of 800 yards, not the most accurate distance for the Martini-Henry rifle. Dunne noted, however, that the men on the south wall

> dropped many of the foremost causing the remainder to swerve away to their left and thus move to the front of our position.[17]

Private Hitch meanwhile kept up a running commentary to Lieutenant Bromhead, noting the increasing concentration of Zulu warriors in the caves and informing Bromhead that they would be 'all around us in a very short time'.[18] Padre Smith also nervously watched as the Zulu took rapid possession of the 'rocks overlooking our buildings and the barricades at the back with the caves and crevices quickly filled – from these the enemy poured down a continuous fire upon us'.[19]

The Main Battle Commences
(4.45–5p.m. approximately)

At 500-600 yards range, the advancing Zulu uThulwana regiment experienced their first serious casualties. Surgeon Reynolds was somewhat frustrated by the continuing inef-fectiveness of these opening volleys, as the Zulu 'seemed quite regardless of the danger'. What again struck Reynolds and many other members of the garrison as 'most strange' was that 'not only was there no war-cry but nor did they at this time fire a single shot in return'.[20] The British rifle fire was initially 'a little wild'. This was undoubtedly due to battle nerves, the common problem of establishing range, and possibly some hesitation as, according to Lyons, the men were told 'not to fire without orders... this... was to make sure that the advancing force was really Zulus'.[21] It was an extremely tense beginning, Reynolds reaffirming that 'we were little put to it by the impotence of our volley'.[22]

Zulu casualties quickly mounted, however, as a few yards further on they were met by a much more 'steady and deliberate fire'. Gunner Howard, stationed in the hospital and borrowing sick Sergeant Maxfield's Martini-Henry rifle, commenced opening fire at 400 yards. His initial battle nerves were very evident:

> When I beheld the swarm I said to myself, 'all up now', but I was wrong and we all agreed to fight until two were left and these were to shoot themselves. Great execution was done as when the Zulus were about 400 yards off, like a wall coming on, we fired the first volley. The rifles being Martini-Henrys our firing was very quick, and, when struck by the bullets, the niggers would give a spring in the air and fall flat down. The enemy advanced to within 300 yards and then it did not seem healthy to come any nearer…[23]

A similarly tense Trooper Harry Lugg 'told off in my turn' to take a loophole and, saddled with a broken Martini-Henry carbine, the stock 'bent' and tied up with a rein, personally opened fire at 350 yards. He

> had the satisfaction of seeing the first I fired at roll over… and then my nerves were as steady as a rock. I made sure, almost before I pulled the trigger. There was some of the best shooting at 450 yards I have ever seen.[24]

Demonstrating great initiative, Corporals Lyons and Allen and Private Dunbar played a key role in breaking up the impetus of this first Zulu assault. Lyons, Allen and several other men formed a cohesive unit to 'check the fire from the enemy's right flank as it was thought the crack shots would go up there. We all consider we did good service.' Alongside these men was the stirring sight of their indefatigable officer Lieutenant Bromhead 'on the right face, firing over the mealies with a Martini-Henry'.[25] Private Dunbar excelled himself, and in several accounts emerges as the real hero of this opening phase of the battle. A crack shot, he scored several hits at 500–600 yards, including 'a chief on horseback'.[26] The early loss of a leading Zulu commander probably came as a distinct shock to many of the Zulu attackers. One can only speculate on the major impact on Zulu morale if the other horseman, almost certainly the senior commander Dabulamanzi, had been the victim. Private Hook later claimed that Dunbar 'shot no fewer than nine Zulus... one of them being a chief'.[27] Padre Smith gave Dunbar a slightly smaller tally: 'eight Zulus, killed with consecutive shots as they came round the ledge of the hill'.[28]

This first Zulu onslaught was not as wild or reckless as some contemporary commentators have suggested. Several of the garrison remembered the prolonged disciplined and methodical pattern of the traditional Zulu attack, with snipers providing covering fire. Private Hitch remembered: 'they attacked us in the shape of a bullocks horn and in a few minutes were all around us'.[29] Harry Lugg also marvelled at the cohesiveness of their formation, as the Zulu 'came on first in sections of four then opened out skirmishing order and up came their reserve and then they were on us.'[30] All were impressed by the excellent use of the terrain by the advancing Zulu. Hook recalled:

> During the fight they took advantage of every bit of cover there was; ant hills, a tract of bush, that we had not time to clear away, a garden or sort of orchard which was near and a ledge of rock and some caves (on the Oskarberg) which were only about 100 yards away. They neglected nothing...![31]

Surgeon Reynolds cursed the tactical disadvantages of the garden and shrubbery which the Zulu skilfully used to

> pour in upon us a galling fire. It was a frightful oversight – the leaving of that garden and shrubbery. Heavens! they rained lead on us at the distance of a cricket pitch or two.[32]

In fact, the garrison had little or no time to clear the area before the Zulu arrival, the main focus necessarily being on strengthening the core inner defences. As Chard later reported:

the bush grew close to our wall and we had not time to cut it down. The enemy were thus able to advance under cover close to our wall, and in this part soon held one side of the wall while we held the other.[33]

At fifty yards, the first Zulu wave was truly decimated by all-out volley fire from the defenders which forced them to divert to the left and complete the encirclement of the garrison as well as probe for any weaknesses in the perimeter. The men in the loopholed store were accordingly able 'to do great execution at that side', while 'semi–flank fire from another part of the laager played on them destructively'.[34] Also, the 'loop-holes in the hospital were made great use of so that the combined fire had the affect of keeping the Zulus at bay'. Harry Lugg recalled the terrible impact of this enfilading fire on the first Zulu echelon, comprised of the relatively young inDluyengwe regiment: 'They were caught between two fires, that from the hospital and that from the storehouse and were checked'. Nevertheless, the Zulu used cover well, 'gaining the shelter of the cookhouse and delivering many heavy volleys'.[35] Both Corporal Francis Attwood and Lieutenant Adendorff played a crucial role here, Attwood firing from an upper window in the storehouse wall and Adendorff from another loophole 'flanking the wall and Hospital – his rifle did good service'. As Attwood wrote to his father,

> I made an awful mess of one fellow; he was running towards the house in a slightly sloping position, when I let fly at him and struck him in the crown of the head, the effect of which was to blow the entire side of his head away... I was at an upper window, the only one in the Barn I call it.[36]

Assegai Against Bayonet: The Initial Battle at the Barricades (5–6p.m. approximately)

It was a soldiers battle – each man fighting for his own hand.
Assistant Commissary Dunne, *Waggoner*, RLCM

Along most sections of the outside perimeter, both sides were now pitched eyeball to eyeball, and the nerves of the British soldiers and their Zulu protagonists were to be tested to the utmost. Until then, the British, deploying their devastating volley fire, clearly had technical superiority, but with close-quarter fighting at the barricades, in which assegais, knobkerries, rifle butts and bayonets were the dominant weaponry, the two sides were more equally matched.

Over the next hour or so:

> reinforced by some hundreds they made desperate and repeated attempts to break through our temporary defences, but were repulsed time and again. To show their fearlessness and their contempt for the red coats and small numbers, they tried to leap the parapet, and, at times, seized our bayonets, only to be shot down. Looking back, one cannot but admire their fanatical bravery.[37]

Individual British soldiers now demonstrated extraordinary coolness and courage. Hitch, realising that the Zulu were now too close for rifle fire, slid down the thatch and dropped down into the laager area taking his position in an uncompleted open space, 'as the deadly work now commenced'.[38] At this second stage of the battle, the bravery of three particular garrison members stood out – Dalton, Byrne and Scheiss. Mr Dalton remained inspirational, rapidly moving through the barricades 'fearlessly exposing himself… cheering the men and using his own rifle most effectively'. When one Zulu ran up near the barricade, Mr Dalton called out 'pot that fellow' and himself aimed over the parapet at another.[39]

The sheer voracity of the Zulu attacks in this period belied their alleged fatigue. The north-west line of mealie bags beside the hospital came under the most sustained pressure. Here Dalton shot a Zulu who was in the act of assegaiing a corporal of the Army Hospital Corps, the muzzle of whose rifle he had seized. Chard testified to the relentless pressure exerted on this section of the garrison by the endless waves of Zulu warriors:

A series of desperate assaults was made on the hospital and extending from the hospital as far as the bush reached; but each was most splendidly met and repulsed by our men, with the bayonet. Each time as the attack was repulsed by us, the Zulus close to us seemed to vanish in the bush, those some little distance off keeping up a fire all the time. Then, as if moved by a single impulse, they rose in the bush as thick as possible, rushing madly up to the wall (some of them being already close to it), seizing, where they could, the muzzles of our men's rifles or their bayonets, attempting to use their assegais and to get over the wall. A rapid rattle of fire from our rifles, stabs with the bayonets, and in a few moments the Zulus were driven back, disappearing in the bush as before, and keeping up their fire. A brief interval, and the attack would be again made, and repulsed in the same manner. Over and over again this happened, our men behaving with the greatest coolness and gallantry.[40]

For a while, the battle stabilised in these static positions, but the garrison was already taking unnecessarily high casualties, not at the barricades but from the Zulu snipers stationed high up on the Oskarberg terraces. Although clearly unfamiliar with the Martini-Henry rifles which they had already looted from the Isandlwana camp, the effect of concentrated fire in such a small area was bound to result in serious injuries or death.[41] Determined to 'check' the flank firing as much as possible, Corporal Lyons, with his neighbour Corporal Allen, found a good counter-sniper position:

we fired many shots and I said to my comrade 'They, the Zulus are falling fast over there' and he replied 'yes we are giving it to them'. I saw many Zulus killed on the hill.[42]

Smith in particular noticed the deadly affect of Zulu snipers on the exposed front wall position, with five men 'shot dead in a very short space of time'.[43] Such losses were to represent nearly one-third of the garrison's final death toll. Chard was acutely aware of the garrison's vulnerability at this stage of the battle:

The fire from the rocks and caves on the hills behind us was kept up all the time and took us completely in reverse... although very badly directed many shots came amongst and caused us some loss.[44]

Thus, Private Hitch

saw one of my comrades – Private Nichols – killed; he was shot through the head, his brains being scattered all about us... He had, up to his death, been doing good service with his rifle.[45]

Under such intense pressure, the 'thin red line' began to briefly waver and the first Zulu were able to penetrate the defences and push right up to the hospital porch. A ferocious struggle took place, in which one British weapon, the bayonet, had an unexpected shock impact on the Zulu attackers. Hitch provided the main account of this critical juncture in the battle:

The Zulus pushing right up to the porch, it was not until the bayonet was freely used that they flinched at least a bit. Had the Zulus taken the bayonet as freely as they took the bullets, we could not have stood more than fifteen minutes. They pushed right up to us and not only got up to the laager but got in with us, but they seemed to have a great dread of the bayonet, which stood to us from beginning to end.[46]

Why this should be so is a mystery, but it is quite possible that some Zulu were unnerved by their inexperience with this unfamiliar weapon. Indeed, these Zulu regiments had largely been bystanders at the battle of Isandlwana and were historically unfamiliar with this weapon, which was not used by their more familiar Boer enemy. In addition, the shorter stabbing spear may have proved less flexible when pitched against the deeper and considerably longer thrusts of the combined rifle and bayonet. The Zulu frustration as to how to deal with this weapon may also have been reflected in the constant eyewitness accounts of their often futile attempts to wrench the hated bayonets from the muzzles of the rifles. Padre Smith recalled at least two instances when intrepid Zulu warriors 'succeeded in wrestling them off the rifles, but the two bold perpetrators were instantly shot'.[47]

It was indeed a life-and-death struggle in a most brutal sense. Private Hitch provided a rare vignette of the sustained intensity and ferocity of the hand-to-hand combat within the porch area:

> During that struggle there was a fine big Zulu see me shoot his mate down – he sprang forward, dropping his rifle and assegais seizing hold of the muzzle of my rifle with his left hand and the right hand hold of the bayonet. Thinking to disarm me, he pulled and tried hard to get the rifle from me, but I had a firm hold of the small of the butt of my rifle with my left hand. My cartridges on the top of the mealie bags enabled me to load my rifle and (I) shot the poor wretch while holding on to his grasp for some few moments.[48]

Corporal Attwood was astonished by the raw courage of the Zulu:

> They do not seem to have much fear. They are very daring, coming right up to the guns, such horrid-looking brutes, quite naked except a thong of something about their loins.

Behind this struggle along the front barricade and particularly the hospital porch, Chard and Bromhead were again seen demonstrating enormous courage and initiative, actively plugging gaps and reinforcing any perceived weak points in the perimeter defences. Their role became particularly crucial as the Zulu gradually extended their attacks further leftwards along the front wall. At one point, it seemed that the Zulu would even scale the wall behind the biscuit boxes, so Chard was forced to

> run back with two or three men to this part of the wall and was immediately joined by Bromhead with two or three more. The enemy stuck to this assault most tenaciously.[49]

Dalton and Scheiss were now proving veritable Herculean figures in the midst of the tumult of battle, with Dalton dropping a man each time he fired his rifle. As the Zulu pressed against the front barricades, Padre Smith witnessed the already wounded 'giant' Corporal Scheiss, incensed when his hat was blown off by a shot from a Zulu rifleman, commencing a frenzied assault on a group of Zulu cowering beneath the parapet. Scheiss instantly

> jumped upon the parapet and bayoneted the man, regaining his place, and shot another, and then repeated his former exploit, climbed up on the sacks and bayoneted a third.[50]

Such exceptional demonstrations of military prowess from men such as Hitch and Scheiss must have impressed, if not demoralised, the attacking Zulu. Even more surprising for the enemy was the overt defiance directed towards them even by severely wounded British defenders. After Dalton was wounded firing over the parapet and treated by Surgeon Reynolds for a bullet wound above the right shoulder, he continued to direct the fire of the men around him. His rifle was given to Acting Storekeeper Louis Byrne, 'who used it well'. Soon after, NNC Corporal Scammell, although mortally wounded by a Zulu bullet in his spine, still managed to crawl a short distance from the storehouse to Lieutenant Chard to hand him the remainder of his cartridges. As Byrne nobly fetched water at the request of this dying man, he was also shot through the head, dying close beside him. When Private Hitch and Corporal Allen were later badly wounded and 'incapacitated from using their rifles', they still continued to serve their comrades with ammunition under fire.[51] Comradeship and self-sacrifice was the order of the day in this epic action.

Non-combatants were also present in the thick of the fight, playing a vital role in maintaining the garrison's logistical supplies: water, food and above all ammunition. Surgeon Reynolds and Padre Smith were particularly active in supplying ammunition, Smith also providing great comfort and cheer to the soldiers on the ramparts (tempered with Christian zeal!). Lieutenant Stafford, in conversation with Lieutenant Adendorff four years after the battle, recorded this colourful story of Smith's activities during the siege:

> He told me that the Reverend W. Smith was a great help. You'll always find that in a tight corner there is a hard case and there was one at Rorkes Drift. This man was cussing all the time. The Reverend Smith went to him and said 'please my good man stop that cussing. We may shortly have to answer for our sins'. The reply he got was 'alright minister, you do the praying and I will send the black B's to hell as fast as I can.'[52]

Even General Wolseley, not known (as we shall see) for his admiration of the Rorke's Drift action, expressed his grudging admiration for the 'fighting Missionary' of Rorke's Drift, who had 'not fired on a Zulu himself but had gone round our men sending out ammo and telling them to fire low'.[53]

It was, however, to take more than religion to save the garrison hospital, now in Dunne's words subjected to the 'heaviest attack'. At around 6p.m., after one-and-a-half hours of fighting, and with signs of severe over-stretch along the extended front perimeter, Chard called 'all the men inside our entrenchment'. Thirty mostly sick men, trapped inside the hospital, now faced the full wrath of the Zulu attackers.

7

Nadir: The Hospital Fight (6p.m.–10p.m.)

We were pinned like rats in a hole.

Private Hook, Silver Wreath, *p.64*

Dusk fell. As the night closed in, the struggle decisively deepened and the battle for Rorke's Drift entered a new, even more deadly phase. The British retreat to the inner 'biscuit box' enclosure from the hospital area, and the subsequent Zulu infiltration of the hospital, represented the most critical stage of the battle for both sides. For Dabulamanzi and his subordinate *indunas*, it represented their greatest opportunity, not only to fatally divide the garrison, but also to 'break its back' by overrunning the retreating red line. Nearly one-quarter of Chard's men were literally 'pinned like rats in a hole' in the now isolated hospital – over thirty sick and barely half a dozen able-bodied men – Privates William and Robert Jones, Robert Cole, Henry Hook, William Horrigan, John and Joseph Williams and John Walters. As the dispersed red line rapidly retreated to the safety of the biscuit box barricade, the Zulu mounted a massive attack to both overrun the hospital and annihilate the retreating soldiers. With the 24th Regulars falling back, Padre Smith observed, at 6p.m., the emergence of scores of Zulu who jumped over the abandoned mealie bags to get into the building.[1] Private Hitch, caught in the middle of this major onslaught, was horribly aware of the potential for disaster at this point:

> Again this was just before they tried to fire the other building, they seemed to me as if they had made up their minds to take Rorke's Drift with this rush. They rushed up madly, notwithstanding the heavy loss they had already suffered.[2]

Many Zulu were, indeed, shot down by combined fire, emanating from both the hospital and the soldiers repositioned on the new inner defences, comprising Chard's biscuit box barricade: 'nearly every man perished in that fatal leap but they rushed to their death like demons, yelling out the war cry of 'Usuto', Usuto!'.[3] A good many other Zulu undoubtedly closed with the momentarily disorientated defenders carrying out their retreat from the outer perimeter, and 'it was in this struggle' that Private Hitch was shot. Hitch, defending a position on the right of the second line of defence with Bromhead in the centre, was exposed to crossfire. He recalled his deadly encounter with the Zulu as he desperately tried to fend off several assegai thrusts:

> They pressed us very hard, several of them mounting the bar-ricade. I knew this one had got his rifle presented at me but at the same time I had got my hands full in front and I was at the present when he shot me through my right shoulder blade and [it] passed through my shoulder which splintered the shoulder bone very much.

Hitch was the last of six men shot in this exposed area (four killed and two wounded). Once again the irrepressible Bromhead arrived to save the day: 'I tried to keep my feet, but could not, he could have assegaied me had not Bromhead shot him with his revolver.' The following brief exchange between Bromhead and Hitch yet again illustrated the high morale, strength of comrade-ship and fighting spirit which pervaded this tiny garrison:

Zulu!

Bromhead seemed sorry when he saw me down bleeding so freely, saying 'Mate, I am very sorry to see you down'. I was not down more than a few minutes, stripping [to] my shirt sleeves with my waist belt on and valise straps. I put my wounded arm under my waist belt. I was able to make another stand, getting Bromhead's revolver and, with his assistance in loading it, I managed very well with it.[4]

As if this latest Zulu 'thunder clap' was not enough, the defenders were dealt another major psychological blow. After penetrating the hospital entrance, several intrepid Zulu attackers proceeded to fire the thatch at the furthest end of the hospital. The thirty-odd men occupying the hospital were now trapped in a maze of tiny cramped rooms with, in many cases, extremely thin walls and doors and, worst of all, no communicating corridor. They were in a terrible plight. In Hook's words:

[it] meant that we were either to be massacred, or burned alive, or get out of the building. To get out seemed impossible; for if we left the hospital by the only door which had been left open, we should instantly fall into the midst of the Zulu.[5]

This dilemma, largely reflecting the poor state of the hospital's inner defences, formed an interesting focal point of Chard's later battle report. Within this report, in a rare moment of criticism of his own men, Chard pinpointed a glaring weakness in the hospital defence arrangements:

All this time the enemy had been attempting to fire the hospital and had at length set fire to its roof and got in at the far end. I had tried to impress upon the men in the hospital the necessity for making a communication right through the building – unfortunately this was not done. Probably at the time the men could not see the necessity, and doubtless also there was no time to do it.[6]

Chard lamented the absence of his cherished Royal Engineer sappers who, earlier that morning, he had already unknowingly left to be massacred at Isandlwana camp, and who could have effectively transformed the inner hospital defences. He chose his words carefully:

> Without in the least detracting from the gallant fellows who defended the hospital and, I hope, I shall not be misunderstood in saying so, I have always regretted, as I did then, the absence of my poor sappers, who had only left that morning for Isandlwana and arrived there just to be killed.[7]

Despite these defensive shortfalls, the subsequent heroic struggle and defence of the hospital was to provide a crucial turning point in the fortunes of the garrison. In Colonel Whitton's words:

> there were gallant deeds done at Rorke's Drift that day but for courage and devotion to duty nothing can exceed the conduct of the half dozen Privates of the 24th Regiment left, as the garrison of the doomed building.[8]

Gunner Howard, located with sick patient Private Adams in the far front corner room, arguably the most exposed position of the hospital defences, could only offer limited resistance after the Zulu had burst in through the front entrance porch. In the ensuing mêlée, Howard took the opportunity to run out of the front of the hospital and managed to conceal himself in the long grass on the other side of the store wall below the front parapet. In company with a dead pig and four deceased horses, shot earlier where they were tethered, he lay undetected throughout the night, the Zulu masses swirling over and above him. It was to be the first of several miraculous escapes. The less daring Private Adams stayed and paid with his life, shot or assegaied in the room itself. Surgeon Reynolds later elaborated on his terrible fate, recalling that Adams, while 'well able to move about... could not be persuaded to leave his temporary refuge in a small room and face the danger of an attempt to escape to the laager'. He paid with his life.[9]

Private Hook – who has provided the most detailed account of this phase of the battle – was able, through a succession of gallant deeds, to save the lives of many sick patients. Occupying his post in a room at the far end of the hospital with Private Thomas, 'Old King' Cole and one sick African patient, Hook was subjected to the full terror of the hungry flames licking the thatched roof above him, combined with the nightmarish sounds of his furious Zulu protagonists pounding against the walls and doors outside. In later years, he vividly recalled the 'extraordinary rattle as the bullets struck the biscuit boxes and queer thuds as they plumped into the bags of mealies'. Hook's previous combat experience undoubtedly helped him to control his nerves in this critical situation, the 'whiz and rip of the assegais' reminding him of his recent 'experiences in the Kaffir campaigns of 1877 to 1878'.[10]

Worse was to follow. Soon, Private Hook became the only able-bodied defender left in his room, as the nerve of Private Cole finally broke. After abruptly informing Hook he 'was not going to stay', he went outside 'and was instantly killed by the Zulu'.[11] His subsequent death was witnessed by Padre Smith:

> A whisper passes round amongst the men; 'Poor Old King Cole is killed'. He had reached the front wall where a bullet passed through his head, and then struck the next man upon the bridge of his nose.[12]

Hook's only company now was the injured African patient, apparently a native of Umlunga's tribe who had been shot through the thigh during the earlier fight at Sihayo's kraal. His leg was broken and he kept crying out 'take my bandages off so that I can come!' Padre Smith recalled the bravery of this particular man, who defiantly cried out that he 'was not afraid of the Zulus and wanted a gun'.[13] Astonishingly, Private Hook continued to be unperturbed by this terrible predicament, as 'it was impossible to do anything but fight, and I blazed away as hard as I could'. His defence of this room was short-lived, however, as flames and dense, choking smoke crept in the room and his post became unsustainable. Hook was forced to exit 'by means of the front door to join his comrades, Privates Connolly and eight patients in an adjoining room'. Tragically, it proved impossible to take the African patient with him and he was left, in Hook's words, 'to an awful fate but his death was at any rate a merciful one'. Hook heard the Zulu briefly interrogate him but he was apparently killed as he 'tried to tear off his bandages and escape'.[14]

Next door, for over an hour, Privates Horrigan, John Williams and Joseph Williams had been hard put to defend their room and the five patients in their care against the fierce assaults of their Zulu attackers. A failure of ammunition apparently sealed the fate of several of these men. In the thick smoke, the escaping Hook thus came across a distressed Private John Williams, who blurted out the news of Private Williams' terrible fate: 'the Zulus are swarming all over the place. They have dragged Joseph Williams out and killed him'.[15] With no cartridges left, Joseph Williams had, in fact, been grabbed by several enraged Zulu who had promptly disembowelled him alive in front of his horrified comrades. Poor Private Joseph Williams had probably paid dearly for his earlier successes, the historian Moodie recording the later discovery of up to fourteen Zulu dead below his firing position outside his window and others along his line of fire. Zulu vengeance had been swift. Within minutes, Private Horrigan was also stabbed to death and two helpless patients, including Private Garrett Hayden, were assegaied in their beds. Drummer Hayden was later found stabbed in sixteen places, his belly cut open in two places and part of his cheek cut off. Meanwhile, the surviving Private John Williams, with two patients, had managed to break through the thin mud wall of his room using a navvy's pick, thereby achieving a successful link-up with the beleaguered Private Hook.

Besieged by Zulu from outside the back wall and now emerging from the two rooms abandoned by Private Hook and John Williams, the 'fire fight' within the hospital reached a new intensity. In such a confined space, the mode of fighting was again reduced to assegai, bayonet and rifle butt. Horrific injuries were inflicted upon both defender and attacker alike. Hook himself had a narrow escape, as assegais 'kept whizzing towards us' and one struck him in the front of his helmet, which 'tilted back under the blow' making 'the spear lose its power so that I escaped with a scalp wound'. While this 'did not trouble me much then', it 'has often caused me illness since'. As Hook fought desperately to defend the exposed doorway, the ever-resourceful Private John Williams again hacked through a side wall to reach the next room where eight sick patients and Privates Connolly, Savage, R.C. Cole, Waters and others were located.

Private Waters of the 1st/24th soon opted for an equally daring escape strategy. Teaming up with the already injured Private Beckett, he discovered, in the adjoining room, an ingenious place of refuge. Five months after the battle he recounted his experiences to the *Cambrian Newspaper*:

> While I was there, I took refuge in a cupboard and Private Beckett, an invalid, came with me. As they [Zulu] were going out (after firing the roof) I killed many of them and as I could not stay there long, the place being suffocating, I put on a black cloak which I found in a cupboard and which must have belonged to Mr Witt, and ran out in the long grass and lay down. The Zulus must have thought I was one of their dead comrades as they were all round about me and some trod on me.[17]

Lieutenant Chard, interviewing Waters after the battle, was able to complete the story. Waters eventually made his way to the cookhouse where he found 'the Zulus were occupying this and firing at us from the wall nearest us'. It was 'too late to retreat', so Waters 'crept softly to the fireplace and standing up in the chimney, blackened his hands and face with the soot. He remained there until the Zulus left'.[18] His sick colleague, Beckett, was less fortunate. Leaving the cupboard about half an hour earlier, he was 'assegaied right through the stomach'. Discovered next morning, he died soon after treatment from Doctor Reynolds who 'did all he could to save him but did not succeed'.[19] The ensuing epic struggle in the back rooms was again carefully left on record by Hook who, like Hitch, was one of the few men to record their actual face-to-face encounters with the enemy:

> Only one man at a time could get in at the door. A big Zulu sprang forward and seized my rifle and I tore it free and, slipping

a cartridge in, I shot him point blank. Time after time the Zulus gripped the muzzle and tried to tear the rifle from my grasp, and time after time I wrenched it back because I had a better grip than they had.[20]

All this time, Private John Williams was dragging the sick patients through the adjoining wall to the next ward which faced the hill and which was occupied by Privates Robert and William Jones and about four patients, including a semi-conscious, fever-ridden Sergeant Maxfield. Maxfield and another sick patient, Private Connolly (called mistakenly Conley by Hook), who suffered from synitus due to a partial dislocation of his left knee in a wagon-loading accident, posed a severe problem in the evacuation procedure. Connolly's heavy build forced a desperate Hook to drag him so violently through the hole that his leg was consequently re-broken. There was, as Hook recalled, 'no help for it. As soon as we left the room, the Zulus burst in with furious cries of disappointment and rage'.[21] The delirious Sergeant Maxfield, who had stubbornly refused to either be dressed or evacuated, had to be left behind and was brutally stabbed to death on his bed. Years later, the terrible fate of the helpless Maxfield continued to haunt the minds of members of the Rorke's Drift garrison:

> We had to leave him there to be killed. Ah! Poor Fellow! and sometimes, thinking it over, I cannot help feeling that I might somehow or another have devised escape for him. I can't help feeling it. But it is hard to think coolly in a rush of that kind![22]

Private Robert Jones did return in a desperate last attempt to save Sergeant Maxfield, but could only watch helplessly as he was stabbed by the Zulu as he lay in his bed. Private Jobbins also long lamented the death of 'poor Sergeant Maxfield' who was 'insane' and 'was burnt alive or then killed and burnt'.[23] Soon Hook, Williams and their eight patients reached a 'dead end', the last back room valiantly defended by Private Robert and William Jones.

In this final defensive position, a small window at the end of the hospital presented the only realistic means of escape. Beyond the window was a courtyard requiring a thirty-yard perilous dash to rejoin the rest of the anxious garrison, who were now fully entrenched in their new defensive positions behind the line of biscuit boxes. There was no alternative to this potential ordeal, as Zulu were all around and casualties had rapidly mounted in this room-to-room struggle for survival, with 'one poor fellow' (Jenkins) having prematurely ventured through one of the holes, being 'also seized and dragged away'.[24] As the two Joneses heroically 'kept at it with bullet and bayonet', the remaining soldiers and their patients alternatively dashed, hobbled, or even crawled across the 'courtyard of death'. One man, Trooper Hunter of the Natal Mounted Police, inexplicably and fatally hesitated. Hunter, a 'very tall young man', clearly inexperienced and possibly suffering from battle shock, or as Chard concluded:

> dazed by the glare of the burning hospital and the firing that was going on all around,... was assegaied before our eyes, the Zulu who killed him immediately afterwards falling.[25]

Surgeon Reynolds provided a different account of Hunter's demise, describing how as he reached the inner laager he was 'shot dead while crossing over to the biscuit boxes by... fire from the enemy from behind mealie sacks'.[26] Lugg recalled his fellow trooper Hunter, 'ill with rheumatism and being assegaied in the kidneys and exhibiting five wounds in the chest',[27] though most of these stab wounds were probably inflicted later on his body as the Zulu reoccupied the area. In the event, Trooper Hunter was fortunately the only man to be killed in the desperate retreat across the hospital yard.

Three other patients involved in this final dash to safety experienced mixed fortunes: Corporal Mayer (also NNC) was wounded under the knee by an assegai at the earlier skirmish at Sihayo's kraal; artillery man Bombardier Lewis, whose leg and thigh were much swollen from a wagon incident, and Trooper S. Green (Natal Mounted Police), also a patient, escaped through the little window. It was a painful exit, Padre Smith recalling their ordeal:

> The window being high up and the Zulus already within the room behind them, each man had a fall in escaping and then had to crawl (for none of them could walk) through the enemy's fire inside the entrenchment.[28]

While attempting this, Green was hit in the thigh with a spent bullet. A few other patients tried to escape from the front of the hospital, running round to the right of the entrenchment, but 'two or three were assegaied as they attempted it'.[29] After successfully crossing to the inner barricade, the surviving sick and wounded were quickly escorted to the relative safety of the veranda in front of the storehouse where Surgeon Reynolds again excelled himself doing 'everything he could for them' in the midst of continual 'heavy fire and clouds of assegais'.[30]

8

The Final Ordeal
(10p.m.–8a.m.)

The rest is just a story of sticking to it. We stood up face to face,
white and black, and blazed at each other… they broke in on us
and we drove them back. They hammered at us and we struck
the hammer up. And then God sent the night and the flag was
still flying,.

AMCM, Surgeon Reynolds, How VCs are Won

For the rest of the garrison, situated only yards away from the
hospital, the situation was one of great anxiety, coupled with
a profound feeling of helplessness, as they watched their compatriots desperately struggling to reach the barricade. All they
could do in this potentially catastrophic situation was to provide
covering fire or reach over the biscuit boxes and pull their comrades to safety. As the fight continued, the Zulu had, by firing the
hospital roof, unknowingly bequeathed the defenders a small but
distinct tactical advantage. As Sergeant Smith explained:

the light from the burning hospital was of the greatest service
to our men lighting up the scene for hundreds of yards around,
although before 10pm it had burnt itself out.[1]

For two or three hours at least, it provided a terrible 'killing ground', as the brave Zulu attackers 'lighted themselves up for us in lurid flames against the darkness, and we poured in death upon them with a rush that swept them away'.[2] During the two hours or so between around 10p.m. and midnight, further major assaults were launched by the Zulu against the shrunken garrison perimeter. Again showing his great tactical awareness, Chard recognised this period as the probable final test or reckoning, as he later analysed the battle in terms of three stages or phases of intensity: the 'first onslaught'; the retreat to the biscuit box line; and the time after it when the 'Zulus had gained greater confidence by their success at the hospital'.[3]

The exceptional determination of Dabulamanzi, his commanders and their already battle-worn regiments was clearly revealed in the decision to continue the battle through the hours of darkness. Night fighting was a rare Zulu tactic and was never repeated again in the course of the Anglo-Zulu war. Again, the decision of the Zulu commanders to persevere after six hours of almost continual fighting throws doubt, as we shall see, upon recent theories as to their high level of battle fatigue and their status as a mere raiding party.

Behind the mealie and biscuit box barricades, Chard, Bromhead and the rest of the garrison were made uncomfortably aware of their dire predicament and complete encirclement, as in the darkness they heard the demoralising sounds of the Zulu 'wrecking the camp of the 24th', a veritable orgy of looting accompanied by the exultant cries of the Zulu attackers. In one rare, amusing moment, Chard observed the strenuous efforts of his fellow Royal Engineer and Batman, Driver Robson, who persistently focused his fire on one particular group of Zulu plunderers in a futile attempt to keep them 'off this wagon in which, were, as he described it "our things"'.[4]

This lighter incident belied the continued grim situation confronting the weary garrison, so tightly hemmed into their tiny laager. Dabulamanzi and his subordinate commanders now launched their final wave of major assaults to finish off the remainder of the garrison. This time, the focus of the Zulu commanders was on the cattle kraal and the store building, fire from which had earlier caused considerable casualties in their ranks. In their final murderous assault, still exposed by the dying flames of the hospital, the Zulu paid a heavy price. Trooper Lugg recalled:

> At about 10 they came on in tremendous force, sweeping the fellows before them and causing them to retreat to the store. But Providence favoured us. The thatched roof… burst out in flames… and made it as light as day and, before they had time to retreat, we were pouring the bullets into them like hail. We could see them falling in scores.[5]

Gunner Howard was more ebullient:

> when the flames burst out it was all the better for us for we could see the niggers and their movements although they could not see us. Didn't we give it to them anyhow.[6]

By midnight, Zulu morale was clearly faltering, as the pace of the attacks slowed up and more time was taken to regroup. Private Hook recalled the futility of such brave Zulu forays, increasingly punctuated by retreats into the bush for morale-building war ceremonies:

> We could see them coming and they could not rush us and take us by surprise from any point… so they went away for ten or fifteen minutes of war-dance. This roused them again and their excitement was so intense that the ground fairly seemed to shake. Then when they were goaded to the highest pitch they would hurl themselves at us again.[7]

But the garrison itself was also rapidly weakening, as individual Zulu attackers came close to setting fire to the store roof, a tactic which could have proved disastrous as it would have deprived them of the one remaining area of complete shelter. Fortunately, all the attacks failed, with one intrepid Zulu warrior being shot ('I believe by Lieutenant Adendorff') just as the light was 'almost touching the thatch'.[8]

The potential for disaster presented by such incidents forced Chard to reorganise and order one more key tactical change – the construction of a final redoubt, both to act as a sanctuary for the more seriously wounded and ultimately to provide a final firing position. In his report, Reynolds recognised Chard's construction of this 'cone shaped stack of mealies' as 'last stand' strategy. Chard, in his view, had again showed great foresight and 'shined in resource' by 'anticipating the Zulus making one more united dash for the fort and possibly making an entrance'.[9] It was a strenuous task, as assisted by Commissary Officer Dunne and other men: the core of an immense stack of mealies was rapidly decapitated and a number of sacks removed from the heart of what remained. This task was 'hard work for the bags of mealie weighed 200 pounds each', which created a sheltered space 'sufficient to accommodate 40 men and in a position to make good shooting',[10] as well as to provide a second elevated line of fire. It was, apparently, a surreal period in the battle, as 'overhead small birds, disturbed from their nests by the turmoil and smoke flew hither and thither confusedly',[11] a scene reminiscent of the First World War trenches, where soldiers were similarly distracted by such small comforting signs of nature amidst the horror and carnage.

The Zulu attackers enjoyed a greater degree of success along the eastern perimeter outside the permanent wall of the kraal. After a protracted struggle and several repulses of their Zulu attackers, the exhausted British defenders were slowly forced back, inch by inch, to the middle and, then, to the inner wall. The Zulu then rapidly occupied the middle wall as the British were forced to abandon it. However, here the position was at last stabilised, as the middle wall proved

> too high for them to use it to effectively to fire over and a Zulu no sooner showed his head over it than he was dropped, being so close it was almost impossible to miss him.[12]

By now, the defenders had experienced nearly eight hours of almost continual fighting, and the heavy toll on men and equipment was becoming starkly apparent. Lieutenant Bromhead, continually touring the positions of his men, was particularly worried about the high expenditure of fire, 'keeping a strict eye on the ammunition and telling the men not to waste one round as we were getting short'.[13] A number of the vital weapon, the otherwise 'fine' Martini–Henry rifles, were also showing ominous signs of wear and tear:

> we did so much firing that became hot, and the brass of the car-
> tridges softened, the result being that the barrels got very fouled
> and the cartridge chamber jammed.

Hook's own rifle 'jammed several times and I had to work away with the ramrod till I cleared it'.[14] Even some of the 'very fine', three-sided 'lunger' bayonets, with their deadly long, thin blades, were proving to be of indifferent quality and had

> either twisted or bent badly. Several were like that after the fight;
> but some terrible thrusts were given, and I saw dead Zulu who
> had been pinned to the ground by the bayonets going through
> them.[15]

The British defenders were themselves exhibiting significant signs of battle fatigue. In the early hours of the morning, an already seriously wounded Private Hitch, wearily leaning against the bis-cuit boxes, recalled his somewhat fatalistic conversation with a fellow 24th soldier, Private Deacon:

> 'Fred, when it comes to the last should I shoot you?' I declined,
> 'no, they have very nearly done for me and they can finish me
> right out when it comes to the last'. Hitch added, tellingly, 'I don't
> remember much after that'.[16]

Water became a pressing need, and for many their desperate thirst was undoubtedly enhanced by the terrible psychological and emotional stresses of such unrelenting combat. Unfortunately, in the rush to retreat from the hospital, the water cart had been left isolated beyond the barricades and alongside the hospital wall. Private Hitch soon became so 'thirsty and faint that he could not do much'.[17] As in the hospital, Private Hook was to again emerge as a saviour of the situation. Having taken up his new post alongside a barricade in the inner fort area, where two men had already earlier been shot, Hook felt compelled to take drastic action:

> All this time the sick and wounded were crying for water but it was just by the deserted hospital and we could not hope to get it until the day broke when the Zulus might begin to lose heart and to stop in their mad rushes. But we could not bear the cries any longer and three or four of us jumped over the boxes and ran and fetched some water in.[18]

For the scores of dying and wounded Zulu littered inside and immediately outside the perimeter, and effectively isolated from their comrades, the situation must have been far worse. At least their comrades in the bush would presumably have had a ready supply of water from the nearby Buffalo or Mzinyathi river.

The collapse of the hospital defences and the occupation of half the kraal area represented the high tide of Zulu successes. By midnight, crippled by such terrible losses, the intensity of their attacks took a rapid downturn. Lieutenant Chard recalled the noticeable reduction in pressure during the early hours of the morning of the 23rd:

> About midnight or a little after, the fire slackened, and after that, although they kept us constantly on the alert by feigning, as before, to come on at different points, the fire was a desultory character… a few shots from the Zulus replied to by our men – again silence broken by the same thing repeated.[19]

Other accounts confirmed the rapidly declining scale of attack, Gunner Howard noting how after the great pre-midnight assaults they 'sheered off, all but a few hung about us all night'.[20] Padre Smith noted that while the enemy fire definitely slackened after midnight, desultory fire continued 'from the bank and garden in front'.[21] Surgeon Reynolds also recalled a relapse to 'desultory firing... but no big rushing attack', while Trooper Lugg also recalled how 'they kept up the attack all night with no better luck'.[22]

There was, however, no possibility of relaxing with the ever-present danger of a renewed Zulu attack. Dunne, for instance, felt curiously unnerved by the long pregnant silences after midnight:

> broken only by the words of command of the Zulu leaders which sounded strangely close. How we longed to know what they said! Every man was then on the alert straining eyes and ears to detect the rush which was sure to follow, only to be checked each time by a withering volley.[23]

It was in fact highly fortuitous for the garrison that no major Zulu assault took place during these last fateful hours. In his subsequent report on the battle, Chard strikingly revealed that by early morning, while 'each man' still 'had a good supply of ammunition in his pouches we had only a box and a half besides'.[24] In fact, at about this time, Chard had felt compelled to send a frightened fugitive 'Kaffir' messenger to Helpmekaar, outlining his predicament and urgently calling for aid. For Dabulamanzi, it had been the great missed opportunity, and one final major assault before dawn might have proved successful. It was not to be.

The garrison put these periods of lull in the fighting to great use. Lieutenant Chard, again demonstrating his endless energy, detailed a working party to rebuild the strength of the remaining defences, mainly by raising the walls and placing sacks of mealie on top of the biscuit boxes. In a wise move, the thatch was removed from the Commissariat Store 'to avoid being burnt out in case of another attack'.[25]

Patrolling around the perimeter, 'collecting the arms and ammunition of the dead Zulus', Chard was both horrified and intrigued by their odd dispositions and the terrible damage inflicted by Martini–Henry rounds:

Some of the bullet wounds were very curious. One man's head was split open, exactly as if done with an axe. Another had been hit just between the eyes, the bullet carrying away the whole of the back of his head, leaving his face perfect, as though it were a mask, only disfigured by the small hole made by the bullet passing through. One of the wretches we found had one hand grasping a bench that had been dragged from the hospital, and sustained thus in the position we found him, while in the other hand he still clutched the knife with which he had mutilated one of our poor fellows, over whom he was still leaning.[26]

Other parties were detailed to collect and destroy the scores of muskets and assegais strewn across the ground, while a third party had 'the painful task of decently laying out our dead in a corner of the enclosure'.[27] Walking around, Dunne found 'everywhere dead Zulus – all ring kops that is married men who alone wear a black ring woven into the hair of the head'.[28] The cold light of dawn revealed distressing scenes in what must have seemed like a landscape from hell:

The scene we beheld was a strange and sad one! On one side stood the blackened walls and still smouldering ruins of the hospital. Around it and in front of that side of the barrier lay the bodies of Zulus in rows, as if literally mown down, showing how brave had been the assault and how unerring the fire that had laid them low. Inside were our own dead comrades – stark and cold, one still kneeling in a natural position at the wall – while the wounded excited pity by their sufferings patiently borne. The ground was strewn with trampled grain which had run from the bags pierced by bullet or assegai, and every face was black with smoke and sweat of toil and battle.[29]

The sense of horror that pervaded the garrison was only equalled by the sense of gratitude for their survival so far. As the severely wounded hospital survivor Private Walters put it:

I got up at daybreak having expected every minute my life would be taken and then saw my comrades on top of the mealie sacks and I said 'thank God I have got my life'.[30]

The battle, however, was not quite over – it was still to be a couple of hours before relief would finally arrive. One false alarm occurred in the early morning (around 5a.m. according to Dunne). Several lookouts spotted a cloud of dust on the road some miles away in the direction of the British outpost of Helpmekaar. Some of the men claimed they saw redcoats, and the ensuing loud cheers apparently astonished the Zulu and, according to Dunne, even caused 'the enemy to pause', as if to 'know what it meant' but, sadly, the dust was dispersed by the wind and the longed for help never came'.[31] The blow to morale must have been consider-able. Later, after the battle, Lieutenant Chard speculated on the circumstances surrounding this event:

> It is very strange that this report should have arisen amongst us, for the two companies 24th from Helpmekaar did come down to the foot of the hill, but not I believe in sight of us. They marched back to Helpmekaar on the report of Rorkes Drift having fallen.[32]

The *Official History* confirms also how two companies of the 24th had approached the garrison but, seeing flames from the post and presuming disaster, had promptly retreated to the Helpmekaar post.[33]

At around 7a.m., another sighting, this time of a large group of the enemy, provided a further test for the garrison's mettle. A 'large body' of the enemy appeared on hills to the south-west. As the signallers on the store roof frantically alerted the rest of the garrison to their presence, Hook recalled the 'awful time of suspense... we looked everywhere for sign of relief but saw nothing and our hearts sank'.[34]

By contrast, Chard, using his past experience, was convinced of the unlikelihood of any major Zulu attack:

> I thought at the time they were going to attack us, but what I know from Zulus, and also of the number we put 'hors de combat', I do not think so. I think that they came up on the high ground to observe Lord Chelmsford's advance; from there they could see Column long before it came in sight of us.[35]

The garrison was astonished by one last admirable act of enemy defiance:

> One Zulu had remained in the Kraal and fired a shot among us (without doing any damage) as we stood on the walls, and he ran off over the hill and in the direction of the river – although many shots were fired at him as he ran, I am glad to say the plucky fellow got off.[36]

It was the last moment of tension, and at about 8a.m., as the enemy disappeared again, Chelmsford's relief column came into sight. The terrible ordeal for the Rorke's Drift garrison was at last over.

9

Aftermath: Relief, Recovery and Retribution

> We broke into roar after roar of cheering, waving red coats and white helmets... we cheered again and again
>
> *Private Hook, Holme, Silver Wreath*

> I thank you all for your gallant defence
>
> *Lord Chelmsford, RLCM, Dunne Account*

The sight of Chelmsford's approaching relief column did not immediately inspire confidence within the Rorke's Drift garrison. Some suspected it was a typical Zulu ruse. Surgeon Reynolds was one of the sceptics:

> For a long time and even after red coats were distinguished through our field glasses, we believed them to be the enemy, some of them perhaps dressed in the kits of those who had fallen at Isandlwana.[1]

Lieutenant Chard also shared his initial caution as the column came into sight:

There were a great many of our native levies with the Column, and the number of red coats seemed so few that, at first, we had grave doubts that the force approaching was the enemy.[2]

Such concerns permeated through to the rank and file of the garrison. As Private Hook put it:

We saw their flags going wildly. What was it? Everybody was mad with anxiety to know whether it could be friends to relieve us, or more Zulus to destroy us. We watched the flags flapping, and then learnt that signals were being made in reply. We knew we were safe and that friends were marching up to us.[3]

Thus, with the help of an improvised white flag and an exchange of signals, the wonderful moment of relief finally dawned. Nevertheless, after so many false alarms, Reynolds waited until the last minute – not until the mounted infantry in the advance party had 'crossed the Buffalo Drift' were he and others totally 'convinced of our relief'.[4] Private Jobbins expressed his profound relief and sense of security in simple but telling words: 'We did not at first recognise them, but after a bit we could see the welcome red coats retiring on us from the other unfortunate camp. Then we all gave a hearty cheer, as we felt safe where we were altogether'.[5] Private Hook was equally joyful: 'there was not a living soul who was not thankful to find that the Zulus had had enough of it and were disappearing over the hill to the south-west'.[6]

The approaching column, having seen the glow of the burning hospital and anticipating another massacre, were extremely tense after their miserable journey to Rorke's Drift from the wrecked Isandlwana camp earlier that morning. Astonishingly, on their journey from Isandlwana, they had experienced a head-on but bloodless encounter with thousands of Zulu who had streamed silently past them on the left side of the road. Lieutenant Milne accordingly reported that, within some three miles of the Drift: 'the enemy were seen in large bodies (some three thousand or four thousand) returning from the river'.[7] Both weary columns, however, passed each other in silence, the Zulu and their walking wounded painfully exiting from Rorke's Drift in defeat, and the already demoralised British column mistakenly believing they were a victorious *impi* who had just sacked the post. Consequently, neither side had any inclination to fight. Lieutenant Harford vividly recalled this incredible stand-off between two erstwhile bitter enemies:

> Contrary to all expectations, Dabulamanzi with his impi made no attempt whatever to interfere with the Column, though some hundreds of warriors sat and stood within a few yards of us on the right of the road, simply gazing at us like sightseers at a revue... I... and... many others... were absolutely dumbfounded at this extraordinary spectacle and could scarcely believe our eyes. Personally, I felt very suspicious about it all and thought a trap was being laid, especially as a few hundred yards below on our left, just above the Buffalo River, great masses of Zulu were coming directly from Rorke's Drift who could easily have swept up the hills, joined Dabulamanzi's men and come down like an avalanche from the rear on our straggling Column.[8]

The first glimpse of the Rorke's Drift garrison was probably the most traumatic moment. Lieutenant Harford again takes up the story:

> As we approached the Drift and reached the hill overlooking the river and the Post, the excitement became intense, all eyes were strained and field-glasses raised, to see if there was any sign of life in the fort. Then as we drew nearer a man was seen on the bared roof of one of the buildings, signalling with a flag, which was hailed with a tremendous cheer from the whole Column as we knew then that the garrison had not been wiped out.[9]

As the column came into sight at 8a.m. (8.15a.m. by Lieutenant Milne's more precise calculation), the last of the Zulu on the Shiyane or Oskarberg hill disappeared again to the south-west. The first men to arrive at the post were Major Cecil Russell and Lieutenant Walsh. They led the mounted infantry, who were duly 'received by us with a hearty cheer'. Chelmsford and his staff soon followed, literally galloping up to the Fort. Chelmsford, still clearly traumatised by the loss of his camp, 'thanked us all with much emotion for the defence we had made'.[10] The rest of the column then slowly inched its way in to the post via the ponts. Captain Hallam Parr recorded the 'startling' scene that greeted the first men of the relief column:

> Hundreds of Zulu lying around the building and parapets in every conceivable attitude and posture. In some places they had fallen in heaps over one another – some with the most ghastly wounds from having been so close to the muzzle of the rifles which killed them; others having been consumed by fire from having fallen into the flames of the hospital, as they were killed or wounded. The 24th men, all blackened, torn and weary, many wounded and bleeding, some dead or dying.[11]

A traumatised Corporal Attwood informed his uncle:

> We killed 390... we found them on the ground the next morning.... such a sight met our eyes, all the white men that were killed were cut open and their entrails protruding.

Trooper Symons also vividly remembered the scenes of carnage:

> around the burned hospital lay in heaps the dead bodies of the Zulus. Under the trees in front of the hospital lay three horses still tied to a trunk of the tree.[12]

Lieutenant Harford's less disciplined Natal Native Contingent were the last to enter the post. Wild, excited scenes ensued as his African levies suddenly broke ranks and 'for some time it was quite impossible to keep the men in hand'. They were

> all around the surroundings of the Fort in a second, crowding about the Zulu dead who were lying thick everywhere, partly, no doubt, from curiosity but I dare say some may have been looking

out to identify friends or relations as many of the Natal Kaffirs are refugees from Zululand.[13]

As the General and his staff occupied the post, a deeply fatigued Chard and Bromhead, relieved temporarily of their onerous responsibilities, were at last able to take time off. Joining their exhausted but exultant men, Chard was

> glad to seize an opportunity to wash my face in a muddy puddle in company with Private Bush, 24th, whose face was covered in blood from the wound in the nose caused by the bullet which had passed through and killed Private Cole, 24th.

It must have been a touching scene, emphasising the deep bonds forged between officers and men after this twelve-hour struggle for survival, as

> with the politeness of a soldier… he lent me his towel, or rather a very dirty half of one, before using it himself, and I was very glad to accept it.

There was an unexpected treat for the two parched officers. In the midst of his wrecked and looted wagon, Chard discovered, to his delight, a forgotten bottle of beer. The contents were eagerly consumed by both officers who 'drank it with mutual congratulations on having come safely out of so much danger'.[14]

There were other, greater surprises. As the relief column marched in, several more survivors, in addition to the hospital escapees, staggered in after experiencing a similar night of terror. Two experiences stood out. One involved the escape of the servant of Colonel Harness RA, who had been left behind sick at Rorke's Drift when the column had crossed into Zululand. He had been unfortunately left isolated outside the barricades at the precise moment when the Zulu made their major rush on the hospital. Harford completed the story of his miraculous escape:

As he would certainly have been shot down by the fire of our own men had he attempted in the darkness to run in and clamber back again, he quickly bolted under a small handcart that had been accidentally left propped up outside against the back of the hospital wall and which (lucky for him but unfortunate for the garrison), was in such a position as to be completely out of the line of fire. Here he remained throughout the night wrapped up in his blanket with the Zulus swarming all around him – many of them actually jumping onto the cart to try and get onto the roof of the hospital... But none of them, curiously enough, made any attempt to move the cart, in which case he would have been done for. In the morning, however, when the Zulus had decamped and all firing had ceased, to the great astonishment of the garrison, he walked in safe and sound, after about as terrifying an experience as any man could have gone through.[15]

Another who had survived 'a terrifying an experience as any man could have gone through' was Lieutenant Chard's own wagon driver, a Cape (coloured) man who had been tasked with caring for the mules outside the garrison perimeter at the start of the battle. He had, understandably, 'lost his courage on hearing the first firing around the hill'. Abandoning his mules, he had retreated into one of the caves in the Oskarberg Hill. His personal nightmare then began, as:

> he saw the Zulus run by him and, to his horror, some of them entered the cave he was in, and lying down commenced firing at us. The poor wretch was crouching in the darkness, in the far depths of the cave, afraid to speak or move, as our bullets came into the cave, actually killing one of the Zulus. He did not know from whom he was in the most danger, friends or foe, and came down in the morning looking more dead than alive.

Chard gratefully recalled how the mules were 'recovered... quietly grazing by the riverside'.[16] Such joyful moments were, however, matched by far more tragic scenes, as, for instance, poor Private

Beckett was also discovered that morning, only to die a few hours later from assegai wounds to the stomach.

After these initial exuberant, even chaotic scenes, a new sombreness returned to the men of the garrison and the relief force. In Hook's words: 'there was no time to sit down and mope…'.[17] With fears of a renewed Zulu attack, three vital tasks had to be implemented. Ironically, the first priority was to feed the starving men of the relief column, and the irrepressible Commissariat officers, Dunne and Dalton, found time and energy to haul out and open up several biscuit boxes for 'us hungry souls'. Captain Harford recalled 'what a God-send it was as it was over two days and two nights since most of us had a mouthful of food'. He added, thankfully:

> hunger, however, luckily does not affect one like thirst, and one could have gone on much longer as there was plenty of good water.[18] [with the Zulu retreat there was a ready access to the water of the Buffalo river].

The second essential task was to strengthen the badly damaged defences, for the General and his staff feared another Zulu attack that very evening. Lieutenant Milne recalled that 'as soon as the Column had had some food they were immediately set to work to improve the defences'.[19] The parapets were heightened further and continued to the edge of the hospital, the remains of the thatched roof of the store were removed and, significantly and belatedly, all the trees in close vicinity were finally cut down, denying the Zulu cover in any future attack. The firepower of the garrison could now be massively increased, with three of the column's four seven-pounders brought inside to strengthen the perimeter, and these were targeted towards the river. The fourth gun was located by the right of the Krantz and in the direction in which the Zulu had come the previous night. While Colonel Russell and a few men rode on to Helpmekaar and 'communicated by letter' the good news of the relief to Sir Bartle Frere, several parties of mounted men were deployed to reconnoitre the area.

The third and perhaps most pressing priority was the burial of the dead. The hundreds of putrefying corpses clearly presented a major threat of disease to the reinforced garrison, 'as decomposition comes on quickly under the hot African sun'.[20] This 'mopping-up' process, in particular the treatment of the Zulu wounded, has, as we shall see, become one of the most controversial episodes in the history of the Rorke's Drift action. The men of the relief column continued to be staggered by the sights within the terrible killing ground in and around the Rorke's Drift post. Lieutenant Harford, hungrily munching his biscuit ration and casually wandering about the Fort, was struck by the appearance of the corpses, coupled with the feeling of a

> devastation after a hurricane, with the dead bodies thrown in, the only thing that remained whole being a circular miniature fortress constructed of bags of mealies in the centre.

Examining the few British dead still remaining where they had fallen, Harford was particularly struck by the sight of 'one of them — a youngster in the Natal Mounted Police — a very fine specimen of humanity'[21] (almost certainly Trooper Hunter, killed during the retreat from the hospital). For a weary Lieutenant Smith-Dorrien, returning from Helpmekaar, where he had spent the night after his miraculous escape from Isandlwana, the scene confronting him was one of

> sheer devastation, his own wagon some two hundred yards away riddled and looted... dead animals and cattle everywhere.[22]

The burying of the Zulu dead lasted up to two days, the first day being a particularly 'stiff, day... officers and men working together with picks and shovels'. For Captain Hallam Parr, assigned to supervise the burial parties, it proved to be a most repulsive task: 'It was disagreeable work handling the dead naked bodies, many with awful looking wounds'. He added that, although there were sufficient numbers of the Native Natal Contingent to supply strong working parties, it was the British regulars who had to

directly dispose of the corpses, as 'the natives have great repug-
nance to touch a dead body'.[23] With no carts or even horses, the
dead Zulu had to be hauled by 'reims' (ropes of hide) over the
ground or carried in rough stretchers. Hallam–Parr recorded the
conversations of his soldiers engaged in this unpleasant task:

> 'Come on, you black devil', I heard a man mutter to a dead Zulu he
> was hauling over the grass, as the body caught against a stone; 'I'm
> blamed if you don't give more trouble dead nor alive…. It's your
> turn now, comrade, now we've cleared the rubbish out of your way'
> said another 24th man to a dead soldier, who was found with two or
> three Zulus stretched almost upon him. 'I'm main sorry to put you
> away, mate,' continued he, laying the end of a torn sack gently over
> the dead man's face, 'but you died well and had a soldier's end'.[24]

Few of the Zulu wounded were spared. Many were finished off
by their own assegais, bayonets or rifle butts, a method designed
to conserve ammunition. It was a process which had started even
as the relief column arrived, Lieutenant Milne noting 'firing still
going on at wounded men trying to escape'.[25] For at least one
contemporary commentator, these apparently callous acts have
been described as constituting a major war crime and, moreover,
conducted within an official policy of 'total war'.[26]

A closer examination of the sources, however, suggests that not
only did the British have sound military reasons for these otherwise abhorrent practices, but that 'other parties' probably carried
out the bulk of the killing. Near the end of the battle, Private
Hook had experienced an encounter with an apparently wounded
Zulu which was repeated elsewhere, and convinced many of the
garrison that a policy of taking Zulu prisoners or rescuing Zulu
casualties had become a perilous task. Hook recounted the incident, which occurred as he strolled around the garrison perimeter
collecting Zulu weapons, 'my own rifle in my right-hand and a
bunch of assegais over my left shoulder'. Soon he

> came across an unarmed Zulu lying on the ground, appearing dead
> but bleeding from the leg. Thinking it strange that a dead man

should bleed, I hesitated and wondering whether I should go on, as other Zulu might be lurking about. But I resumed my task. Just as I was passing, the supposed dead man, seized the butt of my rifle and tried to drag it away. The bunch of assegais rattled to earth. The Zulu suddenly released his grasp of the rifle with one hand and, with the other, fiercely endeavoured to drag me down. The fight was short and sharp; but it ended by the Zulu being struck in the chest with the butt and knocked to the ground.

Hook added, cryptically: 'the rest was quickly over'.[27]

After such dangerous incidents, Hook recalled that we were 'not allowed to go on with our task except in twos and threes'.[28] Hallam-Parr reaffirmed the tough policies now adopted when dealing with what was perceived to be a dangerous and fanatical enemy:

When it is remembered that even to count the dead after an action with the Zulus was a service of considerable danger, on account of the wounded Zulus attacking unawares those engaged in this duty, and that in some cases it was on this account actually forbidden, some idea will be formed of the difficulty in extending to the brave but savage enemy precisely the same rules that are observed in civilised warfare.[29]

There were other exceptional, but less justifiable reasons for what would appear to be cruel and unnecessary behaviour – namely revenge and retribution. Many amongst both the garrison and the relief force were already incensed at the news of atrocities brought to them by the survivors of Isandlwana. One Rorke's Drift defender, Sergeant Smith of the 1st/24th, became a ready believer in such possibly exaggerated stories, and in a letter home, despatched two days after the battle, justified the mood of retribution:

The Zulus took one of the band boys and hung him up by his chin on a hook and cut him up in bits… I cannot tell you one quarter of the horrors that have taken place… we have counted the number of blacks that were killed and shot by my company, there were over 800, so that they paid dearly for what they killed of our men.[30]

Private James Cook, a 2/24th member of the relief column, also angrily wrote home:

> The sight at the camp was horrible. Every white man that was killed or wounded was ripped up and their bowels torn out.[31]

Several other Rorke's Drift defenders had been clearly traumatised by the horrendous deaths of several of their comrades, notably Private Joseph Williams, disembowelled alive outside the hospital, and Drummer Haydon and Sergeant Maxfield, practically dismembered alive in their hospital beds. Such sights almost certainly reinforced their beliefs in the earlier horror stories emanating from Isandlwana survivors.

The resulting extreme anger also manifested itself in the several lynchings of captured Zulu and Zulu civilians that took place during the days after the battle. Lieutenant Smith-Dorrien had been shocked, on his return from Helpmekaar, to find his reim gallows, designed for drying buffalo hides, used as an execution site:

> I saw two Zulus hanging on my gallows and was accused by the Brigade Major Clery… of having given the order.

He was, however, exonerated:

> when it was found it was a case of lynch-law performed by incensed men who were bitter at the loss of their comrades.[32]

Although these acts were even less excusable than the killing of the wounded, there was an understandable element in the actions of often incensed British soldiers, for whom the Zulu enemy 'appeared to us to be possessed of savagery beyond description' and who 'fought to kill and undoubtedly killed the wounded and mutilated the bodies'.[33] Moreover, it was clear from this account by Smith-Dorrien that senior British officers at least were opposed to such practices and were trying to restore order to the situation.

There was also considerable evidence to suggest that only a minority of British soldiers were involved in these practices, and that many Zulu wounded died at the hands of African allies serving in the Natal Native Contingent. Captain Hallam-Parr reported that although

> strict orders were given on the subject it was impossible to prevent the Natal Natives who were slipping away to their homes, killing, according to their custom, any wounded they came across on their way.[34]

His view was supported by the NNC Commandant, Captain Hamilton-Browne, who recalled his personal experiences during the immediate aftermath of the Rorke's Drift battle:

> During the afternoon it was discovered that a large number of wounded and worn-out Zulus had taken refuge or hidden in the mealie fields near the laager. My two companies of Zulus with some of my non-coms, and a few of the 24th, quickly drew these fields and killed them with bayonet, butt and assegai. It was beastly but there was nothing else to do. War is war and savage war is the worst of the lot.[35]

Above all, it is clear that these incidents were not part of a total war or genocidal policy against the Zulu. In his 1878 Regulations for Field Forces, the Commander-in-Chief Lord Chelmsford had laid out strict orders that:

> natives will be treated with kindness. Commanding Officers will exert their influence with all ranks to prevent their being in any way molestation or oppression.[36]

Strict penalties were laid down for British troops and their African allies. Moreover, in retrospect, the actions of often emotion-ally charged soldiers at Rorke's Drift, fighting a savage enemy who quite obviously would give no quarter, differs little from, for instance, American and British treatment of their fanatical Japanese enemy during the Second World War at a time in which a much higher level of morality might have been expected.[37]

Whatever the arguments advanced to explain these tragic situations, the consequence was that probably up to 600 Zulu died during or immediately after the Rorke's Drift action. To Lieutenant Chard's official figure of 351 Zulu dead must be added many more who died during the mopping-up operations, or who suffered a lingering death in remote caves, dongas and fields.[38] Sergeant Smith's own estimate of 800 may, in fact, be a more realistic assessment of Zulu losses. Overall, the Zulu probably suffered a 12-15 per cent mortality rate, proportionately comparable to official British losses consisting of seventeen dead (fifteen in action with two, Private W. Beckett and Lance-Sergeant T. Williams, dying later of their terrible wounds) amounting to around 12 per cent fatalities.

For many of the brave survivors of Rorke's Drift, the ordeal was not yet over. The often horrific battle wounds took weeks to heal. Thus, Corporal William Allen wrote from Helpmekaar, where many of the wounded were transferred:

> I am getting the better of my wound, more rapidly than could be expected. We got here (that is the sick and wounded) on the 26th of January and have been waiting [for] an ambulance to convey us down the country, which is expected every day. My arm is mending quickly, though I am sorry I cannot say the same for the other wounded men, who appear to be making no progress towards recovery. I feel very thankful to God for leaving me in the land of the living.[39]

In the extremely overcrowded, heavily reinforced and cramped conditions of Rorke's Drift and Helpmekaar, it was not long before the 'fourth horseman of the Apocalypse' – pestilence – duly arrived. Thus Captain Walter Parker Jones wrote home disconsolately:

We are still waiting at this beastly unhealthy place until reinforcements come from England. One of my men died from diar-
rhoea yesterday and that and fever have knocked nearly all my
men over. Quite half of the company is in hospital, really ill, it
is most depressing… of course, being crowded together in a fort
with rotten meal and other stores, and difficulties about sanitary
arrangements, has something to do with the question.[40]

An early casualty was the indomitable Lieutenant Chard himself,
who nearly died from fever and was transferred by ambulance
to Ladysmith.

A few miles away at Rorke's Drift, at which the defences
were now transformed by an eight-foot stone wall, conditions
were equally bad and possibly exacerbated by inadequately
buried Zulu dead or the still undiscovered corpses outside the
perimeter. Lance-Corporal Adams, 2/24th, wrote home from
the newly named Fort Melvill (Rorke's Drift building) on 6
March:

We have not received any pay this year yet – we have about forty
men in the hospital, sixty more attending the hospital, all sick of
dysentery and fever, resulting from un-healthiness because of so
many dead being buried around… we generally have about two
men die every week.[41]

Lieutenant Harford blamed a combination of the atrocious wet
weather and poor administration:

This terrible state of things, living in such slush, caused a lot
of sickness from fever and dysentery which carried off a large
number of men and one or two of the officers. Notwithstanding
this and the knowledge that the fort was over-crowded, Colonel
Glyn declined to have any tents pitched outside to relieve matters being afraid that the Zulus might sweep down on the place
again… no one but the officers and NCOs of the Contingent
were allowed outside the fort.[42]

In such dark days there were a few moments of light. The morale of B Company was undoubtedly uplifted by gifts and money donated by many grateful Natal citizens. Sergeant Smith wrote:

> the people of Pietermaritzberg are so well pleased at the manner in which my company kept the stores from being taken by the enemy that they think they cannot do enough for us. They have subscribed £150 for us to buy the troops a lot of clothing, and pens, ink and paper, matches, pipes and a lot of everything, and sent them to us to be given to the troops at Rorke's Drift. They also sent word that they consider we have been the means of saving the whole of the colony from being taken by the Zulus, and I don't think they were far wrong, for if we had left the place and let the enemy take it, nothing would have saved the other parts of the colony from the Zulus' raid.[43]

There were other small fillips to morale which became a foretaste of what was to follow. In the quagmire and filth that dominated the fort for two months after the siege, and in which men possessed no more than 'a blanket and the clothes that he stood up in', a special

> exception was made… with 13 Company, 2nd Battalion 24th Regiment, who had made such a gallant defence, and they were housed in the attic of Rorke's house with a tarpaulin thrown over the rafters (from which the thatch had been removed) to shelter them from the wet, a well-deserved honour.

This did not prevent both Harford and Surgeon Reynolds being 'literally washed out of our sleeping place' on 'one particular night'. A retreat to the eaves of B Company's roof failed to save them, as

> presently swish came about half a ton of water clean on top of us – B Company were emptying their tarpaulin!![44]

One wonders if this was a pre-meditated prank by B Company directed against their officers.

An equally amusing incident, an excellent example of 'Tommy' humour in adversity, helped relieve the post-siege misery. Private Hook became the subject of a long-running, hilarious episode, being taken on as a servant by Major Wilsone-Black, whose shrill voice with its Scotch accent could be heard above the fort calling for 'H–o–o–k!', as

Many times a day… the men had their little joke. Whenever Hook was called for they themselves shouted for Hook and then yelled out, 'I think he's hooked it, sir!', which always caused great merriment.[45]

Major Wilsone-Black was soon to be entrusted with a much more sombre task, as Rorke's Drift became a main base for the recovery and burial of the Isandlwana dead. On 4 February he led a small patrol which discovered the assegaied but still well-preserved bodies of Lieutenants Melvill and Coghill, while Harford himself recovered the Queen's Colour case and next day, nearby, in a quiet pool, the tattered remains of the silk Colour itself. Harford vividly recalled the earlier scene when Melvill and Coghill were found:

Both were clearly recognisable. Melvill was in red, and Coghill in blue, uniform. Both were lying on their backs about a yard from each other, Melvill at right angles to the path and Coghill parallel to it, a little above Melvill and with his head uphill. Both had been assegaied, but otherwise their bodies had been left untouched. Major Black at once said 'Now we shall see whether they have the Colours on them', and proceeded to unbutton Melvill's serge while I opened Coghill's patrol jacket but there were no Colours. Presently Major Black said, 'I wonder if Melvill's watch is on him, he always carried it in the small waist pocket of his breeches!', and on looking there was his gold watch which was subsequently sent to his widow. Nothing was found on Coghill, but his bad knee was still bandaged up. Undoubtedly, Melvill must have stuck to him and helped him along, otherwise he never could have got so far over such terrible ground.[46]

A second, larger patrol visited the battlefield of Isandlwana itself on 14 March, 'a horrid scene of desolation' as the 'still-tainted air' filled their nostrils. Most of the Zulu dead had long been removed by their victorious compatriots, but over 100 wagons were left intact, the bodies of the 24th lying in

> all conditions of horrible decay. Some were perfect skeletons, others that had not been stripped, or only partially so, were quite unapproachable and the stench was sickening; but with few exceptions it was impossible to recognise anyone and the only officer that was seen was discovered by his clothes. Of the regular soldiers the largest found in one place was sixty-eight.[47]

A much larger patrol, led by Colonel Drury Lowe, comprising a contingent mainly of the 17th Lancers and accompanied by several journalists, arrived at the Isandlwana camp site on 21 May 1879. By then, oats and mealies spilled from the food wagons and had sprouted around and through the deliquescent corpses. Charles Norris-Newman of the *London Standard* discovered his own tent, 'or rather the disjecta membra of what had once been mine', and behind it the dried-up bodies of his servants and the skeletons of his horses. The site of Durnford's last stand on the Nek was also examined and the body of Durnford himself was identified in a patch of long grass, the distinctive long moustache still clinging to the withered skin of his face. He was easily recognisable:

> as he had on his Mess waistcoat, from the pocket of which Shepstone took a small pocket knife with his name on it; two rings were taken from the dead man's hand and presented with his knife... to his family.[48]

Perhaps the most distressing account of the massacre site was provided by Archibald Forbes, correspondent of the *Daily News*:

> The line of retreat towards Fugitives Drift lay athwart a rocky slope to our right front with a precipitous ravine at its base. In this ravine dead men lay thick – mere bones, with toughened, discoloured

skin like leather covering them and clinging to them, the flesh all wasted away. Some were almost dismembered heaps of clammy yellow bones. I forbear to describe the faces with their blackened features and beards blanched by rain and sun. Each man had been disembowelled. Some were scalped and others subjected to yet ghastlier mutilation. The clothes had lasted better and helped to keep the skeletons together. All the way up the slope I traced, by the ghastly token of dead men, the fitful line of flight. Most of the men hereabouts were infantry of the 24th. It was like a long string with knots in it, the string formed of single corpses, the knots of clusters of dead where... little groups might have gathered to make a hopeless gallant stand and die. I came on a gully with a gun limber jammed in its edge, and the horses, their hides scarred with assegai stabs, hanging in their harnesses down the steep face of the ravine. A little further on was a broken and battered ambulance wagon, with its team of mules, mouldering in their harness, and around lay the corpses of soldiers, poor helpless wretches, dragged out of an intercepted vehicle and done to death without chance of life.

On the crest or saddle 'the slaughtered ones lay thick so that the string became a broad belt. Many hereabouts wore the uniform of the Natal Police... A strange dead calm reigned in this solitude of nature; grain had grown luxuriantly round the wagons, sprouting from the seed that dropped from the loads, falling in soil fertilised by the life-blood of gallant men... As one strolled aimlessly about one stumbled in the grass over skeletons that rattled to the touch. Here lay a corpse with a bayonet jammed into the mouth up to the socket, transfixing the head and mouth a foot into the ground. There lay a form that seemed cosily curled in a calm sleep, turned almost on its face, but seven assegai stabs have pierced the back. Most, however, lay flat on their backs with the arms stretched out and hands clenched. I noticed one dead man under a wagon with his head on a saddle for a pillow and a tarpaulin drawn over him, as if he had gone to sleep and died so... Close beside the dead, at the picquet line, a gully traverses the ground in front of the camp. About 400 paces beyond this was the ground of the battle before the troops broke from their formation and on both sides of the gully the dead lie thickly. In one place nearly fifty of the 24th lie almost touching as if they had fallen

in rallying square. The line of straggling rush back to camp is clearly
marked by skeletons all along the front.[49]

Even hardened veterans were profoundly shocked by the scenes
of devastation, in which even many camp pets had been killed
by the rampant *impis*. A few escaped and survived, some arriving
starved and exhausted at Rorke's Drift in the days following the
disaster. They included Colonel Pulleine's pony and Lieutenant
Daly's dog, 'Ponto'.[50]

The scenes were equally poignantly captured in the memoirs
of a Zulu boy, living close by the massacre site:

> we returned to Isandlwana. We arrived early in the morning – we
> went to see the dead people – we saw a single warrior dead, staring
> in our direction, with his war shield in his hand… we saw count-
> less things dead. Dead was the horse, dead too, the mule, dead was
> the dog, dead was the monkey, dead were the wagons, dead were
> the tents, dead were the boxes, dead was everything, even to the
> very metals…. We saw white men dead (they had taken off their
> boots, all of them) and the people also who had served with them
> and fought with them, and some Zulus, but not many…[51]

Tragically, it was to take nearly six months before the last of the
garrison dead were buried. On 28 June 1879 the last scattered
remains were interred, appropriately by 240 of their own regimental colleagues.

For the Rorke's Drift survivors, at least rewards were soon
forthcoming. An unprecedented eleven VCs were awarded to:
Lieutenants Chard and Bromhead, Assistant Commissary Dalton,
Corporal Allen, Privates Hook, Hitch, John Williams, William
and Robert Jones, Surgeon Reynolds and Corporal Scheiss.[52]
Five men received the Silver Medal for Distinguished Conduct:
Colour-Sergeant Bourne, 2/24th, Second Corporal Attwood,
Army Service Corps, Private Roy, 1/24th, Second Corporal
McMahon of the Army Hospital Corps and Wheeler John
Cantwell of N/3 Battery Royal Artillery.

Composition of the British Force

Lieutenant J.R.M. Chard, 5th (Field) Company, Royal Engineers, commanding:
Staff: Sergeant G.W. Mabin

'N' Battery, 5th Brigade, Royal Artillery

Bombardier T. Lewis
Wheeler J. Cantwell
Gunners: A. Evans and A. Howard

5th (Field) Company, Royal Engineers

Driver E. Robson

1st Battalion, 24th (2nd Warwickshires) Regiment of Foot

Sergeant E. Wilson
Privates: W. Beckett; P. Desmond; W. Horrigan; J. Jenkins; E. Nicholas; T. Payton; W. Roy;
H. Turner; J. Waters

2nd Battalion, 24th (2nd Warwickshires) Regiment of Foot

Lieutenant G. Bromhead
Colour-Sergeant F.E. Bourne
Sergeants: H. Gallagher; R. Maxfield; G. Smith; J. Windridge
Lance-Sergeants: J. Taylor; T. Williams
Corporals: W.W. Allan; G. French; (1112) J. Key; A. Saxty
Lance-Corporals: W. Bessell; W. Halley
Drummers: P. Galgey; P. Hayes; J. Keefe; J. Meehan
T. Chester; J. Chick; T. Clayton; R. Cole; T. Collins; J. Connolly; A. Connors; T. Connors; W.
Cooper; G. Davies; W.H. Davis; T. Daw; G. Deacon; M Deane; J. Dick; W. Dicks; T. Driscoll;
J. Dunbar; G Edwards; J. Fagan; E. Gee; J. Hagan; J. Harris; G. Hayden; F. Hitch
Privates: R. Adams; J. Ashton; T. Barry; W. Bennett; J. Bly; J. Bromwich; T. Buckley;
T. Burke; J. Bushe; W.H. Camp; A.H. Hook; J. Jobbins; E. Jones; R. Jones; W. Jones; P.
Judge; P. Kears; M. Kiley; D. Lloyd; T. Lockhart; J. Lodge; T.M. Lynch; (1441) J. Lyons; J.
Mauley; J. Marshall; H. Martin; C. Mason; M. Minehan; T. Moffatt; A. Morris; F. Morris;
T. Morrison; J. Murphy; W. Neville; R. Norris; W. Osborne; S. Parry; W. Partridge; S. Pitts;
T. Robinson; J. Ruck; E. Savage; J. Scanlon; A. Sears; G. Shearman; J. Shergold; J. Smith; T.
Stevens; W. Tasker; F. Taylor; T.E. Taylor; J. Thomas; P. Tobin; W.J. Todd; R. Tongue; (1395) J.
Williams; (934) J. Williams; (1398) J. Williams; C. Woods

90th (Perthshire Volunteers) Light Infantry

Corporal J. Graham

COMMISSARIAT AND TRANSPORT DEPARTMENT
Assistant Commissary W.A. Dunne; Acting Assistant Commissary J.L. Dalton; Acting
Storekeeper L.A. Byrne

ARMY SERVICE CORPS
Second Corporal F. Attwood

ARMY MEDICAL DEPARTMENT
Surgeon J.H. Reynolds; Mr Pearce (surgeon's servant)

ARMY HOSPITAL CORPS
Corporal R. Miller; 2nd Corporal M. McMahon; Private T. Luddington

HONORARY CHAPLAIN, WEENEN YEOMANRY
The Rev G. Smith, Vicar of Escort

NATAL MOUNTED POLICE
Troopers: R. Green; S. Hunter; H Lugg

NATAL NATIVE CONTINGENT
Lieutenant J. Adendorff
Corporals: M. Doughty; J.H. Mayer; C. Scammel; C.F. Scheiss; J. Wilson
Native Private (Name Unknown)

CIVILIAN
Mr Daniells (Ferryman)

British and Colonial Casualties: Killed in Action

1st Battalion, 24th (2nd Warwickshires) Regiment of Foot
Privates: W. Horrigan; J. Jenkins; E. Nicholas

2nd Battalion, 24th (2nd Warwickshires) Regiment of Foot
Sergeant R. Maxfield
Privates: R. Adams; J. Chick; T. Cole; J. Fagan; G. Hayden; J. Scanlon; J. Williams

COMMISSARIAT AND TRANSPORT DEPARTMENT
Acting Storekeeper L.A. Byrne

NATAL MOUNTED POLICE
Trooper S. Hunter

NATAL NATIVE CONTINGENT
Native Private (Name Unknown)

British and Colonial Casualties: Wounded in Action

1st Battalion, 24th (2nd Warwickshires) Regiment of Foot

Private W. Beckett, mortally wounded. Died of wounds 23 January 1879
Private P. Desmond, slightly wounded
Private J. Waters, severely wounded

2nd Battalion, 24th (2nd Warwickshires) Regiment of Foot

Lance-Sergeant T. Williams, mortally wounded. Died of wounds, 25 January 1879
Corporal W.W. Allan, severely wounded
Corporal J. Lyons, dangerously wounded
Drummer J. Keefe, slightly wounded
Private J. Bushe, slightly wounded
Private F. Hitch, dangerously wounded
Private A.H. Hook, slightly wounded
Private R. Jones, slightly wounded
Private J. Smith, slightly wounded
Private W. Tasker, slightly wounded

COMMISSARIAT AND TRANSPORT DEPARTMENT
Acting Assistant Commissary J.L. Dalton, severely wounded

NATAL MOUNTED POLICE
Trooper R. Green, slightly wounded

NATAL NATIVE CONTINGENT
Corporal C. Scammell, dangerously wounded
Corporal C.F. Scheiss, slightly wounded

British and Colonial Casualties: Killed

Corporal W. Anderson (By British fire)

Zulu Casualties

500 killed or mortally wounded. At least two prisoners taken alive who were subsequently hanged.

Honours and Awards

The Victoria Cross

Lieutenant J.R.M. CHARD, Royal Engineers and Lieutenant G. BROMHEAD, 2nd/24th Regiment of Foot

For their gallant conduct at the defence of Rorke's Drift on the occasion of the attack by the Zulus on the 22nd and 23rd January 1879.

The Lieutenant-General commanding the troops reports that, had it not been for the fine example and excellent behaviour of these two Officers under the most trying circumstances, the defence of Rorke's Drift post would not have been conducted with that intelligence and tenacity which so essentially characterised it.

The Lieutenant-General adds that its success must, to a great degree, be attributable to the two young Officers who exercised the Chief Command on the occasion in question.

Supplement to the *London Gazette*, 2 May 1879

Private John WILLIAMS, 2nd/24th Regiment of Foot

Private John Williams was posted with Private Joseph Williams and Private William Horrigan, 1st Battalion, 24th Regiment, in a distant room of the hospital, which they held for more than an hour, so long as they had a round of ammunition left: as communication was for the time cut off, the Zulus were enabled to advance and burst open the door; they dragged out Private Joseph Williams and two of the patients, and assegaied them. While the Zulus were occupied with the slaughter of these men, a lull took place during which Private John Williams (who along with two patients were the only men now left alive in this ward), succeeded in knocking a hole in the partition and in taking the two patients into the next ward, where he found Private Hook.

Supplement to the *London Gazette*, 2 May 1879

Private Henry (*sic*) HOOK, 2nd/24th Regiment of Foot

These two men together, one man working while the other fought and held the enemy at bay with his bayonet, broke through three more partitions, and were thus enabled to bring eight patients through a small window into the inner line of defence.

Supplement to the *London Gazette*, 2 May 1879

Private William JONES and Private Robert JONES, 2nd/24th Regiment of Foot

In another ward, facing the hill, Private William Jones and Private Robert Jones defended the post to the last, until six out of the seven patients it contained had been removed. The seventh, Sergeant Maxfield, 2nd Battalion, 24th Regiment, was delirious from fever. Although they had previously dressed him, they were unable to induce him to move. When Private Robert Jones returned to endeavour to carry him away, he found him being stabbed by the Zulus as he lay on his bed.

Supplement to the London Gazette, 2 May 1879

Corporal William ALLEN (*sic*) and Private Frederick HITCH, 2nd/24th Regiment of Foot

It was chiefly due to the courageous conduct of these men that communication with the hospital was kept up at all. Holding together at all costs a most dangerous post, raked in reverse by the enemy's fire from the hill, they were both severely wounded, but their determined conduct enabled the patients to be withdrawn from the hospital, and when incapacitated by their wounds from fighting, they continued, as soon as their wounds had been dressed, to serve out ammunition to their comrades during the night.

Supplement to the London Gazette, 2 May 1879

Surgeon-Major James Henry REYNOLDS, Army Medical Department (Promoted to Surgeon-Major, 23 January 1879)

For the conspicuous bravery, during the attack at Rorke's Drift on the 22nd and 23rd January 1879, which he exhibited in his constant attention to the wounded under fire, and in his voluntarily conveying ammunition from the store to the defenders of the hospital, whereby he exposed himself to a cross-fire from the enemy both in going and returning.

The London Gazette, 17 June 1879

Acting Assistant Commissary James Langley DALTON, Commissariat and Transport Department

For his conspicuous gallantry during the attack on Rorke's Drift Post by the Zulus on the night of the 22nd January 1879, when he actively superintended the work of defence, and was amongst the foremost of those who received the first attack on the corner of the hospital, where the deadliness of his fire did great execution, and the mad rush of the Zulus met its first check, and where by his cool courage he saved the life of a man of the Army Hospital Corps by shooting the Zulu, who, having seized the muzzle of the man's rifle, was in the act of assegaing (*sic*) him.

This Officer, to whose energy much of the defence of the place was due, was severely wounded during the contest, but still continued to give the same example of cool courage.

The London Gazette, 18 November 1879

Corporal (C.F.) SCHIESS, Natal Native Contingent

For conspicuous gallantry in the defence of Rorke's Drift Post on the night of the 22nd January 1879, when, in spite of his having been wounded in the foot a few days previously, he greatly distinguished himself when the Garrison were repulsing, with the bayonet, a series of desperate assaults made by the Zulus, and displayed great activity and devoted gallantry throughout the defence. On one occasion when the Garrison had retired to the inner line of defence, and the Zulus occupied the wall of mealie bags which had been abandoned, he crept along the wall, without any order, to dislodge a Zulu who was shooting better than usual and succeeded in killing him, and two others, before he, the Corporal, returned to the inner defence.

The *London Gazette*, 2 December 1879

The Silver Medal for Distinguished Conduct in the Field

Regiment/Corps	Name	Date of Submission
2nd/24th Foot	Colour-Sergeant F.E. Bourne	28/7/1879
Army Service Corps	Second Corporal F. Attwood	29/7/1879
1st/24th Foot	Private W. Roy	22/10/1879
Army Hospital Corps	Second Corporal M. McMahon	15/1/1880 (Award Cancelled)
'N' Battery, 5th Brigade Royal Artillery	Wheeler J. Cantwell	11/2/1880

Sources: J. Young, *They Fell like Stones: Battles and Casualties of the Zulu War, 1879* (Greenhill 1991), pp.85-94 and N. Holme, *The Silver Wreath* (Samson Books, 1979), p.85

Legacies and Lessons: The Military, Social and Political Significance of Rorke's Drift

The battle of Rorke's Drift fully deserves its elevated status in the annals of British military history, if only as one of the most heroically fought and efficiently conducted small-scale military actions of the last 100-odd years. The British were, from the outset, vastly outnumbered by up to thirty to one by their Zulu protagonists. In the context of the relatively confined space of the garrison, and the considerable opportunities for enemy concealment in the shrubs, bushes and caves outside and overlooking the garrison, British technical superiority had been much more limited than some observers have suggested. After the initial, albeit destructive volleys fired against the first wave of Zulu attackers, much (if not the majority) of the fighting was at close quarters. The survival of the garrison depended at its most critical times as much on rifle butts and bayonets as it did on the efficacy of the Martini-Henry box 45 cartridge. The successful withdrawal from the hospital, for instance, was conducted largely at bayonet and assegai point. Indeed, the incredible closeness and intensity of the fighting was graphically testified to by Lieutenant Chard himself during his post-war extended audience with Queen Victoria in October 1879: 'The fight was at such close quarters that the Zulus actually *took* the bayonets out of the rifles'.[1]

Battle Analysis

It is possible to evaluate command and control and the overall conduct of the battle more precisely in terms of both modern British military doctrine and the views of contemporary experts, notably Major William Penn Symons. A broad comparison of the events of the Rorke's Drift battle with the key principles of war laid down in the current British Army Hand Book (selection and maintenance of aim, maintenance of morale, offensive action, surprise, concentration of force, economy of effort, security, flexibility, co-operation and overall sustainability) is instructive.[2]

Selection and Maintenance of Arms

In terms of 'selection and maintenance of aim', after the initial debate about whether to evacuate the garrison to Helpmekaar, Chard, Bromhead and Dalton collectively and clearly defined and selected their defensive aims with commendable speed, only minutes after hearing the news of the Isandlwana disaster and the approach of the Zulu Undi Corps. In such a short time, the arrangement of the strategic defences was a masterpiece, with full use made of artificial and natural features. The stone and mud walls of the kraal, hospital and storehouse were fully utilised with a formidable mealie bag barricade along the perimeter, and the front perimeter was also given excellent elevation by its construction along the three-foot rocky ledge. These defensive aims were thus attainable and precisely prepared with a number of subsidiary aims, notably a secondary line of defence or fall-back position constructed of biscuit boxes. The broad strategic aim was, moreover, sustained throughout the battle, its defensive principles widely disseminated throughout the garrison, and made the main focus of activity for all the able-bodied men, who were fully briefed on their tasks at their designated posts along the barricades.

Maintenance of Morale

The principle of 'maintaining morale' was also clearly fulfilled, bearing in mind the terrible and unique battle conditions, in which so few British soldiers faced a ferocious enemy who had not only just annihilated a force twelve times their size, but who patently gave no quarter. In terms of morale, Assistant Commissary Dalton, by his experience, exceptional energy and raw courage, proved to be perhaps the most inspiring figure for the rest of the garrison. Thus Hook admiringly wrote: 'He had formally been a Sergeant-Major in a Line Regiment and was one of the bravest men who ever lived',[3] a man who had been seen at the start of the battle literally taunting the Zulu and beckoning them to come on. Bromhead's clear popularity and extremely close rapport with his own B Company soldiers also played a key role in the resilience and survivability of the garrison – he constantly patrolled the perimeter, reinforcing weak points and always giving stirring encouragement to his men. Thus, for instance, Bromhead had given sympathy and even loaned his revolver to the seriously wounded Private Hitch, their bond or comradeship continuing well after the battle, as Bromhead 'brought his Lordship to see me and was my principal visitor and nurse while I was at the Drift'.[4] Lieutenant Chard also attracted universal admiration from officers and men for his coolness under fire and the competence of his defensive preparations. Of the officers, Dalton clearly occupied a special place in the hearts of the men of B Company. Major-General Molyneux thus recorded a moving incident which occurred at the end of the war:

> After the war, the company of the 24th that had defended Rorke's Drift was marching into Maritzburg amidst a perfect ovation. Among those cheering them was Mr Dalton, who, as a conductor, had been severely wounded there; 'Why, there's Mr Dalton cheering us! We ought to be cheering him; he was the best man there' said the men, who forthwith fetched him out of the crowd and made him march with them. No-one knew better the value of this spontaneous act than that old soldier. The men are not

supposed to know anything strategy, and not much about tactics, except fire low, fire slow, and obey orders; but they do know when a man has got his heart in the right place, and, if they had a chance they will show him that they know it. Mr Dalton must have felt a proud man that day.[5]

Offensive Action

The outstanding performance of the officers instilled a high degree of determination, confidence and defensive spirit, evident throughout the battle. In terms of the principle of 'offensive action', both Chard and Bromhead managed the battle exceptionally well and instinctively understood that 'a sustained defence, unless followed by offensive action will only avert defeat temporarily'.[6] Thus Bromhead organised mobile bayonet parties, a crude human form of 'mobile weapons platforms', which were constantly deployed to repel Zulu breakthroughs, thereby effectively depriving them of initiative. 'Fire mobility' was thus fully sustained throughout the siege.

Surprise and Concentration of Force

'Surprise' was also a principle which was well exploited by all the officers commanding the garrison of Rorke's Drift. The frequent change of tactics, from sustained volley fire at the start of the siege and the potent use of enfilading fire from the storehouse throughout the siege, followed by the sudden retreat from the hospital perimeter to the well-prepared biscuit box barricades, continually wrong-footed the attacking Zulu force. Allied to this tactic was the extensive use of 'concentration of force' at decisive times and places, which accompanied this use of deception. Hence Chard's and Bromhead's constant switching of their soldiers from the front and rear barricades in the first two hours of the siege confused and distracted the Zulu attackers in their constant search for weak points along the perimeter.

Economy of Effort

The efficient, at times frugal, use of resources — was also applied extremely well. Lieutenant Bromhead was the pivotal man in terms of the distribution of the 20,000-round ammunition supply. Constantly reminding his men of the need to conserve rounds during the later stages of the siege, both he and Chard kept meticulous accounts of the allocation and quantity of ammunition.

Overall Security

In this way 'overall security' was achieved, with Chard always guarding an adequate reserve. The judicious allocation of troops and resources was therefore at a premium in the Rorke's Drift siege. In summary, in regard to the three interrelated principles of concentration of force, economy of effort and security, Lieutenants Chard and Bromhead and Acting Commissary Officer Dalton achieved a high level of excellence.

Flexibility

'Flexibility' was also ably demonstrated by the commander, Lieutenant Chard. Without undermining his overall defensive aim, Chard brilliantly modified his plan to rescue the much more dangerous and precarious situation occurring after the retreat from the hospital. In this new tactic, part of the garrison's effort was redeployed using the lulls in the fight after midnight to construct a last bastion of defence, the mealie-bag redoubt. This manoeuvre demonstrated both elasticity of mind and resourcefulness at this critical last stage of the battle. It was a simple but highly effective solution, designed to both protect the wounded and provide a final elevated concentration of fire for up to forty soldiers.

Co-operation

'Co-operation' or teamwork was also ably demonstrated by all members of the garrison. All four 'services' or units present at the siege – the Commissariat, the army regulars, the chaplain and even the Army Hospital Corps – each massively supported one another and adapted to one another's requirements; key 'players' such as Byrne, Reynolds, Dalton, Dunne, Padre Smith, Bromhead and Chard all worked closely together to carry out essential duties ranging from close-quarter fighting at the barricades to the distribution of food and ammunition. Surgeon Reynolds was, perhaps, the most outstanding example, both attending to the wounded and supplying the hospital under fire with much-needed ammunition. His VC citation very much recognised this achievement.

Overall Sustainability

Overall 'sustainability' was definitely achieved. Chard and Bromhead kept an exceptionally fine balance between 'teeth and tail', wholly maintaining both the physical and psychological condition of the soldiers in order to maintain morale. It was an important achievement, bearing in mind the inexperience and youth of a good many of the garrisons' 2/24th regulars.

Major Penn Symons' contemporary (1890) battle analysis prepared for the Commander-in-Chief the Duke of Cambridge, while giving full credit to the role of the officers at Rorke's Drift, reserved its highest praise for the NCOs and men and, in particular, the heroic deeds of half a dozen private soldiers. He stressed:

> It must be understood that it was essentially a soldiers fight. Given all credit to the officers who used the best judgement under the circumstances and exhibited prompt action and readiness of resources, given also the confidence with which Lieutenants Chard and Bromhead, young officers both inspired their men, we repeat that it was a fight at long odds of one white man to thirty black savages frenzied with success and slaughter – each individual soldier stood to his post, did his work and duty grandly.[7]

Aside from the commissioned officer, Penn Symons selected seven men whose heroic exploits had played an exceptional role in saving the garrison.

In the hospital fight, four men had been outstanding. Privates Hook and John Williams had fought from room to room, Private Hook being 'last man to leave the hospital'. Privates William and Robert Jones had also excelled far beyond the call of duty and had 'defended their post to the last', with 'six out of seven of their patients being saved'. In short, it was 'owing to the personal pluck and exertion of these four men that the last of the patients escaped'.[8]

Penn Symons also singled out both Acting Assistant Commissary Officer Dalton, 'badly wounded in the shoulder', and the impressive Corporal Scheiss, who 'deserved the highest praise for their cheery encouragement of the soldiers and the good work they performed in defence'. He again recalled how Dalton 'who had charge of the wagon barricade stood up on one of the wagons and jeered at the Zulus, daring them to come on and that when… he had no more ammunition left he threw his helmet at some of them crouched behind the covers'. Corporal Scheiss had 'fought like a little tiger – he could not restrain himself but more than once dashed over the barricade, bayoneting a Zulu and got back again'.[9]

Two other men, Corporal William Allen and Private Hitch, Penn Symons asserted:

> must also be mentioned for their courageous work and initiative. It was chiefly due to these two men that contact with the hospital was kept up at all. Holding, at all cost, a most dangerous part at the north-east corner of the hospital, raked in reverse by the enemy fire from the hill, they were both severely wounded, but their determined conduct enabled the patients to be withdrawn from the hospital. When incapacitated from their firing themselves they continued, as soon as their wounds had been dressed, to serve out ammunition for their comrades during the fight.

Overall, it had been 'a gallant defence'. The young soldiers 'backed each other up and fought splendidly'. They 'never wavered for an instant' and, despite only a few months of training and influence of esprit de corps, had become the best and pluckiest 'Warwickshire Lads' and gloriously upheld the traditions of the old 24th.[10]

Aside from their own survival instincts and loyalty to their officers, loyalty to 'mates' or comrades constituted a prime motivator for both the NCOs and rank and file. This had been demonstrated repeatedly during the hospital fight, as men fought to rescue their wounded colleagues, and displayed constantly outside on the barricades as men fought shoulder to shoulder, and also on one famous occasion, led by Private Hook, formed a bayonet party and risked their lives to fetch water for their exhausted and wounded comrades.[11] Such was the intensity of comradeship and 'battlefield bonding' that some men had even sworn to die in mutual suicide pacts rather than surrender to such a merciless enemy (notably Gunner Howard and his comrades in the storehouse at the start of the attack, and Privates Hitch and Deacon, stationed on the barricades).[12] Regimental pride was also an important motivating factor for some, especially the NCOs. Thus, Corporal Lyons recalled how: 'we were all determined to sell our lives like soldiers and to keep up the credit of our Regiment'.[13] Colour-Sergeant Bourne exuded regimental pride in his account of the battle:

> now just one word for the men who fought that night; I was moving about them all the time, and not for one moment did they flinch, their courage and their bravery cannot be expressed in words; for me they were an example all my soldiering days.[14]

After the débâcle at Isandlwana, recovering regimental honour was clearly at a premium in many men's minds. All men, including the NCOs such as Colour-Sergeant Bourne, later took enormous pride in royal honours bestowed on the regiment, notably Queen Victoria's award of the 'Wreath of Immortelles' now preserved in the Regimental Chapel at Brecon Cathedral.[15] Closely associated with regimental pride was the much less attractive but perhaps understandable motive of seeking revenge for their dead comrades at Isandlwana. Sergeant Smith noted how the Zulu 'paid dearly for what they killed of our men'.[16] Religion played a role at this time of great adversity, hence the frequent references to gratitude to God and Providence for saving their lives in many of the battle accounts.[17] While all the individuals mentioned earlier received the Victoria Cross, there were clearly many other unsung heroes amongst the garrison. Lieutenant Chard himself singled out 'Corporal Lyons, Private McMahon, Army Hospital Corps, Privates Roy, Deacon, Bush, Cole, Jobbins of the 24th and many others'.[18]

In any assessment of the military significance of Rorke's Drift, a key question is the degree of threat presented by the Zulu enemy to the garrison and to the wider region. At least one recent writer has played down the status of the attacking Zulu force to a mere 'raiding party' with the very limited aims of attacking a few border farms in Natal. Thus Professor Laband writes:

> In reality the defence of Rorke's Drift merely diverted a large Zulu raiding party from going about its short term business of ravaging the Buffalo River valley in the vicinity, and not from marching on Pietermaritzburg.[19]

In fact, the 'raiding party' was a full Zulu Corps (the Undi Corps), up to one-fifth of the main Zulu army engaged earlier at Isandlwana. It was a force of 4,000 men, at least four times greater than one would expect to comprise an over-large Zulu raiding party. It included the crack uThulwana regiment, reportedly the king's favourite regiment. Moreover, the Zulu demonstrated exceptional courage and resilience by sustaining a prolonged attack, which included at least six major assaults sustained over a period of up to eight hours (far longer than their compatriots at Isandlwana and at proportionately comparable human cost [casualties of between 10 and 15 per cent]). No 'raiding party' would even have contemplated such a heavy major sustained attack, particularly after the heavy losses resulting from the initial British volleys. By their very nature, raiding parties engage in only light 'hit-and-run' tactics over a wide area and do not tolerate large casualties.

Contrary to suggestions that the Undi Corps was an already fatigued force,[20] there is plenty of contrary evidence to show that it was 'battle-ready'. As the Zulu reserve at Isandlwana, the Undi Corps had spent most of the morning of 22 January as virtual spectators of the battle, as their comrades annihilated the British garrison. They had time to eat and rest, probably, as in Zulu tradition, with their backs to the fight. At the most they had been engaged at the tail end of the battle in a few light mopping-up operations, killing isolated fugitives on their slow journey to attack the mission station at Rorke's Drift. As one key Zulu eyewitness recalled:

> the Mbzankomo [uThulwana] regiment merely remained at the Ingwebini river. They danced and just ate merrily. Presently they said 'Oh! let's go and have a fight at Jim's' [the Zulu name for Rorke's Drift]. [21]

As the distinguished historian Webb further confirms: 'the main body of the Undi lagged behind the other Zulu regiments when the battle began. During the course of the fighting they circled round Isandlwana and moved on to Rorke's Drift'.[22]

Moreover, the ten-mile route to Rorke's Drift from Isandlwana Camp had been conducted at a leisurely pace for a Zulu regiment with, as we have seen, frequent manoeuvrings and stops for traditional snuff-taking and to burn isolated farms. Thus the historian Moodie records their slow progress, the three companies of the Undi Corps advancing in open order from Isandlwana, 'going through various exercises… remaining a long time on the river… and sitting down to take snuff'.[23] In short, the Zulu regiments that so ferociously attacked Rorke's Drift were an extremely confident, fit unit, anxious to engage in a prolonged battle with the garrison and desperate to gain the full battle honours of their comrades at Isandlwana. In Dabulamanzi's own words, he 'wanted to wash the spears of his boys'.[24]

The Zulu longer-term objectives were, it can also be argued, potentially very serious, extending far beyond those of a raiding party, and were aimed, if some sources are to be believed, at overrunning large parts of Natal Colony. Although Cetshwayo had initially ruled against extending the war beyond the Natal border, there is

strong evidence, as we have seen, that the Sihayo fight had already
led to a major review of his strategy. Moreover, the notoriously
individualistic, reckless Undi Corps commander Dabulamanzi later
confessed to having his own wider strategic objectives, had Rorke's
Drift fallen. When Lieutenant Stafford visited his kraal a few years
after the war, he significantly asked Dabulamanzi:

> if it had been his intention to invade Natal. He answered that,
> while initially Cetschwayo had told him that the 'flooded rivers
> were a bigger king than he was…, had Rorke's Drift fallen I should
> have taken my army into Natal.[25]

From both the garrison and from contemporary local settler perspectives, the successful defence of Rorke's Drift had been crucial to saving
Natal and the rest of the column. Padre Smith, for instance, wrote:

> It was certainly of the utmost strategic importance that this place
> should not be taken… the safety of the remainder of the Column
> and this part of the Colony depended on it.[26]

The *Times of Natal* echoed his words: 'Had we lost our position
here, I believe the wave of destruction would have gone on into
the Colony.'[27] When, in 1882, the traveller Bertram Mitford asked
Mehlokazulu, a 'sub-chief of the Ngobomakhosi Regiment' and
a veteran of Isandlwana, what he had perceived to be Natal's
strategic position during the war, he replied:

> not much… how easy it would have been for an impi to 'eat
> up' the place and kill everyone in it. They would begin at
> Mkunkundhlovwane (Grey Town) in the morning and finish with
> Mkukundhlovu (Maritzburg) in the evening.[28]

Penn Symons also reaffirmed the strategic importance of the
Rorke's Drift victory:

> It was of the utmost importance that Rorkes Drift should not
> have been captured by the enemy. Had it fallen Helpmekaar would

probably have gone also and not only would a great panic have fallen in the Colony of Natal, probably followed by invasion by a triumphant enemy, but the safety of the remainder of Colonel Glyn's Column would have been imperilled.[29]

As a contemporary memorandum by F. Grenfell (later Field Marshal Lord Grenfell) revealed, Natal had been extremely vulnerable to attack in the aftermath of the Isandlwana disaster: 'We are working day and night at the defence of Natal. There is nothing to prevent an invasion'.[30]

For the Zulu, flushed with the success of Isandlwana, the failure at Rorke's Drift (albeit an heroic failure) was a brutal reminder of the futility of open-order attack on a fortified position. One report from a Zulu witness printed in the *Natal Colonist* and *Mercury* even claimed that some of the Rorke's Drift Zulu commanders had been put to death for 'attacking in the open'.[31] Dabulamanzi had made some serious tactical errors and his generalship was, overall, poor. Weaknesses in the Rorke's Drift perimeter had not been exploited. Colour-Sergeant Bourne, for instance, was mystified by the Zulu failure to literally pierce the mealie-bag wall and thereby collapse it,[32] while several eyewitnesses were amazed at the general Zulu reluctance to use their 'throwing' spears.[33] Harford was also astonished to see how the Zulu commanders had failed to set fire to a haystack near the storehouse, which could have severely compromised the garrison's defences.[34] The resultant losses were proportionately comparable to Isandlwana – 2,000 to 3,000 dead out of a 25,000-strong attacking Zulu force, and 400 to 600 out of a 4,000-strong attacking force at Rorke's Drift. One 'crack regiment', the uThulwana, had been almost destroyed. Even more than the same-day British victory at Inyenzane, Rorke's Drift had been an abject lesson for the Zulu. As one leading colonist put it:

in its unsuccessful attack upon Lieutenant Gonville Bromhead's Garrison of the 2/24th the uTulwana Regiment, Cetchwayo regiment lost half its best men... the uTulwana is a crack regiment, some four thousand strong and their signal repulse after twelve hours fierce fighting by the small force has… much damaged the rejoicing of the Zulu Nation.[35]

The extent of Zulu humiliation and its implication for Zulu morale and prestige was revealed by a contemporary Zulu eyewitness:

the Mbazamkamo (Undi) Regiment was finished up at Jim's – shocking cowards they were too. Our people laughed at them, some said, 'you, you're no men! You're just women, seeing that you ran away for no reason at all like the wind. – 'You marched off. You went to dig little bits with your assegais out of the house of Jim that had never done you any harm'.[36]

After the Rorke's Drift defeat, the

Zulus had no desire to go to Maritzburg. They said 'there are strongholds there'. They thought that they should perish and come utterly to an end if they went there.[37]

The combined casualties of Isandlwana and Rorke's Drift had, indeed, been devastating for the Zulu people. Major-General Molyneux, who visited several Zulu kraals after the war, found in one large kraal, 'a lot of wounded' – one had lost two brothers at Isandlwana (his regiment was the Ngobamakhosi) – while 'the many little mounds outside, covered with stones, told how many poor fellows had crawled home merely to die'.[38] A Dutch trader, Cornelius Vijn, staying at one of Cetshwayo's kraals, recorded the local impact of the news on 25 January of the terrible losses at Isandlwana and Rorke's Drift. As he lay in a hut talking with Ziwedu (Cetshwayo's brother):

our attention was drawn to a troop of people, who came back from their gardens crying and wailing. As they approached I recognised them as persons belonging to the kraal at which I was staying. When they came into or close to the kraal they kept on wailing in front of the kraals rolling themselves on the ground and never quietening down; nay, in the night they wailed so as to cut through

the heart of anyone. As this wailing went on, night and day for a
fortnight; the effect of it was very depressing; I wish I could not
hear it... of the Zulus, according to their account, many thousands
had been left behind on the field – Dabulamanzi told me they
were buried – never more to return to their homes, and still more
were wounded.[39]

The Political and Social Significance of Rorke's Drift

The battle of Rorke's Drift had wider political reverberations
extending to the highest level of the Victorian establishment. The
news of the military catastrophe at Isandlwana on 11 February
1879 had come, as we have seen, as a terrible shock to both the
government and people of Britain. As Hicks Beach's somewhat
ambivalent despatches immediately before the war had indicated,
both Sir Bartle Frere and Lord Chelmsford were likely to pay
a heavy political price if the war was not conducted cheaply
and with minimum casualties. By mid-February 1879, as the full
extent of the tragedy became clear, the 'Izamgoma' ('witch find-
ers') of press and Parliament had commenced a vitriolic campaign
demanding for the recall of both men. It soon became clear that
Disraeli's government needed scapegoats. As one Colonial Office
official, Edward Fairfield, cryptically observed: 'the war and, above
all, the defeat of Isandula have totally changed the case'.[40] The
Times was much more explicit: 'There is, in fact, little room for
doubt that if Lord Chelmsford's invasion had been successful, Sir
Bartle Frere's conduct would have been condoned.'[41]

Given this major military disaster, 'somebody must be fixed for
the blame' as one speaker in the House of Commons so aptly
put it.[42] The Prime Minister, the Earl of Beaconsfield, Benjamin
Disraeli, was particularly stunned by the disaster and, forced to
dispatch urgent and costly reinforcements, was privately furious with both Frere and Chelmsford. The disaster at Isandlwana
would 'change everything, reduce our continental influence and
embarrass our resources'.[43] Moreover, even after the subsequent
Court of Inquiry, held in February 1879, Chelmsford continued
to deny his direct culpability for this disastrous failure of his battle

plans. In a recently discovered memorandum dated 20 February 1879, there was even an attempt by Chelmsford to assign much of the blame for the disaster to his No.3 column commander Colonel Glyn. He wrote:

> I have no desire whatever to shift any of the responsibility which probably belongs to me on to the shoulders of the officers command-ing No.3 Column. At the same time I am anxious to make it clear that, by accompanying No.3 Column, I did not accept the responsibility for the numerous details which necessarily have to be considered by an officer commanding a Column in the field. On arriving at the camp of No.3 Column I myself emphasised personally to Colonel Glyn that I did not wish to interfere in anyway with the Commander of the Column but that, of course, I should be only to glad to talk over with him all matters connected with it, and to give him the benefit of my opinion whenever he required it – I believe that I also said the same of Major Clery my Senior Staff Officer.

While admitting:

> as regards the movement of the Column and the several recon-naissances made by portions of that column, I was entirely responsible... my orders, however, were always conveyed to Colonel Glyn in plenty of time for him to consider and to reflect upon things; and I consider that I have a right to assume that if Colonel Glyn considers that any such orders were any way likely to be injurious to the interest of any portion of his force, or that my proposed movements were in any way hazardous, he would have once have brought the fact to my notice.

He continued further to say that: 'I consider Colonel Glyn was bound to inform me, if at any time his own judgement differed from mine the movement I was anxious to carry out.'

Chelmsford concluded:

> no such objection was ever made and I assume therefore that orders by me received his approval. As regards outposts, patrolling

and the ordinary precautions for the safety of the camp, I, on arriving at the camp of No. 3 Column, considered that for all these arrangements Colonel Glyn was solely responsible and had I interfered in such matters it would have been tantamount to my taking direct command of the Column, a position in which I deprecated from the very first.[44]

It was a view which directly contradicted Clery's earlier private letter, which claimed that Lord Chelmsford had effectively taken over command of the force and had become involved in every minute operational detail.[45]

Another recently discovered, astonishing if unverified piece of evidence supports suggestions that Pulleine may have been fatally compromised by conflicting orders that morning, and that his frantic attempt to remedy this situation was cut short by his own premature death. Caught between the need to support Durnford on the plateau and an order from Chelmsford to strike camp, evidence indicates that Pulleine, faced by large numbers of attacking Zulu, had by late morning finally decided to withdraw to a defensive laager. A War Office memo noted that he had already 'called in the cattle and begun to harness them so as to draw the wagons into a circle',[46] while the recently discovered (last?) but still unverified order issued to Lieutenant Cavaye at 11.30a.m. suggests that Pulleine was aiming to pull his exposed left wing into this defensive circle. The order reads as follows:

Cavaye
Zulus are advancing on your right in force. Retire on camp in order. E Company will support your right. NNC on your left.
H.B. Pulleine
11.30 am, Received 11.45 am 22/01/1879.[47]

Hallam Parr's private letter to Sir Bartle Frere the day after the disaster on the 23 January gives some further credence to this theory that Pulleine's death, occurring in the midst of this intricate manoeuvre, may have contributed to the administrative confusion at this critical time, perhaps just after Durnford left the camp:

In the evening we heard more of the matter. Pulleine, who was shot early had been left with instructions, if attacked, to strike camp, contract his lines and act steadily on the defensive. Durnford alas, came to take the command.[48]

Whoever was responsible at ground level, with both Pulleine and Durnford dead, it was Frere and Chelmsford who were to take the brunt of the blame. In the weeks during and after the Court of Inquiry, both men were subjected to further severe criticism both locally from the Cape and at home in the Houses of Parliament. With the ensuing South African debates in the House of Lords of 26 March 1879, Lord Lansdowne

complained generally of Sir Bartle Frere's conduct and pointed out that if the Government was not satisfied with Sir Bartle Frere's conduct they were bound to recall him. This motion was treated as a motion of censure.[49]

Similarly, Lord Cranbrook made a most effective speech, admitting that Sir Bartle Frere ought to have consulted the government before sending the ultimatum to the Zulu king, and states that Sir Michael Hicks Beach had notified this in very plain terms to Sir Bartle Frere.[50]

In the later Commons 'South African debate', a leading MP, Sir Robert Peel, 'made a really virulent attack on Sir Bartle Frere' and then 'took it into his head to make a still more virulent attack on Lord Chelmsford whom he denounced as being worthy of Admiral Byng'.[51]

These political attacks were paralleled by fierce attacks on Frere and Chelmsford, emanating from within the Victorian military establishment. Before the results of the Court of Inquiry had been convened, the Adjutant General, on behalf of the Duke of Cambridge, the Commander-in-Chief of the British army, had already sent to Chelmsford a highly critical memo for which answers were immediately required. In addition to criticisms of Chelmsford's deployment of camp, including the lack of laagering entrenchment and the splitting of his forces, Chelmsford was also significantly criticised for his deployment of Rorke's Drift supply depot. He was asked

> how did it happen that the post at Rorke's Drift, covering as it did the passage into Zululand, was not put into a state of defence previous to your Lordships advance to Isandula Hill.[52]

General Sir Garnet Wolseley and officers from his 'school' were even more vitriolic in their public and private criticism of both Frere and Chelmsford, but particularly Chelmsford. Thus, General Wolseley wrote to his wife that Chelmsford 'has violated every principle of war in his plan of campaign, and has, in fact, courted disaster'.[53] In his private diary, he was even more scathing in his criticism of not only the tactics of the Isandlwana and Rorke's Drift actions, but also their officers. He wrote:

> Heroes had been made of men like Melville and Coghill who, taking advantage of their having horses, bolted from the scene of action to save their lives. If the 24th had been well handled and had behaved well then the disaster could never had occurred, much as Chelmsford by his ignorance of Zulu tactics, had left them exposed to attack, and it is monstrous making heroes of those who saved or attempted to save their lives by bolting, or, of those who shut in the buildings at Roorke's [*sic*] Drift could not bolt and fought like rats for their lives which they could not otherwise save.[54]

Earlier on 16 July 1879, after presenting Major Chard with his Victoria Cross, he acidly remarked:

> a more uninteresting or more stupid looking fellow I never saw – Bromhead of the 24th Regiment who was the second in command of the post is a very stupid fellow also.[55]

Such scathing comments were, perhaps, to be expected of a man who was later cheated of victory in the Zulu war by Chelmsford, who won the decisive battle that broke Zulu power at Ulundi on 4 July 1879.

Under such a barrage of attacks from both the military and political establishment, both Frere and Chelmsford made maximum use of the Rorke's Drift action to defend their policies and to divert or deflect attention away from the disastrous battle of Isandlwana. In the weeks leading up to the censure debate, Rorke's Drift became a veritable 'political football' between the two sides. Thus on 27 January 1879, only five days after the disaster, Chelmsford informed the Secretary of State for War:

> The defeat of the Zulus at this post and the very heavy losses suffered by them have to a great extent neutralised the effect of the disaster at Isandlwana and it no doubt saved Natal from serious invasion... The cool determined courage displayed by the gallant garrison is beyond all praise... the lesson taught by the defence is most valuable.[56]

In a letter to the Colonial Office, Sir Bartle Frere staunchly echoed Chelmsford's words. Noting that Chelmsford's orders 'were clearly not obeyed on that terrible day at Isandlwana camp', he continued:

> I will not say a word of blame of those who died so nobly but I should ask attention to the defence of that same night of the Rorke's Drift post by a company of Her Majesty's 24th Regiment against an overwhelming force of Zulus. The latter action is most instructive as illustrating what is the real strength as well what is the weakness of Cetewayo's military organisation.[57]

Frere then proceeded to give a long, blow-by-blow account of the action. In this simmering political row Frere and Chelmsford received massive support from both Queen Victoria and the Royal Family in general. Already, on 11 February, as soon as she heard of the Isandlwana disaster, the Queen had, via her private secretary General Ponsonby, sent two simultaneous telegrams to Frere and Chelmsford expressing 'complete confidence' in Frere and 'every hope you will be able to restore the feeling of security in Natal and the Cape Colony'.[58]

Huge pressure was placed on Prime Minister Disraeli and Colonial Secretary Hicks Beach to resist the mounting attacks on both men. On 12 March, however, Disraeli regretfully informed the Queen that 'with the exception of Sir Michael Hicks Beach' his 'whole Cabinet had wanted to yield to the clamours of the Press and Clubs for the recall of Lieutenant Chelmsford'.[59] During her defence of the two men, the Queen and her private secretary General Ponsonby received voluminous correspondence from both Chelmsford and Frere, thanking her for her support but also again stressing the political and strategic importance of Rorke's Drift as a means of vindicating their policies. Thus, on 10 February 1879, Frere wrote the Queen a letter, which blamed Durnford for the débâcle and for 'inducing Pulleine to divide his forces... an officer... brave to rashness', and he once more used Rorke's Drift to salvage the situation:

> yet more pronounced is the Zulu admiration of the defence of the post of Rorke's Drift... a model of a most gallant defence... they defended their post foot by foot from four and half in the evening till five and half next morning.[60]

In his campaign, Frere was ably supported by his most 'political' wife Lady Catherine Frere and daughter Miss Mary Frere. Both women exerted great influence, bombarding General Ponsonby and the Queen with letters defending their father and husband, letters which stressed both the political correctness of his decision to instigate the Zulu war, but also highlighting the importance of the Rorke's Drift action as to how Isandlwana should have been fought and won and how it had saved Natal from invasion. Thus, on 17 February 1879, Frere's wife, Lady Catherine Frere, wrote to General Ponsonby:

> You will have seen the Report of the gallant defence of Rorke's Drift Post – it shows how much could be done and was done there with such materials which lay at hand to keep back a force of desperate savages thirty times the number of the little garrison – we hear that the Zulus are greatly disheartened at their enormous losses in spite of Isandlwana! They say they have not tears enough for [them] all.

The Chief, she reported,

> who commissioned the attack on Rorke's Drift is now a prisoner
> at the Royal Kraal and some reports say has been put to death for
> being beaten by our soldiers.[61]

In a letter of 4 February, addressed to the Queen, Lady Catherine
Frere further reinforced her husband's position on the basis of the
successful defence of Rorke's Drift:

> One of the bright gleams of light which have come through this
> darkness and which your Majesty may have heard by the same
> mail, was the gallant and successful defence of the camp at Rorke's
> Drift (on the Natal side of the Buffalo) by Lieutenant Bromhead
> 2/24th, Lieutenant Chard, Royal Engineers, who barricaded it
> with sacks of mealies (Indian corn) and biscuit tins, and, with
> only so few men, sustained a hand-to-hand fight through the
> whole night against some four thousand Zulus who attacked so
> desperately that they seized the muzzles of the guns. They six times
> got in and six times were driven out of the camp.[62]

Similarly, in a letter addressed to the Queen on 9 March 1879,
Frere himself extolled the use of laagered defences which would
have saved the camp at Isandlwana, had it been

> sufficiently manned by stout hearts and well armed bands, to
> repeat the noble example of the Rorke's Drift post – if Wolseley's
> 'advice' had been earlier followed our present perils might have
> been averted.[63]

Their defence cut no ice with their political superiors, but with
such evidence presented before her in all these letters, the Queen
took an increasingly robust posture against demands for the recall
of both Sir Bartle Frere and Lord Chelmsford. The Queen, for
instance, took particular exception to the 'impertinent remarks'
made in both Houses of Parliament 'about my messages of con-
dolence and encouragement to Lord Chelmsford and Sir Bartle

Frere'.[64] Although not wholly uncritical of Chelmsford's military performance ('Lord Chelmsford ought to have known more and poor Colonel Durnford was too rash'),[65] she felt compelled to defend her two loyal servants who in her view were being abandoned by her government. As the censure debate loomed in late March, under intense pressure from the Queen and no doubt aware of the ambiguities of his pre-war Zulu policy, on 23 March Hicks Beach told the Queen of his unhappiness, especially about the despatches of censure that were 'being forced upon him by the Cabinet'. Telling her he had written a letter of explanation to Sir Bartle Frere, he promised to 'do all in his power to defend him and Lord Chelmsford'.[66] In the event, both men were censured rather than recalled. The wording of the censure despatch constitutes one of the most remarkable documents in British political history, and gives both Frere's position and the Queen's extensive support for him considerable credibility. Thus, while sharply reprimanding Frere for taking 'without their full knowledge and sanction, a course almost certain to result in war' (Sir Michael's support in January for 'an early and decisive war' of course being ignored), it contradicts itself by expressing the government's appreciation of his services with 'no desire to withdraw in the present crisis of affairs the confidence hitherto reposed in you' and 'to bring the South African difficulties to a successful termination', a strange censure indeed![67] It was, in Robert Blake's words, 'a double faced document',[68] and aptly summarised the ambivalence of both Disraeli's and Hicks Beach's pre- and post-war Zulu policies. The despatch was later brilliantly satirised in the House of Commons by Sir William Harcourt, who read out to the House an imaginary letter from Hicks Beach:

> Dear Sir Bartle Frere, I cannot think you are right. Indeed I think you are very wrong; but after all you know a great deal better than I do. I hope you won't do what you are going to do; but if you do I hope it will turn out well.[69]

Even General Wolseley, otherwise a fierce critic of Sir Bartle Frere, later admitted to Hicks Beach's 'gross ignorance upon the subject of the Zululand settlement',[70] resulting in him 'giving him a bit of my mind officially'. Indeed, his overall disenchantment with Hicks Beach's politicking was crudely, but perhaps aptly, expressed in another diary entry: 'if only I had Hicks Beach within reach of my boots, I should enjoy making him feel the stiffness of the soles'![71]

The controversy continued well beyond the censure despatch. On 23 May 1879, the Queen was stunned to receive a telegram from Disraeli, asking her for her views upon the supersession of Chelmsford by General Wolseley as Commander-in-Chief of South Africa, and the restriction of Sir Bartle Frere's powers to the Cape and to the territory adjacent only, with General Wolseley as Her Majesty's High Commissioner in Natal and Transvaal. The telegram provoked one of the few political rows that occurred between the Queen and her favourite minister. While bowing to this political decision, the Queen made her private anger clear in her telegraphed reply to Disraeli. The telegram read:

> I will not withhold my *sanction* although I cannot *approve* it I cannot but feel that such a step will lead to the immediate resignation of both Sir Bartle Frere and Lord Chelmsford. This I would deeply deplore as it would in my opinion lower the country in the eyes of all Europe as well as encourage our enemies in South Africa.[72]

On 26 May, the Queen further declared that she was 'much annoyed' about Sir Garnet Wolseley's appointment, 'not having received any answers or further explanations'.[73] The appointment went ahead, the Queen's preferred candidate, Lord Napier of Magdala, being considered too old. The Queen's rift with Disraeli was complete when Chelmsford, after ignoring Wolseley's orders and completing his final victory at Ulundi, came home to be welcomed with open arms by Queen Victoria, who considered that Ulundi had finally vindicated the reverse at Isandlwana. When Disraeli accordingly refused to invite Chelmsford to his private house at Hughenden, the Queen's deep displeasure was made clear.[74]

Her revenge was sweet. While Disraeli invited Redvers Buller and Sir Evelyn Wood – two other prominent soldiers in the Zulu

campaign – to Hughenden, she publicly fêted Lord Chelmsford on
his return. Equally significantly, the Queen went out of her way to
honour the returning heroes of the Rorke's Drift action, which was
fully publicised across the country and received wide coverage in
the press. In August 1879, the Queen accordingly made a journey
from Osborne House to Netley Military Hospital with General
Ponsonby. Here, a visit was made to the ward of wounded Rorke's
Drift hero 'young Private Hitch of the 2nd 24th', who was

> very severely wounded in the shoulder affecting the use of his right
> arm which he cannot raise to his head… he behaved most gallantly at
> Rorke's Drift defending the Hospital and serving out ammunition to
> the men long after he was wounded till he fell senseless from exhaus-
> tion. He is a tall, good looking young man, with a very determined
> expression, but very modest and bears a high character.[75]

Before leaving, perhaps as a final sop to critics such as Wolseley, she
recorded an extremely rare honour for a private soldier: 'Hitch
was brought to the door for me to give him the VC which I told
him I did as a reward for his great bravery. He could not say a
word and I hear afterwards fainted.'[76]

An equally distinguished royal accolade was afforded to
Lieutenant Chard on his return from South Africa. He was
granted several audiences with the Queen over a three-day period
in October 1879. There, he was asked to give a meticulous verbal
account of the Rorke's Drift action, the Queen using Chard's
earlier despatch to record all the details in her journal. Several
other members of the Royal Family were present, and the Queen
was even duly instructed by Chard on the Zulu use of an assegai
that she had been given earlier as a gift.[77]

It was a fitting epitaph to one of the greatest tragi-heroic episodes in British imperial history. As Robert Blake points out:

> Disraeli's dealings with Frere and Chelmsford constitutes one of
> the least creditable episodes in his premiership. He ought, in the
> summer of 1878, to have examined the correspondence between
> Hicks Beach and Frere more closely, and, as Prime Minister, he

must share some responsibility for the fatal ambiguity of the Government's attitude.[78]

Once the Isandlwana disaster had occurred, Disraeli, and to a lesser extent Hicks Beach, had not only practically ignored the successful defence of Rorke's Drift, but had pushed the Cabinet into a double-faced treatment of both the High Commissioner and the Commander-in-Chief, which, despite their acknowledged shortcomings, can still be considered indefensible. In Blake's words: 'he should either have sacked them or backed them. On this rare occasion of divergence from her favourite Prime Minister the Queen was in the right'.[79]

The Queen's ostentatious celebration of her 'Rorke's Drift heroes' was mirrored across the country, undoubtedly much to the discomfiture of government, severely embarrassed by the earlier Isandlwana defeat, and those parliamentary critics seeking the recall of both Frere and Chelmsford. *Punch* took the lead with a splendid cartoon celebrating the heroic achievements of Lieutenant Chard and Bromhead. Over the next few months the event became a major feature in numerous popular journals, pamphlets and newspapers. Tributes and scores of poems in the Penny Dreadfuls appeared and reappeared. Such accolades were representative of a deeper cultural phenomenon – a new awareness, in an age of distant and poor communication, of the impact of the Empire upon indigenous peoples, if only in a somewhat naive and heroic 'noble savage' tradition. The Victorian public demonstrated a voracious appetite for all things 'Zulu', admiring – even fearing – their enemy for their exploits as much as they admired their compatriots who had fought so valiantly at Rorke's Drift. As Frank Emery observes, 'the moguls of show business were not slow to respond'.[80] Travelling theatre reenacted the battle across the country, including a troupe of 'genuine' Zulu warriors, allegedly veterans of the battles. The show reached Brecon, hard-hit by the Isandlwana losses, but both performances nevertheless attracted healthy audiences (prices ranging from two shillings for front seats and sixpence in the promenade), although the *Brecon County Times* more realistically appraised the show as a circus act of 'Burnt Cork Zulus'.[81] When the show reached

London, however, the continuing and deep political sensitivities of the government became abundantly clear. In an astonishing move, the Home Secretary attempted to ban the show, 'presumably', as Emery succinctly observes:

> because the Disraeli government was still highly sensitive from the confusion into which they had been plunged by the Zulus. No reminder, not even a public entertainment was welcome.[82]

For the general military establishment, the response to the Rorke's Drift victory was equally enthusiastic and longer lasting. The bitter carping of Wolseley and his supporters was ignored and the battle remained a central focus for military displays and re-enactments during and far beyond the Victorian period. The Rorke's Drift veterans were always a central feature of regimental celebrations, especially anniversary dinners, until literally the end of their lives. The last public appearance of two veterans, Colour-Sergeant Bourne and Private Jobbins, probably occurred at the 1934 Ravensworth Castle 'Northern Command Tattoo', where a splendid re-enactment of the battle took place.

The battle's significance was never lost to popular culture, and re-emerged in a spectacular way with the making and release of the acclaimed action film *Zulu* in 1964. The film not only recreated (if often with poetic licence) the events of the battle in Victorian heroic tradition, emphasising coolness and discipline under fire and extreme bravery on the British side, but also reflected the new post-war critical style of film-making, with a strong emphasis upon Zulu culture, gallantry and sacrifice.[83] Both Briton and Zulu are portrayed as, to some extent, tragic victims of a brutal 'imperial war'. In the words of Trevor Willsmer, the film was '*our* epic, a celebration of national courage (but not nationalism with its eyes "wide open")'.[84] Such balanced treatment probably explains the mass appeal of a film which, in 1960s multi-racial Britain:

> reflected the post-war mood of residual pride but one which also carried a new awareness of the harsher realities and consequences of empire-building for both conquerors and conquered.[85]

Conclusion

The political and military significance of the battle of Rorke's Drift has been significantly underestimated. The victory at this post, achieved by a few British soldiers and against massive odds, provided a major deterrent to further Zulu inroads into Natal, at a time when Chelmsford's main column was totally demoralised and Natal's defences severely compromised. The scale and intensity of the fighting fully justified the award of eleven VCs and must be treated in isolation from the earlier catastrophic defeat at Isandlwana. For these reasons, Rorke's Drift was of far more significance than the other British victory at Inyenzane the same day, and decisively demonstrated the efficacy of fortified positions against Zulu open-order attack. Indeed, the battle undoubtedly became a model for the rest of the campaign and subsequent British campaigns against 'native enemies' (notably in the Sudan).[86] The treatment of Zulu wounded was reprehensible but understandable in the context of such a brutalised conflict, in which prisoners were rarely taken by either side. The battle was significant in other ways. It was a major psychological boost to the Victorian public after the Isandlwana disaster and became an enduring symbol of, initially, British heroism, and ultimately Zulu heroism. Its political significance must not be underestimated. The victory played an important role in the post-Isandlwana debate and was extensively used by both Frere and Chelmsford and their supporters to justify their policies. If both men had, in different ways, exceeded or neglected their duties, their subsequent ambivalent treatment by their political masters, in which the military importance of Rorke's Drift was largely ignored or unrecognised, must also be the subject of severe censure.

Postscript: The Post-War Careers of the VC Holders and Other British and Zulu Veterans

John Chard's professional career flourished in the post-war years, matched by his private audiences with Queen Victoria and a hero's welcome in his home town. The people of Plymouth duly presented him with various gifts, including a gold watch and sword of honour. In 1886, after several overseas appointments, he was promoted to Major, to Lieutenant-Colonel in 1893, and, in 1896, was awarded a colonelcy. Tragically, the year 1896 proved to be one of mixed fortune, with the onset of a fatal disease. After several operations for cancer of the tongue, his health further deteriorated and he retired to Hatch Beauchamp, Somerset, where he died on 1 November 1897, aged forty-nine. Queen Victoria had not forgotten her Rorke's Drift hero and sent both a Diamond Jubilee medal and a laurel wreath to his funeral, inscribed 'A mark of admiration and regard for a brave soldier, from his sovereign'.

Gonville Bromhead's post-war career was sadly more short-lived. After a similar hero's welcome and the award of a jewelled dress sword at Lincoln Masonic Hall, he was presented with a revolver by the tenants of Thurlby Hall. After service in the

Burmese Campaign and the East Indies and promotion to Major in 1883, he was tragically struck down by enteric or typhoid fever at Allahabad Barracks, India, on 9 February 1891.

James Dalton enjoyed a brief but colourful last few years after the Rorke's Drift action. He served in Egypt and then returned to South Africa in 1884 to dabble in gold mining in the Transvaal. Soon afterwards, in December 1886, he died suddenly while staying with a friend in Port Elizabeth.

James Reynolds, after receiving his VC from Lord Wolseley at St Paul's, Zululand, enjoyed an illustrious career. In 1879 he was promoted to Surgeon-Major and elected honorary Doctor of Law and honorary fellow of the Royal College of Physicians of Ireland. He retired in 1896, and, in November 1929, attended the VCs' dinner at the House of Lords, convened by the Prince of Wales. He died in London in 1932, aged eighty-two, one of the last of the surviving veterans.

Corporal William Allen, one of the longest-serving veterans, having joined the 24th Regiment at Aldershot in 1859, received his VC from Queen Victoria at Windsor Castle on 9 December 1879. After serving at Colchester as a Sergeant Instructor of Musketry in 1886, he succumbed to influenza in February 1890.

Robert Jones's post-war career was marked by illness and despair, probably resulting from the stresses of the battle and his extensive bullet and assegai wounds. Originally a farm labourer in Monmouthshire, his last years were traumatic, with bouts of mental illness which culminated in suicide in 1898. He left a wife and five children.

William Jones was born in 1839, and having enlisted in the army in 1858, he was awarded his VC by Queen Victoria at Windsor Castle in January 1880. That year, suffering from chronic rheumatism, he was discharged as unfit for service. Reduced to poverty by 1893, he was forced to pawn his VC for five pounds, and as ill-health increased, he experienced nightmares reliving his battle experiences. In 1913 he died, destitute, leaving a wife and seven children.

Frederick Hitch, originally a building labourer and seriously wounded in his left arm during the siege, was, as we have seen, awarded his VC at Netley Hospital by Queen Victoria in August 1879. With his arm permanently disabled, he was soon invalided from the army and worked for many years as a member of the Corps of Commissionaires at the Imperial Institute. In 1901, while working at RUSI, White-Hall, his VC was stolen, but fortunately a replacement was presented to him in 1908. His last years were spent as a taxi driver for the General Motor Cab Company and he died of heart failure on 6 January 1913, aged fifty-six. He left six children.

Henry Hook, born in Gloucester, had only been in army service for two years before Rorke's Drift, although he did have useful combat experience in the Ninth Frontier War. He was one of the few soldiers to be awarded a VC at the original battle site. In 1880, he bought himself out of the army and worked for some years for the British Museum as a cloakroom attendant. In March 1905, he died, aged fifty-five, of pulmonary tuberculosis, soon after recording his memoirs in the *Royal Magazine*. His funeral was more spectacular than most, including representatives from twenty-three regiments.

John Fielding (Williams), born in Abergavenny, had enlisted in the army in 1877 under the assumed name of Williams, ostensibly to escape the disapproval of his father. After receiving the Victoria Cross he served in India and was eventually discharged in 1893. He was attached to the Brecon Civilian Staff until his retirement in May 1920. Returning to Cwmbran, he died of heart failure in 1932 at the ripe old age of seventy-five. His impressive funeral was attended by other survivors (including Private Jobbins), with floral tributes sent by Colonel Bourne and relatives of Privates Hook and Hitch.

Ferdinand Scheiss was born in 1856 at Berne in Switzerland. He was one of the least well known of the Rorke's Drift VC winners and was awarded the Victoria Cross by Lord Wolseley at a parade in Pietermaritzburg in February 1880. After working briefly as a telegraph officer in Pietermaritzburg, he died destitute on board the troop-ship *Serapis* en route to England. He was buried at sea off the west coast of Africa. Sadly, there is no known authenticated photograph or portrait of this gallant veteran.

Of the other non-VC survivors of the garrison, Colour-Sergeant Bourne, Padre Smith and Walter Dunne deserve a special mention. Colour-Sergeant Frank Bourne, after being awarded the Distinguished Conduct Medal for his gallant service at Rorke's Drift, served in Gibraltar, India and Burma and ended his career as Adjutant at the Hythe School of Musketry until his retirement in 1907. He was present at the Northern Command Military Tattoo, Gateshead, in 1934 with other surviving veterans, Sergeant Saxby and Privates William Cooper, John Jobbins and Caleb Woods. By the time of his death in May 1945, possibly the last of the Rorke's Drift survivors, he had left a priceless record of his experiences by speaking on BBC radio on 20 December 1936.

Walter Dunne, like his deceased colleague Louis Byrne, was mentioned in despatches and served in the Transvaal at First Anglo-Boer War (1880–1) and during the Egyptian Campaign (1882). He became a Lieutenant-Colonel in 1888 and was promoted to Colonel in 1897. He died in 1908 at the age of fifty-five.

Padre George Smith, widely praised for his moral and logistical support at Rorke's Drift, was later commissioned as Chaplain to the Forces in January 1880. He served in north-east Africa, including the Egyptian and Anglo-Sudan campaigns. Between 1887 and 1905 he took up domestic appointments in England and eventually died at Fulwood, aged seventy-three, from bronchial trouble.

Sadly, little is known of the fate of the several thousand brave Zulu warriors and their *indunas* who fought at Rorke's Drift. Some were undoubtedly present at the fiftieth anniversary gathering held at Isandlwana in January 1929 and recorded in local Natal newspapers.

We do, however, know of the fate of their commander, Prince Dabulamanzi. During the turmoil of the post-Zulu war settlement, his forces clashed with local Boers during a land dispute in north-eastern Zululand. In the ensuing skirmishes in September 1886, he was shot dead by a Boer commando named Paul van de Berg. This was a tragic end for a brave, if flawed, Zulu commander.[87]

Notes

1 ROAD TO WAR: THE STORM-CLOUDS GATHER 1877-9

1   For discussions of the origins of the Anglo-Zulu War, see especially A. Duminy
    and C. Ballard (eds), *The Anglo-Zulu War: New perspectives* (University of Natal Press,
    Pietermaritzburg, 1981), especially chapters 1-4, and R. Cope, *Ploughshare of War, The
    Origins of the Anglo-Zulu War of 1879* (University of Natal Press, Pietermaritzburg,
    1999).
2   J. Morley, *Life of Gladstone* (London 1903), Vol. 7.
3   A.G. Gardiner, *Life of Sir William Harcourt* (London, 1923), Vol. 1, p.349.
4   For an expanded version of this ensuing discussion, see E.J. Yorke, 'Sir Bartle Frere,
    Sir Michael Hicks Beach and the Zulu Question January 1878 to March 1879',
    unpublished MA thesis (University of London 1977).
5   Colonial Office Files, PRO, Kew (hereafter CO), CO 48. 48s, Carnarvon to Frere,
    2 January 1878.
6   Martineau, *Life and Correspondence of Sir Bartle Frere*, Vol. II (London, 1895), Frere to
    Herbert, 23 December 1878.
7   B.C. Pine, 'Contemporary Review', June 1879.
8   CO 48/482, Shepstone to Carnarvon, 27 May 1877.
9   Frere, 'Nineteenth Century', February 1881.
10 Royal Archives, *Victoria's Journal* (hereafter RA VIC).
11 Sir H. Rider Haggard, *Cetshwayo and his white Neighbours* (London, 1882), chapter 3
    passim.
12 C.W. de Kiewiet, *The Imperial Factor in South Africa* (Cambridge, 1937), p.27.
13 Sir J. Lawrence, Minute (from B. Worsfold, *Sir Bartle Frere*, p.24).
14 Lady Hicks Beach, *Life of Sir Michael Hicks Beach* (London, 1932).
15 C.F. Goodfellow, *Great Britain and South Africa Confederation* (Cape Town, 1966).
16 St Aldwyn (Hicks Beach) Papers, Gloucester Records Office (hereafter GRO,
    PCC), Hicks Beach to Frere, 7 March 1878.
17 GRO, PCC, Hicks Beach to Frere, 4 April 1878.
18 GRO, PCC, Hicks Beach to Frere, 7 March 1878.
19 *Ibid*.

20   CO 48/484, Shepstone to Carnarvon, Oct 1877.

21   Martineau, II, p.233, Sheptstone to Frere, 1 December 1877.

22   *Ibid.*

23   Martineau, II, p.223-4, Frere to Herbert, 18 March 1878.

24   RA,VIC.

25   India Office Library (Political and Secret Memoranda) (hereafter IOL) File A12 Frere, Minute, 6 December 1863.

26   Martineau, II, p.230, Bulwer to Carnarvon, 2 Nov 1876.

27   Goodfellow, pp.166-7.

28   GRO, PCC/22, Hicks Beach to Frere, 7 March 1878.

29   *Ibid.*

30   GRO PCC/22 Hicks Beach to Frere, 4 April 1878.

31   GRO PCC/22 Hicks Beach to Frere, 11 June 1878.

32   CO 48/486, Pearson Minute, 24 Sept 1878.

33   CO 48/486, Wingfield Comment, 24 Sept 1878.

34   CO 48/486, Frere to Hicks Beach, 5 Sept 1878.

35   Worsfold, p.91, Frere to Hicks Beach, 30 Sept 1878.

36   CO 48/486, Wingfield Note, 16 Sept 1878.

37   CO 48/486, Herbert Note, 16 Sept 1878.

38   CO 48/486, Hicks Beach to Frere, 5 Oct 1878 (Tel).

39   GRO PCC/22 Hicks Beach to Frere, 10 Oct 1878.

40   G Buckle, *The Life of Benjamin Disraeli*, Vol.VI, p.420, Disraeli to Lady Bradford, 27 Sept 1878.

41   CO 48/486, Chelmsford to Secretary of State for War (hereafter SOS War) 27 Oct 1878.

42   GRO PCC/23, Frere to Hicks Beach, 25 Apr 1879.

43   *Ibid*; for Frere's anxiety over Boer discontent see voluminous correspondence in CO 468/487.

44   GRO PCC/13, Hicks Beach to Disraeli, 17 Oct 1878.

45   GRO PCC/13, Hicks Beach to Disraeli, 3 Nov 1878.

46   CO 48/487, Frere Memorandum, 13 Nov 1878.

47   CO 48/487, Pearson Minute to Herbert, 16 Nov 1878.

48   CO 48/487, Herbert Note, 13 December 1878.

49   CO 48/487, Herbert Note, 17 January 1879.

50   For an elaboration of his view, CO 48/487, Fairfield Minute, 10 March 1879.

51   CO 48/487, Fairfield Minute, 10 March 1879.

52   GRO PCC/22, Hicks Beach to Frere, 11 December 1878.

53   *Ibid.*

54   GRO PCC/13, Hicks Beach to Disraeli, 13 January 1879.

55   *Ibid.*

56   *Ibid.*

57   For details of the Ultimatum see J.Young, *They Fell Like Stones* (London, 1991), pp.22-3.

57   Martineau, p.266, Frere to Herbert, 23 December 1878.

58   Moodie, *Moodie's Zulu War,* pp.7-8.

2 PREPARATIONS FOR WAR: THE TWO OPPOSING ARMIES

1   For detailed studies of the British army in the Victorian period see, especially, E. Spiers, *The Late Victorian Army 1868–1902* (MUP 1992) *passim* and Correlli Barnett,

Britain and Her Army 1509–1970 (London, 1970) pp.272-299.

2 For a comprehensive treatment of the military and their role in social order in Britain see, especially, C. Townshend, *Taking the Peace: Public Order and Public Security in Modern Britain* (OUP, 1993) and A. Babington, *Military Intervention in Britain: From the Gordon Riots to the Gibraltar incident* (London, 1990).

3 See, for instance, F. Emery, *The Red Soldier,* pp.18-22, for an excellent discussion of the literacy levels of 1879 British soldiers.

4 For a detailed discussion of British army equipment see, for instance, M. Barthorp, *The British Army on Campaign 1816–1902,* 4 vols (London, 1987–8).

5 F. Emery, *The Red Soldier: The Zulu War 1879* (Johannesburg, 1983), p.49.

6 A. Preston (ed.), *Sir Garnet Wolseley's South African Journal 1879–80* (Capetown, 1973) p.73.

7 For detailed treatments of the Zulu society and army in 1879 see J. Laband, *The Rise and Fall of the Zulu nation* (London, 1995) especially chapters 1-4, J. Guy, *The destruction of the Zulu Kingdom* (London, 1979) pp.3-39.

8 Guy, *Zulu Kingdom,* p.21.

9 War Office, *Precis of Information regarding Zululand,* HMSO 1885 p.87.

10 See Chapter 1, p.19.

11 War Office, *Precis* p.87.

12 *Ibid.*

13 *Ibid.,* p.88. For oral source material on Zulu war rituals see, especially, C. de B. Webb and J.B. Wright (eds), *The James Stuart Archive* Vol. III (hereafter *JSA*), Statement, 99 Mpatshana Ka Sodondo pp.296-329.

14 War Office, *Precis* p.89.

15 Webb and Wright, JSA, III, p.317.

16 H.L. Hall, 'With Assegai and Rifle'.

17 War Office, *Precis* p.88.

18 *Ibid.,* p.87.

19 As Chelmsford informed Frere early in the campaign: 'We shall occupy a large extent of Zululand, and shall threaten the portion which remains to the King… we shall oblige Cetshwayo to keep his army mobilised, and it is certain that his troops will have difficulty in finding sufficient food'. Chelmsford, Memorandum to Frere, 16 January 1879 (encl. Frere to Hicks Beach, 16 January 1879), J. Laband and I. Knight (eds) *Archives of Zululand,* Vol I, p.628.

20 War Office, *Precis* pp.87-8.

21 For a deeper examination of Chelmsford's battle plans see E.J. Yorke, 'Isandlwana, 22 January 1879' in *Battle Plans, Before and After* (Helicon Books, 1998) pp.165-178.

22 PRO WO33/33, G.O.C. (Lord Chelmsford) to S.O.S. War, 11 Nov 1878.

23 PRO WO33/33 G.O.C. to Surveyor General of Ordnance, 12 Aug 1878. For an excellent study of Zulu war transport problems, see I. Bennett, *Eyewitness in Zululand* (London, 1989).

24 Hall, *With Assegai and Rifle,* p.196.

25 *Ibid.*

26 H. Smith-Dorrien, *Forty-eight Years Service* (London, 1923) p.8.

27 *Moodie's Zulu War,* p.75.

28 *Ibid.,* p.76.

29 For full roll-call of the officers and men of Rorke's Drift including other units and regiments see pp.129-131.

30 See ch. 9, pp.182-4 and ch.10 pp.213-4 for VC citations and post-war careers.

31 Harford, *Zulu War Journal,* pp.16-17.

32 Emery, *Red Soldier,* p.72.

33 Hallam Parr, *Sketches*, p.180.

34 Harford, *Zulu War Journal*, p.17.

35 Lock and Quantrill, *Red Book*, p.22, *Natal Times*, 11 January 1879.

36 Hallam Parr, *Sketches*, p.183.

37 Harford, *Zulu War Journal*, p.19.

38 Emery, *Red Soldier*, pp.74-5; Coghill (to mother?).

39 Hallam Parr, *Sketches*, pp.184-5.

40 J. Martineau, *The Life of Sir Bartle Frere*, p.272, Chelmsford Memorandum, 8 January 1879.

41 Hallam Parr, *Sketches*, p.185.

42 Emery, *Red Soldier*, Coghill, Diary, 9 January 1879.

43 RRWM, Clery Memorandum, 17 February 1879.

44 Harford, *Zulu War Journal*, pp.22-3.

45 RRWM, Historical Records of the Second Battalion 24th Regiment, Secunderabad, 1884.

46 Hallam Parr, *Sketches*, p.188.

47 Harford, *Zulu War Journal*, p.24.

48 *Ibid.*, p.24.

49 RRWM Clery Memorandum, 17 February 1879.

50 *Ibid.*

51 Hallam Parr, *Sketches*, pp.189-90.

3 THE ISANDLWANA MASSACRE: DAY OF THE AASVOGELS

1 C.F. Molyneux, *Campaigning in South Africa and Egypt* (London, 1896) pp.112-13.

2 Royal Regiment of Wales (South Wales Borders) Museum Archives, Brecon (hereafter RRWM) Kilvert diary, 11 February 1879.

3 F.W.D Jackson, 'Isandlwana, 1879 – the sources re-examined, Journal of the Society For Army Historical' Research, vol. 43 (1965) p.39. His account, published in three articles, remains one of the best accounts of the battle and the units engaged.

4 RRWM Pulleine note, 22 January 1879.

5 Holme, *Silver Wreath*. p.48, Pte E. Wilson's account.

6 Holme, *Silver Wreath*, p.46, Pte J. Bickley's account.

7 *Illustrated London News* (hereafter *ILN*) 17 March 1879, Isandlwana Ct Inquiry, Lt Essex evidence.

8 NAM, Stafford Papers.

9 *ILN* 17 March 1879 Isandlwana Ct of Inquiry, Lt Cochrane evidence.

10 I. Knight, *Isandlwana and Rorke's Drift* (Greenhill Books, London, 1992) p.62.

11 NAM, Stafford Papers.

12 Holme, *Silver Wreath*, p.48, Wilson account.

13 Moodie, *Moodie's Zulu War,* p.640.

14 Holme, *Silver Wreath*, p.47, Bickley account. See also Williams account, p.47.

15 NAM, Chelmsford Papers, J.N. Hamer account.

16 NAM, Chelmsford papers, Lt C. Raw account.

17 NAM, Stafford papers.

18 Clements, *Glamour and Tragedy*, p.59.

19 Holme, *Silver Wreath*, p.48, Pte Williams account.

20 *ILN*, 17 March 1879, Isandlwana Ct of Enquiry, Capt Nourse evidence.

21 Holme, *Silver Wreath*, p.47, Pte D. Johnson account. See also Grant and Trainer accounts, pp.46-7.

22   *ILN*, 17 March 1879, Isandlwana Ct of Inquiry, Essex evidence.
23   H. Smith-Dorrien, *Memories of Forty-eight years Service* (London, 1925), p.13-14.
24   J.A. Brickhill, 'The Isandhlwana Massacre', in A.F. Hattersley, *Later Annals of Natal* (London 1938), p.153.
25   The *Times*, 2 April 1879, Essex letter.
26   Morris, *Washing of the Spears*, p.367.
27   Holme, *Silver Wreath*, p.46, Bickley account.
28   NAM, Stafford Papers.
29   NAM, Chelmsford Papers, Malindi evidence.
30   Moodie, *Moodie's Zulu War*, p.25-6.
31   NAM, Chelmsford Papers, Hamer evidence.
32   Morris, *Washing of the Spears*, p.375.
33   Norns Newman, *In Zululand*, p.82.
34   NAM, Stafford Papers.
35   NAM, Chelmsford Papers, Hamer evidence.
36   Norris Newman, *With the British... Zululand*, p.83.
37   Emery, *Red Soldier*, p.84.
38   *Narrative of Field Operations – Zulu War 1879*, p.38.
39   Norris Newman, *In Zululand*, p.83.
40   Emery, *Red Soldier*, p.85.
41   *Ibid.*, p.84.
42   Hallam Parr, *Sketch*, p.221.
43   Harford, *Journal*, p.34.
44   See Brickhill, 'Isandlwana Massacre', Hattersley, *Later Annals* and Holme, *Silver Wreath*, p.48, Williams account.
45   WO33/33, Ct of inquiry, Curling Evidence.
46   RRWM Clery Memorandum, February 1879.
47   *The Imperial Club Magazine* (1929), p.129, Colour Sgt Gittins 2/24th account.
48   Streatfield, *Reminiscences of an old 'un*, p.155-7, Lonsdale account.
49   *Imperial Club Magazine* , p.131, Gittins account.
50   *The Graphic*, 29 March 1879, Crealock report.

4 BATTLE ANALYSIS: THE LESSONS OF THE ISANDLWANA DISASTER

1   *Moodie's Zulu War*, pp.43-44, Molife account.
2   Hallam Parr, *Sketch*, pp.211-12.
3   Smith-Dorrien, *Memoires*, p.14.
4   Norris-Newman, *In Zululand*, p.63.
5   Hattersley, *Later Annals of Natal*, p.154, Brickhill account.
6   Holme, *Silver Wreath*, p.46, Bickley account.
7   *Ibid.*, p.46, Grant account.
8   *Ibid.*, p.47-8, Williams account.
9   *Ibid.*, p.48, Wilson account.
10   *Ibid.*, p.46, Bickley account.
11   *Ibid.*, p.47, Williams account.
12   C.T. Atkinson, *The South Wales Borderers, 24th Foot* pp.332-3, Lt Mainwaring account.
13   Norris-Newman, *In Zululand*, p.220, Wilsone-Black report.
14   Knight, *Isandlwana and Rorke's Drift*, p.84.
15   Hattersley, *Annals*, p.261.
16   Emery, *Red Soldier*, p.87.

17   *Ibid.*, p.84.
18   Norris-Newman, *In Zululand*, pp.78-9.
19   *Ibid.*, p.83.
20   For several key articles on the continuing ammunition controversy see my own extended article, 'Isandlwana 1879, further reflections on the ammunition controversy', *Journal of Society for Army Historical Research* (hereafter *JSAHR*), Jackson, Isandlwana (*JSAHR*, March, Sept and December, 1965) and Knight.
21   NAM, Stafford Papers.
22   J.C. Laband (ed.), *Lord Chelmsford's Zululand Campaign*, Chelmsford to Frere, 23 January 1879, p.78.
23   Laband, *Zululand Campaign*, pp.92-3.

5 THE FLIGHT FROM ISANDLWANA: PRELUDE TO RORKE'S DRIFT

1   NAM, Stafford Papers.
2   *ILN*, 17 March 1879, Isandlwana Ct of Inquiry, Curling evidence.
3   NAM, Chelmsford Papers, Malindi evidence.
4   Clements, *Glamour and Tragedy*, p.63.
5   Smith-Dorrien, *Memories*, pp.16-17.
6   Moodie, *Moodie's Zulu War*, p.26.
7   NAM, Stafford papers.
8   Moodie, *Moodie's Zulu War*, p.27.
9   Smith-Dorrien, *Memories*, pp.21.
10   Holme, *Silver Wreath*, p.63, Pte Hook account.
11   *Ibid.*, p.62, Pte Hitch account.
12   Museum of the Army Medical Corps (hereafter AMCM), *How VCs are Won; A tale of Rorke's Drift* (told by its last VC), Reynolds interview, USA 1903.
13   Holme, *Silver Wreath*, p.63. Hook account.
14   *Ibid.*, p.59, Colour-Sgt Bourne account.
15   *The Waggoner*, April 1991, Acting Assistant Commissary Walter Dunne, 'Reminiscences of Campaigning in South Africa 1877-81'.
16   Smith-Dorrien, *Memories*, pp.8-10.
17   Holme, *Silver Wreath*, p.49, Chard account.
18   *Ibid.*
19   *Ibid.*
20   See WO 32/7738 for Chelmsford's later defence of Spalding's actions.
21   AMCM, *How VCs are Won*, Reynolds Interview.
22   AMCM, *JHR*, Reynolds, 'Report of the Defence of Rorke's Drift'.
23   *Ibid.*
24   Holme, *Silver Wreath*, p.50. Chard account.
25   Lt Adendorff has been portrayed as a deserter from both Isandlwana and Rorke's Drift, but Chard's, Stafford's and other sources confirm his positive role at Rorke's Drift.
26   Holme, *Silver Wreath*, p.50. Chard account.
27   *Ibid.*, p.59, Pte Waters account.
28   *Ibid.*, p.63, Hook account.
29   *Ibid.*, p.50, Chard account.
30   *Ibid.*, p.63, Hook account.
31   AMCM, Reynolds. 'Report'.
32   Holme, *Silver Wreath*, p.50, Chard account.

33   *Ibid.*, p.63, Hook account.
34   *Ibid.*, p.50, Chard account.
35   *Waggoner*, Dunne, 'Reminiscences'.
36   Holme, *Silver Wreath*, p.50, Chard account.
37   *Ibid.*, p.60, Bourne account.
38   *Ibid.*, p.50, Chard account.
39   AMCM, Reynolds, 'Report'.
40   *Ibid.*
41   *Waggoner*, Dunne, 'Reminiscences'.
42   Emery, *Red Soldier*, p.132.
43   Holme, *Siver Wreath*, p.50, Bourne account.
44   Emery, *Red Soldier*, p.126.
45   Emery, *Red Soldier*, p.132, Lugg account.
46   *Ibid.*, p.50 Chard account.
47   Hallam Parr, *Sketch*, p.237.
48   AMCM, Reynolds, 'Report'.
49   *Waggoner*, Dunne.

6 THE FIRST ZULU ASSAULTS

1   AMCM Reynolds, 'Report'.
2   *Ibid.* Chard took a more charitable view, noting that Smith had 'elected to remain with us', Holme, *Silver Wreath*, p.50, Chard account.
3   The man killed was in fact Corporal W. Anderson: 'His heart must have failed him when he saw the enemy and heard the firing and got over the parapet and tried to make his escape on foot, but a bullet from the garden struck him and he fell dead within 150 yards of our front wall.' *Lummis*, Smith Diary, p.51.
4   Trooper F. Symons, Natal Carbineers, one of the relief force, later wrote: 'on reaching the house, the first body we saw was that of a native auxiliary who was shot for deserting in the hour of need'. Hattersley, *Later Annals,* p.150, Symons account.
5   Holme, *Silver Wreath*, p.60, Bourne account.
6   *Ibid.*, p.50, Chard account.
7   *Ibid.*, p.63, Hook account.
8   AMCM, *How VCs are Won*, Reynolds interview.
9   Holme, *Silver Wreath* p.62, Hitch account.
10   AMCM, *How VCs are Won*, Reynolds interview.
11   *Waggoner*, Dunne, 'Reminiscences'.
12   Holme, *Silver Wreath* p.60, Bourne account.
13   *Ibid.,* p.61, Lyons account.
14   *Ibid.,* p.59, Waters account.
15   *Ibid.,* p.62, Hitch account. Also Emery, *Red Soldier*, p.136.
16   *Ibid.*
17   *Waggoner*, Dunne, 'Reminiscences'.
18   Holme, *Silver Wreath*, p.62, Hitch account.
19   Canon W.M. Lummis, *Padre George Smith at Rorke's Drift* (Wensum Books, 1978) p.52, Smith Diary.
20   AMCM, Reynolds 'Report'.
21   Holme, *Silver Wreath*, p.61, Lyons account.
22   AMCM, *How VCs are Won*, Reynolds interview.
23   Emery, *Red Soldier*, p.134 Howard account.

24   *Ibid.*, p.132, Lugg account.

25   Holme, *Silver Wreath*, p.61, Lyons account.

26   Holme, *Silver Wreath*, p.51, Chard account.

27   Holme, *Silver Wreath*, p.63, Hook account.

28   Lummis, p.52 Smith Diary.

29   Holme, *Silver Wreath*, p.6, Hitch account.

30   Emery, *Red Soldier*, p.132, Lugg account.

31   Holme, *Silver Wreath*, p.63, Hook account.

32   AMCM, *How VCs are Won*, Reynolds interview.

33   Holme, *Silver Wreath* p.51, Chard account.

34   AMCM, Reynolds 'Report'.

35   Emery, *Red Soldier*, p.132, Lugg account and *ibid.*, p.127, Hook account.

36   Holme, *Silver Wreath*, p.50, Chard account and Attwood Papers.

37   *Ibid.*, p.60, Bourne account.

38   Holme, *Silver Wreath*, p.63, Hook account.

39   Lummis, *Padre Smith*, p.52.

40   Holme, *Silver Wreath*, p.51, Chard account.

41   Colour-Sergeant Bourne noted how the Zulu 'had collected rifles from the men they had killed at Isandhlwana and had captured the ammunition from them so our own arms were used against us'. In fact, the Undi Corps were absent from the main part of the battle and probably secured no more than a few score Martini-Henry rifles from fugitives killed on the way to Rorke's Drift. Nevertheless, these were enough, as Bourne recalled, to cause serious losses to the garrison. Holme, *Silver Wreath*, p.60, Bourne account.

42   Holme, *Silver Wreath*, p.61, Lyons account.

43   Lummis, p.53, Smith Diary.

44   Holme, *Silver Wreath*, p.8, Chard account.

45   Emery, *Red Soldier*, p.136-7, Hitch account.

46   Holme, *Silver Wreath*, p.62, Hitch account.

47   Lummis, p.52, Smith Diary.

48   Holme, *Silver Wreath*, p.62, Hitch account.

49   *Ibid.*, p.51, Chard account and Attwood Papers.

50   See several accounts, notably Lummis, p.52, Smith Diary and Holme, *Silver Wreath*, p.52, Chard account.

51   *Ibid.*, p.50, Chard account.

52   NAM, Stafford Papers.

53   A. Preston (ed.), *Sir Garnet Wolseley's South African Journal 1879-80* (Capetown 1973), p.145.

7 NADIR: THE HOSPITAL FIGHT (6P.M.–10P.M.)

1   Lummis, p.53, Smith Diary.

2   Holme, *Silver Wreath*, p.62, Hitch account.

3   Lumiss, p.53, Smith Diary.

4   Holme, *Silver Wreath*, p.62, Hitch account.

5   *Ibid.*, p.64, Hook account.

6   *Ibid.*, p.51, Chard account.

7   *Ibid.*, p.51, Chard account.

8   F. E. Whitton, *Deeds which Should not Pass Away* (Edinburgh, 1939).

9   AMCM, Reynolds report 64.

10   Holme, *Silver Wreath*, p.63, Hook account.
11   *Ibid.*
12   Lummis, p.52, Smith Diary. See also Lyons account.
13   *Ibid.*
14   Holme, *Silver Wreath*, p.63, Hook account.
15   *Ibid.*
16   *Moodie's Zulu War*, p.82.
17   *Ibid.*, p.59, Waters account (originally from *The Cambrian,* 13 June 1879).
18   *Ibid.*, p.53, Chard account.
19   *Ibid.*, Water's account, p.59.
20   Holme, *Silver Wreath*, p.64, Hook account.
21   *Ibid.*, p.64, Hook account. After the battle, Private Connolly gave a different version of his escape.
22.   AMCM, Reynolds 'Report'.
23.   Holme, *Silver Wreath*. p.65, Jobbins account.
24.   Lummis, p.52, Smith diary.
25.   Holme, *Silver Wreath*, p.51, Chard account.
26.   AMCM, Reynolds report.
27.   Emery, *Red Soldier*, p.132, Lugg account.
28.   Lurrins, p.54, Smith diary.
29.   *Ibid.*
30.   Holme, *Silver Wreath*, p.64, Hook account.

8 THE FINAL ORDEAL (10P.M.–8A.M.)

1   Holme, *Silver Wreath*, p.161, Sgt Smith account.
2   AMCM, *How VCs are Won*, Reynolds interview.
3   Holme, *Silver Wreath*, p.52, Chard account.
4   *Ibid.,* p.52.
5   Emery, *Red Soldier*, p.132, Lugg account.
6   *Ibid.,* p.134, Howard account. See also C.E. Calwell, *Small Wars*, p.495.
7   Holme, *Silver Wreath*, p.64, Hook account.
8   *Ibid.,* p.51, Chard account.
9   AMCM, Reynolds report.
10   RLCM, *Waggoner*, Dunne account.
11   *Ibid.*
12   Holme, *Silver Wreath*, p.52, Chard account.
13   *Ibid.,* p.60, Hitch account.
14   *Ibid.,* p.64, Hook account.
15   *Ibid.,* p.62, Hitch account.
16   *Ibid.*
17   *Ibid.*
18   *Ibid.,* p.64–5, Hook account.
19   *Ibid.,* p.19, Chard account.
20   Emery, *Red Soldier*, p.134, Howard account.
21   Lummis, p.55, Smith diary.
22   Emery, *Red Soldier*, p.132, Lugg account.
23   RLCM, *Waggoner*, Dunne account.
24   Holme, *Silver Wreath*, p.53, Chard account.
25   *Ibid.*

26 *Ibid.,* p.52.
27 *Ibid.*
28 RLCM, *Waggoner*, Dunne account.
29 *Ibid.*
30 Holme, *Silver Wreath*, p.59, Waters account.
31 RLCM, *Waggoner*, Dunne account.
32. Holme, *Siver Wreath*, p.52, Chard account.
33. War Office, *Precis*, p.47.
34. Holme, *Silver Wreath*, p.65, Hook account.
35. *Ibid.,* p.52, Chard account.
36. *Ibid.*

9 AFTERMATH: RELIEF, RECOVERY AND RETRIBUTION

1   AMCM, Reynolds report.
2   Holme, *Silver Wreath*, p.53, Chard account.
3   *Ibid.,* p.65, Hook account.
4   AMCM, Reynolds report.
5   Holme, *Silver Wreath*, p.65, Jobbins account.
6   *Ibid.,* p.65, Hook account.
7   PRO ADM 16486, Report on the proceedings of 21, 22 and 23 January 1879, by Lt B. Milne.
8   Harford, *Zulu War Journal*, p.35.
9   *Ibid.,* p.36.
10 Holme, *Silver Wreath* p.65, Hook account.
11 Hallam Parr, *Sketch*, p.243.
12 Hattersley, *Annals of Natal*, p.150, Trooper F. Symons account.
13 Harford, *Zulu War Journal*, p.36.
14 Holme, *Silver Wreath*, p.53, Chard account.
15 Harford, *Zulu War Journal*, p.41.
16 Holme, *Silver Wreath*, p.53, Chard account.
17 *Ibid.,* p.65, Hook account.
18 Harford, *Zulu War Journal*, p.36-7.
19 ADM 16486, Milne Report.
20 Hallam Parr, *Sketch,* p.260.
21 Harford, *Zulu War Journal*, p.37.
22 Smith-Dorrien, *Memories,* p.19.
23 Hallam Parr, *Sketch,* p.261.
24 *Ibid.,* pp.261-2.
25 ADM 16486 Milne Report.
26 See M. Lieven, 'Butchering the Brutes all over the Place: Total War and Massacre in Zululand, 1879 , *History* 84, 286 October 1999.
27 Holme, *Silver Wreath* p.65, Hook account.
28 *Ibid.*
29 Hallam Parr, *Sketch,* p.264.
30 Smith to wife, 24 January 1879 (and in Emery, *Red Soldier*, p.139-40), also in Holme, *Silver Wreath*, p.61.
31 Emery, *Red Soldier*, p.98, Cook to father, 1 February 1879.
32 Smith-Dorrien, *Memories*, p.19. See also Harford, p.48, *Zulu War Journal* for a report of another lynching.

33   Hallam Parr, *Sketch*, p.264.

34   *Ibid.*, p.263.

35   G. Hamilton-Browne, *A Lost Legionary in South Africa* (London, 1912), p.152.

36   Regulations Field Forces S. Africa (Pietermaritzburg, 1878).

37   See R. Holmes, *Firing Line* (1987), pp.380-4.

38   See for instance Hallam Parr, *Sketch*, p.246: 'Their actual loss we shall never know but must have far exceeded five hundred, as very many bodies were carried away and thrown into *dongas* by the Zulus.' On page 262 he adds, 'Though most of the dead Zulus were buried by the 24th it was very hard to get at the dead who had crept away in the long grass partially wounded, to die, and, for days and days afterwards bodies of men would be found, which had defied previous search!'

39   Emery, *Red Soldier*, p.141, Allan to wife, 4 February 1879.

40   *Ibid.*, p.141, Capt. W.P. Jones to wife (?), 25 February 1879.

41   *Ibid.*, p.143-4, Lance-Corporal Adams to mother, 6 March 1879.

42   Harford, *Zulu War Journal*, pp.38-9.

43   *Ibid.*, p.140, Sergeant Smith to wife, February 1879.

44   Harford, *Zulu War Journal*, pp.49-50.

45   *Ibid.*, p.41.

46   Harford, *Zulu War Journal*, pp.49-50.

47   Norris-Newman, p.123.

48   *Ibid.*, p.183.

49   Moodie, *Moodie's Zulu War*, pp.251-2.

50   RRM, Heaton diary.

51   *Natalia*, December 1978, 'A Zulu Boy's recollections of the Zulu War', p.13.

52   See pp.182-4 for details of the VC citations.

10 LEGACIES AND LESSONS: THE MILITARY, SOCIAL AND POLITICAL SIGNIFICANCE OF RORKE'S DRIFT

1   RAQVJ, 12 October 1879.

2   *The Application of Force: An Introduction to British Army Doctrine and to the Conduct of Military Operations,* MOD 1998, pp.206-218.

3   Holme, *Silver Wreath*, p.63, Hook account.

4   *Ibid.*, Hitch account, p.62.

5   Molyneux, *Campaigning in South Africa*, p.206-7.

6   *Application of Force*, p.2-9.

7   RRWM, Penn Symons, Memorandum to Duke of Cambridge, 21 February 1890. Curiously his memorandum included the caveat: 'not to be published until after the death of Chelmsford'.

8   *Ibid.*

9   *Ibid.*

10   *Ibid.*

11   See Chapter 8, p155.

12   See Chapters 6, p.131 and 8, p.154.

13   Holme, *Silver Wreath*, p.61, Lyons account.

14   *Ibid.*, p.60, Bourne account.

15   *Ibid.*, p.60-1.

16   *Ibid.*, p.61, Smith account.

17   See for instance Holme, *Silver Wreath*, p.65, Jobbins account 'All that night a Minister was praying in the fort they would go away. God helped us and gave us

the victory', and Reynolds, chapter 8, page i.

18   Holme, *Silver Wreath*, p.51, Chard account.

19   Laband, *Kingdom and Colony at War*, chapter 5, p.111.

20   Laband, *Kingdom and Colony at War*, p.115.

21   Webb, 'A Zulu Boy's Recollections', p.12.

22   *Ibid.*, p.20.

23   Moodie, *Moodie's Zulu War*, p.77.

24   W.R. Ludlow, *Zululand and Cetywayo* (London, 1882), p.61.

25   NAM, Stafford Papers. See also R.A.VIC/034/67 South Africa III, Mary Frere to
      Ponsonby, 6 May 1879, whose interview with Hamu, Cetshwayo's half-brother,
      confirmed that the 'Zulus were on the road to Natal when checked at Isandlwana
      and Rorke's Drift'.

26   Lummis, *Padre Smith,* p.55.

27   Lock and Quantrill, *Red Book*, p.70, Eyewitness account.

28   Mitford, *Through the Zulu Country*, p.81.

29   RRWM, Penn Symons, *Memorandum,*.

30   RRWM, F. Grenfell, Memorandum, 3 February 1879.

31   Lock and Quantrill, *Red Book,* p.102. See also Laband, *Kingdom and Colony,* p.110.

32   Holme, *Silver Wreath*, p.60, Bourne account.

33   Holme, *Silver Wreath* and Emery, *Red Soldier, passim.*

34   Harford, *Zulu War Journal*, p.41.

35   Chelmsford Papers, Chamberlain to father, 7 February 1879.

36   Webb, 'A Zulu Boy's Recollections', p.12-13.

37   *Ibid.*

38   Molyneux, *Campaigning in South Africa*, p.196-8.

39   C.Vijn, *Cetshwayo's Dutchman*, pp.28-9.

40   CO 79/126, Minute, Fairfield to Bramston, 10 March 1879.

41   The *Times*, 12 February 1879.

42   Goodfellow, *'Great Britain and South African Confederation',* p.43. Disraeli to Her
      Majesty (hereafter HM), quoted in RA QUJ, 12 February 1879.

44   Wilson-Black Papers, Philip Barlow private collection (hereafter WBP),
      Chelmsford, Memoranda, Durban, 20 February 1879.

45   See Chapter 2.

46   Memorandum on the Isandlwana Disaster, 11 February 1879, RA VIC/033/92.

47   WBP, Barlow collection. The mistaken reference to E Company, Cavaye's own
      company, probably reflects confusion on Pulleine's part as the battle was clearly
      intensifying at this point.

48   RA VIC/033/118, South Africa (II) Hallam Parr to Frere, 23 January 1879.

49   RA VIC/034/29, South Africa III, Duke of Richmond to HM, 26 March 1879.

50   *Ibid.*

51   *Ibid.*, Sir Stafford Northcote to HM, 1 April 1879.

52   Chelmsford's Papers, *Adjt General to Chelmsford*, 6 March 1879.

53   Sir G. Arthur, *The Letters of Lord and Lady Wolseley* (London, 1923).

54   Preston, *Wolseley's South African Journal 1879-80*, pp.256-7.

55   *Ibid.*, p.57.

56   CO 48/489, Chelmsford to SOS War, 27 January 1879.

57   *Ibid.*, Frere to Colonial Office, 3 February 1879.

58   See RA VIC 003/86-87 South Africa II (Tels) Ponsonby to Stanley (SOS War), 11
      February 1879.

59   RA QVJ, 12 March 1879.

60   RA VIC/033/80 South Africa (II), Frere to HM, 10 February 1879.

61 *Ibid.*, Lady Frere to Ponsonby, 4 February 1879.

62 Lady Frere to HM, 4 February 1879. RA VIC/033/76.

63 RA VIC/034/7South Africa III, Frere to HM, 9 March 1879.

64 RA QVJ, 19 March 1879.

65 *Ibid.*, 4 March 1879.

66 *Ibid.*, 23 March 1879.

67 CO 48/489 Colonial Office to Frere, 19 March 1879.

68 R. Blake, *Disraeli* (London, 1966), p.671.

69 *Ibid.*

70 Preston, *Wolseley South Africa Journal*, p.236, 22 February 1880.

71 *Ibid.*, 21 February 1880.

72 RA QVJ (tels). Disraeli to HM and HM to Disraeli, 23 May 1879.

73 *Ibid.*, 26 May 1879.

74 Blake, *Disraeli,* pp.673-4.

75 RA QVJ, 12 August 1879.

76 *Ibid.*

77 *Ibid.*, 11, 12 and 13 October 1879.

78 Blake, *Disraeli*, p.674.

79 *Ibid.*, p.674.

80 *Emery, Red Soldier*, p.144.

81 *Ibid.*

82 *Ibid.*, pp.144-5.

83 T. Willsmer, 'Zulu', *Movie Collector* 1:8 (1944: 31).

84 E.J. Yorke, 'Cultural Myths and Realities, The British Army, War and Empire as portrayed on Film 1900-1990' in S.C. Carruthers (ed), *War Culture and the Media* (Flicks Books, 1996).

85 *Ibid.*

86 See, for instance, Lt R.D. Coster, Porter R.E. 'Laagers in the Zulu War', *Royal Engineer Institute Occasional Papers* Vol. IV, 1880, for impact on siege warfare of Rorke's Drift.

87 These brief, limited post-war biographies have relied heavily on Bancroft, *Rorke's Drift 1879,* ch.9 pp.123-47 and Knight, *Nothing Remains but to Fight*, ch.5, pp.117-161.

Select Bibliography

Unpublished Official Sources

PUBLIC RECORD OFFICE, KEW

WAR OFFICE
WO16 Series, Regimental and Corps Pay Lists
WO32/7706-84, WO33/33, Zulu War Correspondence
WO146/1, Submissions for the DCM
War Office Army Lists, January-July 1879, July-December 1879

COLONIAL OFFICE FILES
Cape Colony (CO 48)
482-488: January to December 1878
489: January to April 1879
490: May to August 1879
Admiralty File 1/6486 (1879)

Natal (CO 179)
126-7 : January to December 1878

BRITISH LIBRARY

India Office Library (IOL) London:
A4 – Policy on NW Frontier, Lawrence and Frere Minutes (1863-4)
A12 – Sir B. Frere: Minutes on Sind and Punjab Frontier System

National Army Museums Archive (NAM), London:
Chelmsford Papers File: 6807-386

Stafford Papers File: 8406-49
Miscellaneous Papers

Museum of Royal Regiment of Wales (South Wales Borderers) (R.R.W.M.) Brecon,
Powys, Wales:
Zulu War Boxes 1-3 esp. Heaton Diary and Penn Symons Papers (2C 211, 212, 2/3)

Royal Military Academy Sandhurst, Surrey:
Zulu War Photograph Collection

Army Medical Corps Museum, Aldershot, Hants:
Surgeon Major James Henry Reynolds, MB VC : Report of the Defence of Rorke's
Drift.
Zulu War Boxes: Miscellaneous Material

Royal Logistical Corps Museum Deepcut, Camberley:
The Waggoner – The Zulu War: The Defence of Rorke's Drift, 22-23 Jan 1879 (incl.
accounts by Lt-Col. Walter Alphonsus Dunne, ASC and Corporal Francis Attwood).
Zulu War Box – Miscellaneous correspondence
Private Collections

Royal Archives, Windsor Castle, Berkshire. By gracious permission of HM the Queen
1. Queen Victoria's Journals Jan-Dec 1879 (QVJ)
2. South Africa Files (Correspondence Jan-Dec 1879 [032-4])

Gloucestershire County Records Office, Gloucester:
Earl St Aldwyn (Hicks Beach) Papers (D2455)
PCC/22-3 Hicks Beach to Frere
PCC/13 Hicks Beach to Disraeli
PC/11 Hicks Beach to Queen Victoria
PCC/30 Hicks Beach to Salisbury

Philip Barlow Collection:
(Major) Wilsone-Black Papers

NEWSPAPERS AND JOURNALS

The Times (London), 1879
The Graphic, 1879
The Illustrated London News, 1879
The London Gazette, 1879
Punch, 1879
The Natal Mercury Supplement, 21/1/1929
The Strand Magazine
Journal of the Society for Army Historical Research, JSHR (various dates)
Soldiers of the Queen, The Journal of the Victorian Military Society (various dates)

PUBLISHED BOOKS

Adams, J., *The South Wales Borderers*, London, 1968.

Arthur, Sir G., *The Letters of Lord and Lady Wolseley*, London, 1923.

Ashe, W. & Wyatt-Edgell, E.V., *The Story of the Zulu Campaign*, London, 1880.

Atkinson, C.T., *The South Wales Borderers, 24th Foot 1689-1937*, Cambridge, 1937.

Bancroft, J.W., *Rorke's Drift*, Tunbridge Wells, 1988.

Barnet, C., *Britain and Her Army 1509-1970*, London, 1970.

Barthorp, M., *The Zulu War: A Pictorial History*, Poole, 1980.

Bengough, Major-General Sir H.M., *Memories of a Soldier's Life*, London, 1913.

Bennett, I., *Eyewitness in Zululand*, London, 1989.

Binns, C.T., *The Last Zulu King – The Life and Death of Cetshwayo*, London, 1963.

Blake, R, *Disraeli*, London, 1966.

Blood, Sir B., *Four Score years and Ten*, London, 1933.

Bradford, S, *Disraeli*, New York, 1983.

Buchan, J., *History of the Royal Scots Fuziliers, 1678-1918*, London, 1925.

Butler, W.F., *Sir William Butler, An Autobiography*, London, 1913.

Butterfield, P.H. (ed.) *War and Peace in South Africa 1879-1881: the writings of Philip Anstruther and Edward Essex*, Pietermaritzburg, 1987.

Callwell, Colonel C.E., *Small Wars: a tactical textbook for Imperial Soldiers*, London, rep. 1990.

Carruthers, S.L. and Stewart I., *War, Culture and the Media: Representations of the Military in 20th C. Britain*, Trowbridge, 1996.

Child, D. (ed.), *The Zulu War Journal of Colonel Henry Harford, C.B.*, Pietermaritzburg, 1978.

Clammer, D., *The Zulu War*, London, 1973.

Clements, W.H., *The Glamour and Tragedy of the Zulu War*, London, 1936.

Coghill, P., *Whom the Gods Love*, Halesowen, 1968.

Colenso, F.E., *The Ruin of Zululand*, London, 1884.

Colenso, F.E. and Durnford, E.C.L., *The History of the Zulu War and its Origin*, London, 1880.

Cope, R., *Ploughshare of War: the origins of the Anglo-Zulu War of 1879*, Pietermaritzburg, 1999.

Coupland, R., *Zulu Battle Piece – Isandlwana*, London, 1948.

Dixon, N.F.D., *On the Psychology of Military Incompetence*, London, 1976..

Drooglever, R.W.F., *The Road to Isandlwana*, London, 1992.

Duminy, A. and Ballard, C. (eds), *The Anglo-Zulu War: New Perspectives*, Pietermaritzburg, 1981.

Durnford, E., *A Soldier's Life and Work in South Africa 1872 to 1879. A Memoir of the Late Colonel A.W. Durnford, Royal Engineers*, London, 1882.

Egerton, R., *Like Lions They Fought*, London, 1988.

Elliot, W.J., *The Victoria Cross in Zululand and South Africa and How it was Won*, London, 1882.

Emery, F., *The Red Soldier, Letters from the Zulu War, 1879*, London, 1997.

– *Marching over Africa*, London, 1986.

Fenn, T.E., *How I Volunteered For The Cape and What I Did there*, London, 1879.

French, G., *Lord Chelmsford and the Zulu War*, London, 1939.

Furneaux, R., *The Zulu War: Isandlwana and Rorke's Drift*, London, 1963.

Gardiner, A.G., *Life of Sir William Harcourt*, London, 1923.

Gibson, J.Y., *The Story of the Zulus*, New York, rep. 1970.

Glover, M., *Rorke's Drift – A Victorian Epic*, London, 1975.

Gon, P., *The Road to Isandlwana*, Johannesburg, 1979.

Goodfellow, C.F., *Great Britain and South African Confederation 1870-1881*, Capetown, 1966.

Guy, J., *The Destruction of the Zulu Kingdom*, London, 1979.

Haggard, H. Rider, *Cetshwayo and His White Neighbours*, London, 1912.

Hamilton-Browne, G., *Lost Legionary in South Africa*, London, 1912.

Harris, *A Life in the British Army*.

Hart, H.G., *Army Lists, 1878-80*.

Hart-Synnot, *Letters of Major-General Hart-Synnot*, London, 1912.

Hattersley, A.F. (ed.), *Later Annals of Natal*, London, 1938.

– *Carbineer: the history of the Royal Natal Carbineers*.

Haythornthwaite, P.J., *The Colonial Wars Source Book*, London, 1995.

Hicks Beach, Lady V., *Life of Sir Michael Hicks Beach* (Vol. 1), London, 1932.

Holme, N., *The Silver Wreath – Being the 24th Regiment at Isandlwana and Rorke's Drift, 1879*, London, 1979.

Holt, H.P., *The Mounted Police of Natal*, London, 1913.

Jones, L.T. (ed.), *Reminiscences of the Zulu War by John Maxwell*, Cape Town, 1979.

Knight, I.J., *Zulu: Isandlwana and Rorke's Drift 22-23 January 1879*, London, 1992.

– *Nothing Remains but to fight: the Defence of Rorke's Drift, 1879*, London, 1993.

– (ed.) *There will be an Awful Row at Home About This* (Revised), Shoreham-by-Sea, 1987.

Laband, J.P.C., *Fight us in the Open*, Pietermaritzburg, 1985.

– *The Battle of Ulundi*, Pietermaritzburg, 1985.

– *Kingdom in Crisis: The Zulu response to the British Invasion of 1879*, Manchester UP, 1992.

– *Lord Chelmsford's Zululand Campaign 1878-9*, Army Records Society Vol 10, Gloucestershire, 1994.

– *The Rise and Fall of the Zulu Nation*, London, 1997.

– *Kingdom and Colony at War*, Uni. of Natal Press, 1990.

Laband, J. and Knight, I., *The War Correspondents: the Anglo-Zulu War*, London, 1996.

– *Archives of Zululand: Anglo-Zulu War 1879* (Vols 1 and 2), London, 2000.Laband, J.P.C. and Thompson, P.S., *Field Guide to the War in Zululand and the Defence of Natal 1879* (2nd edition with minor revisions), Pietermaritzburg, 1987.

Laband, J.P.C. and Thompson, P.S., *War Comes to Umvoti: The Natal Zululand Border*, Durban, 1980.

– *The Buffalo Border*, Pietermaritzburg, 1983.

Laband, J.P.C. and Wright, J., *King Cetshwayo KaMpande*, Pietermaritzburg, 1980.

Lloyd A., *The Zulu War*, London, 1973.

Lock, R., Quantrill P. (eds) *Red Book, Natal Press Reports Anglo-Zulu War 1879*, London, 2000.

Lugg, H.C., *Historic Natal and Zululand*, Pietermaritzburg, 1949.

Lummis, W.M., *Padre George Smith of Rorke's Drift*, Norwich, 1978.

MacKinnon, H.J.P. and Shadbolt, S., *The South African Campaign*, London, 1880.

MOD, *The Application of Force: An Introduction to British Army Doctrine and to the conduct of Military Operations*, London, 1998. j230

Martineau J., *Life and Correspondence of Sir Bartle Frere*, London, 1895.

Mitford, B., *Through the Zulu Country: Its Battlefields and People*, London, rep 1992.

Molyneux, W.C.F., *Campaigning in South Africa and Egypt*, London, 1896.

Moodie, D.C.F., *The History of the Battles and Adventures of the British, the Boers and the Zulus in Southern Africa*, Adelaide 1879, repr. *Moodie's Zulu War*, Cape Town, 1988.

Morley, J., *Life of Gladstone* (Vol 7), London, 1903.

Morris, D.R., *The Washing of the Spears*, London, 1966.

Norbury, H.F., *The Naval Brigade in South Africa During the years 1977-78-79*, London, 1880.

Norris-Newman, C.L., *In Zululand with the British Throughout the War of 1879*, London 1880 (reprinted 1988).

Parr, H.H., *A Sketch of the Kafir and Zulu Wars*, London, 1880.

Paton, G., Glennie, F. and Penn Symons, W., *Historical Records of the 24th Regiment*, Devonport, 1892.

Porter, R. da C., *Warfare against uncivilised races; or how to fight greatly superior forces of an uncivilised and badly-armed enemy*, Royal Engineers Professional papers, Prize Essay for 1881, London, 1882.

Preston, A. (ed.), *Sir Garnet Wolseley's South African Journal 1879-80*, Cape Town, 1973.

Prior, M., *Campaigns of a War Correspondent*, London, 1912

Robinson, R. and Gallagher, J., *Africa and the Victorians*, London, 1961.

Smith-Dorrien, H., *Memories of Forty-Eight Years Service*, London, 1925.

Stalker, J. (ed.), *The Natal Carbineers*, Pietermaritzburg and Durban ,1912.

Streatfield, F.N., *Reminiscences of an Old 'Un*, London, 1911.

Tavender, I.T., *Casualty Roll for the Zulu and Basutho Wars: South Africa 1877-79*.

Tomasson, W.H., *With the Irregulars in the Transvaal and Zululand*, London, 1881.

Uys, C.J., *In the era of Shepstone*, London, 1933.

Vijn, C. (trans. and ed. J.W. Colenso), *Cetshwayo's Dutchman*, London, 1880 (reprinted 1988).

War Office: Intelligence Branch, Précis of Information concerning Zululand, HMSO, London, 1885.

War Office, Rothwell, J.S. (compiler), *Narrative of Field Operations Connected with the Zulu War of 1879*, London, 1881 (reprinted 1907 and 1989).

Webb, C. de B., and Wright, J.B., *A Zulu King Speaks: Statements made by Cetshwayo kaMpande on the history and customs of his people*, Pietermaritzburg and Durban 1978

Whitehouse, H. (ed.), *'A Widow-Making War': the life and death of a British officer in Zululand 1879*, Nuneaton, reprinted 1989.

Whitton, F.E., *Deeds Which Should Not Pass Away*, Edinburgh, 1939.

Wilkinson-Latham, C., *Uniforms and Weapons of the Zulu War*, London, 1978.

Wilmott, A., *History of the Zulu War*, London, 1880.

Wood (H.)E., *From Midshipman to Field Marshal*, Vol. II, London, 1906.

– *Winnowed Memories*, London, 1918.

Worsfold, B., *Sir Bartle Frere*, London, 1923.

Young, J., *They Fell Like Stones: Battles and Casualties of the Zulu War, 1879*, London, 1991.

Articles

Hall, H.L., 'With Assegai and Rifle: Reminiscences of a Transport Conductor in the Zulu War', *I have Reaped my Mealies,* Cape Town, 1937.

Jackson, F.W.D., 'Isandlwana 1879: The Sources re-examined', *JSAHR* Vol. XLIII, Nos 173, 175, 176, March, Sept, Dec 1965 (LXXII, No. 292, Winter 1994).

Knight, I., 'Ammunition at Isandlwana 1879': A Reply, *JSAHR* Winter 1995.

Lieven, M., 'Butchering the Brutes all over the Place: Total War and Massacre in Zululand 1879', *History,* Vol. 84, No. 286, Oct 1999, pp.614-32.

Webb, 'A Zulu Boy's Recollections of the Zulu War', *Natalia*, 6. 1978.

Yorke, E.J., 'Isandlwana 1879: Reflections on the Ammunition Controversy', *JSAHR*, Vol. LXXII No. 292, Autumn 1994.

Yorke, E.J. 'Isandlwana 1879, Dividing your Forces', *Battle Plans: Before and After,* Helicon Books, 1998, p.165-77.

List of Illustrations

Index

TEMPUS — REVEALING HISTORY

Private 12768
Memoir of a Tommy
JOHN JACKSON
'Unique... a beautifully written, strikingly honest account of a young man's experience of combat' *Saul David*
£9.99
0 7524 3531 0

D-Day: The First 72 Hours
WILLIAM F. BUCKINGHAM
'A compelling narrative'
The Observer
£9.99
0 7524 2842 X

English Battlefields.
500 Battlefields that Shaped English History
MICHAEL RAYNER
'A painstaking survey of English battlefields... a first-rate book' *Richard Holmes*
£25
0 7524 2978 7

Trafalgar Captain Durham of the Defiance: The Man who refused to miss Trafalgar
HILARY RUBINSTEIN
'A sparkling biography of Nelson's luckiest captain' *Andrew Lambert*
£17.99
0 7524 3435 7

   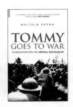

Battle of the Atlantic
MARC MILNER
'The most comprehensive short survey of the U-boat battles' *Sir John Keegan*
£12.99
0 7524 3332 6

Okinawa 1945 The Stalingrad of the Pacific
GEORGE FEIFER
'A great book... Feifer's account of the three sides and their experiences far surpasses most books about war' *Stephen Ambrose*
£17.99
0 7524 3324 5

Gallipoli 1915
TIM TRAVERS
'The most important new history of Gallipoli for forty years... groundbreaking' *Hew Strachan*
£13.99
0 7524 2972 8

Tommy Goes To War
MALCOLM BROWN
'A remarkably vivid and frank account of the British soldier in the trenches'
Max Arthur
£12.99
0 7524 2980 9

If you are interested in purchasing other books published by Tempus, or in case you have difficulty finding any Tempus books in your local bookshop, you can also place orders directly through our website
www.tempus-publishing.com